Art as Expression

Art as Expression

Henry W. Peacock

Foreword by

Frank Goodyear, Jr.

WHALESBACK BOOKS • *Washington, D.C.*

Edited by Thea Clarke
Book and Cover designed by Anne Meagher-Cook
Composition by John Reinhardt Book Design
Printed (alk paper) and bound in Hong Kong

Library of Congress Cataloguing-in-Publication Data

Peacock, Henry W., 1926–
Art as expression / by Henry Peacock; foreword by Frank Goodyear, Jr.
p. cm.
Includes bibliographical references and index.
ISBN 0-929590-14-7
1. Painting--Technique. 2. Painting--Psychological aspects.
3. Visual perception. I. Title.
ND1500.P42 1995 94-37460
750'.1--dc20 CIP

Whalesback Books is an imprint of Howells House
Box 9546, Washington, D.C. 20016

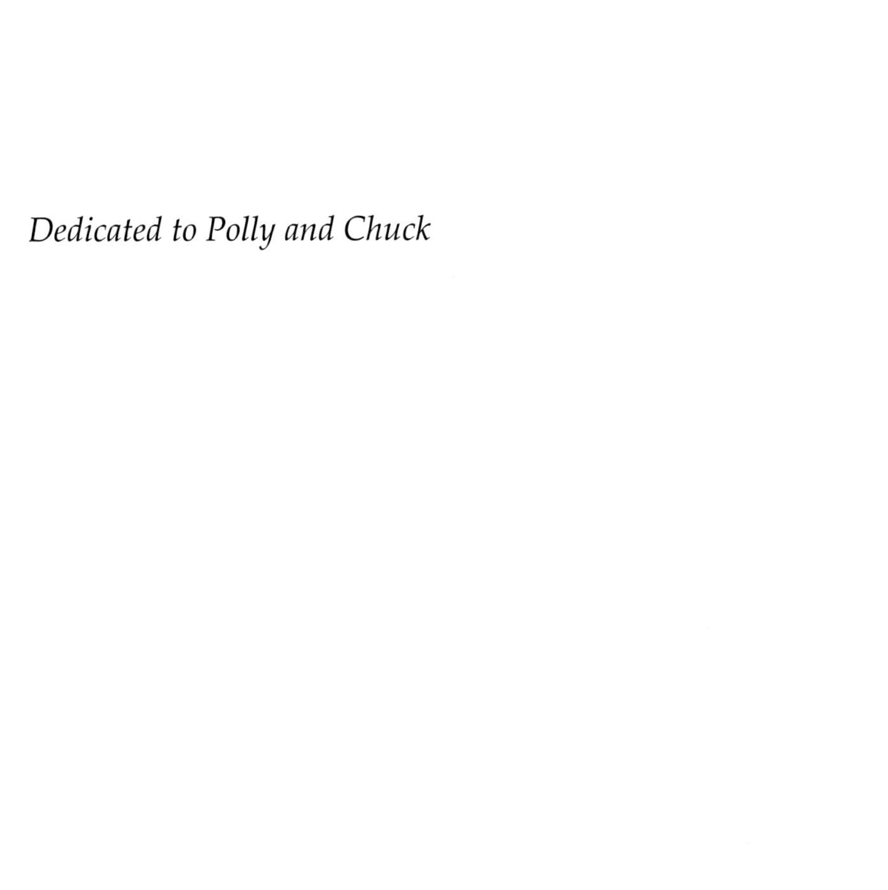

Dedicated to Polly and Chuck

Contents

List of Illustrations

Chapter 1

Chapter 2

Chapter 3

Chapter 4

Foreword

This book reminds me vividly of the many times I have pondered over the process of the making of art and the making of an artist. At a time when I was involved with an art school, I used to be asked by anxious young art students: "What is important to the making of an artist?" A good question indeed, but a difficult one to answer.

In those days, it would have seemed logical to roll out my defense of art schools and the various factors that make art schools valuable learning experiences for students. Not so. While I have always believed in the principle of learning the fundamentals first, I also hesitated to give a blanket endorsement to art schools. The higher truth for me was that art schools do not work for everybody. Sometimes those "fundamentals" end up getting in the way. Sometimes they end up being the end rather than the means. Academic dogma is the mortal enemy of art.

So what, then, is important to the making of an artist? The answer is too simple: whatever works for you. There simply are not any formulas. But if the answer to the question is simple, it is not so simple to find the right answer for any one artist.

I have always advised art students to find something that is their own, to pursue their vision with passion, tenacity, and hard work, and to remain loyal to that vision. Edward Hopper summarized it this way: "Great art is the outward expression of the inner life of an artist, and this inner life will result in a personal vision of the world." Robert Motherwell put it more bluntly: "Much of what passes for art is not different from the rest of society, a series of lies, for exterior reasons, or occasionally from self-delusion, or most often from inherited prejudices and *a priori* conceptions. True originality is that which originates in one's own being." Again, the definition is simple, but the answer for each artist is not.

The making of great art does not come easily, but the rewards are worth the struggle. To create something that emanates from the soul, touches originality, captures an essence, holds broad meaning, and is beautiful all at once is a noble act.

This book provides many useful insights on how to understand the fundamentals of making art, but its real message is that technique is important but is not art, that art is an individual act but is not technique, and that all real art is the expression of the vision and feelings of one human. Too many artists avoid the issue of personal expression and thus delay or entirely miss the rewards of significant artistic achievement. By helping artists reach this stage in their work, this book will be a valuable contribution to them.

—Frank Goodyear, Jr.

Preface

How can I achieve more, go beyond what I know, and become more original with my art? This question confronts anyone searching for a more expressive direction in his painting. *Art As Expression* addresses this question and opens the door to a more fundamental understanding of the inner self in relation to the outer experience of making art.

Self-liberation based on independent thought and action is far removed from the minds of most people, yet it is an important factor for the creative person who seeks to fulfill his potential for making art. This does not just happen. True liberation for the artist begins with the simple need to express feelings with paint. Sincere, original painting, however, cannot be learned quickly. Development as an artist has little to do with "how-to" technical solutions to painting problems, or with a clever, opportunistic expression of "newness" as the result. Time must be paid for, step by step, by increasing inner abilities correlated with an expansion of fundamental perceptions. Creative growth depends on an unshakable, solid foundation.

I have found through many years of making and teaching art that the philosophical mandates that underlie a creative existence should not be separated either from painting or from the teaching of painting. All art is a mirror of its creator's attitudes and beliefs. Consequently, the teaching methods used in this book combine formal principles of drawing, color, and composition with informal observations derived from my own experience and growth in the larger context of making art. Excerpts from notes and lectures, diagrams, sketches, and reproductions of paintings, as well as comments and evaluations about the work of some of the master painters who have shaped twentieth-century art, are used for visual clarification. Many of the fundamentals described in the first chapter, from elementary drawing principles to a more comprehensive understanding of the use of space in making art, are used as a basis for broadening perceptions in the later chapters. Most of learning how to draw and paint well is based on the expansion of individual awareness. Teaching painters to be open, to overcome conditioned visual responses, to see form wholly and with emotion, and to regard vision as the principal means of gaining a more liberated personal expression, is fundamental to personal growth.

Little by little, a visual language has evolved during this century. Because of the rapid changes and developments in modern art, art critics have labeled particular styles of painting and generally have kept up with the escalation of creative expression in its various time frames, forms, and directions. Most of the terminology used in teaching art has been developed because of the need to bridge the gap between audio/literary communication and that which is purely visual. The terms "positive form" and "negative space," for example, have been in use in art schools and colleges since the early 1960s. Today, they are accepted as standard by professional painters and teachers of painting. I have invented a few new terms for further clarification of the creative process in modern painting. These terms are "proportional interchange" (the interactions between proportions in composition); "spatial interval" (the optical interval between two colors); "color/form" and "color/space" (the form and space of color in modern painting); and "visual weight," visual energy," and "visual structure." I hope these terms will be useful to painters and students of painting.

A glossary at the back of the book lists special technical and difficult words that are used in the text, with explanations and comments.

Acknowledgments

This book is the result of my experiences of teaching drawing and painting over three decades. It was encouraged by the receptive responses of many of my students during that period. I acknowledge with gratitude their interest and constructive help, based on their enthusiastic personal journeys with paint and brush.

A special thanks goes to Marion F. T. Johnson, founder and former director of the Art Education program at The Delaware Art Museum. Marion repeatedly gave me valuable support and assistance in developing teaching ideals and helped me formulate the high standards of art education in my studio classes.

I am also indebted to my good friend and wonderfully expressive painter, Alexandra Linett, who spent countless hours helping me simplify and clarify the text. I am most grateful to Lorraine Fry, Louise Christopher, Connie Cowan, Marcy Dunn Ramsey, Frank Elliot, and Neil Welliver, all of whom went out of their way to review and critique the manuscript. Their unselfish cooperation and insights have been invaluable. My deep thanks go to Anne Beals for correcting and typing several drafts of the manuscript.

I feel fortunate to have Dean Howells as my publisher. His curiosity, selfless interest, and guidance improved the manuscript in countless ways, and it has been a pleasure to have worked with him.

Finally, I am eternally grateful to the two most important women in my life: my late mother, who encouraged my art career when I was very young and sustained her support throughout her lifetime; and my wife, Eleanor, who has always been there for me.

1.

The Perception of Visual Structure

The Hex Sign and Reality

Steep, wind-driven waves laced with white foam etch the dark plane of the Chesapeake Bay. Two fishermen are working in the pale lemon-colored early morning light off Swan Point Bar. Their forty-five foot, bay-built work boat is towing two heavily laden twenty-foot batteaus, surfing, zig-zagging, spray-sloshed, as they haul seine nets aboard. Wet slickers and coveralls, orange and yellow, stand out—brilliant colors pushing forward opposing the deep background. On certain days, vision is sharpened. The horizon stands up. Distance advances. This is the view from our front yard at the "Strawberry Factory."

My good-natured, artistic, hard-working wife and I bought the old Kelsh Building in 1976. We renamed it "The Strawberry Factory," and, together with her two sons and my son and daughter, ripped it apart and rebuilt it to serve our purposes. We overlook the bay at Gratitude, a little town at land's end just west of Rock Hall, the largest fishing port on the northern bay. The Factory is our fortress. Crude in appearance and monolithic, it contains some 15,000 square feet that we converted into studio and workshops on the first floor and gallery areas and residence on the second. It is a creative factory for making and enjoying art.

Our view of the bay covers nearly 180 degrees; it extends twelve miles to the south and the Bay Bridge, and seven miles to the west and the entrance to the Patapsco River and distant Baltimore. It also encompasses Swan Point and the entrances to Tavern Creek and Swan Creek to the northwest. Around us is the hustle and bustle of a small boat marina. The factory—aloof, like an island in its midst—is protected by heavy block walls. The downstairs was originally used for cold storage for fish, tomatoes, and strawberries to be shipped by truck and small boat to Annapolis and Baltimore.

Gratitude is far removed from city life by long stretches of flat farmlands. The atmosphere created by the merchants, the boatyard, and particularly the watermen—oystermen, crabbers, clammers, and eelers—provides us with the simplicity and solitude so conducive to creative work. When I look back from this perspective to my student days at The Pennsylvania Academy of the Fine Arts in Philadelphia, I realize how much I conformed to the requirements of the academic regime, to an environment so different from this.

When I returned from World War II in 1946, the academy was a citadel detached from the busy commerce of the surrounding city. To the students, the galleries were sacred. Among its treasures were images of the past, including twenty-foot allegorical paintings by Benjamin West, dark, glowing portraits by Thomas Eakins, and the famous *Fox in the Snow* by Winslow Homer, all cordoned off by maroon velvet ropes in the central rotunda and the main galleries.

Downstairs, beneath the museum, the art school made its own demands for faithful reproduction of subject matter and correct tonal values: "Perhaps a little more rose in the cheeks, Henry," was a kind criticism. These were the methods of the oldest and one of the most prestigious art schools in the country, and they were consistent with a sharpened vision. Realism was paramount. Expressiveness was caged in a mysterious niche and never mentioned. The Academy stressed practice and learning all the techniques; only then could one portray subject matter.

The October sun slanted brilliantly onto my rough sheet of Arches watercolor paper. The goal was to reproduce with scumbled textures, the siennas and ochres shining through the whitewashed fieldstone wall of the old Pennsylvania barn with correct proportions and handling of light. The wood siding was weathered to a silver gray; I worked from light to dark, reproducing each tone and subtle nuance of color. I constructed the wall solidly and then glazed the deep, angled shadow, permitting the underlying texture to shine through. The faded red hex sign toward the top of the barn, which the Amish builders had painted to ward off evil spirits, was the final detail.

A few months later, I did an oil painting of this barn using the earlier watercolor as the basis for the composition. Titled *The Hex Sign*, it was purchased by the Academy for its permanent collection. A few years later, I realized that this

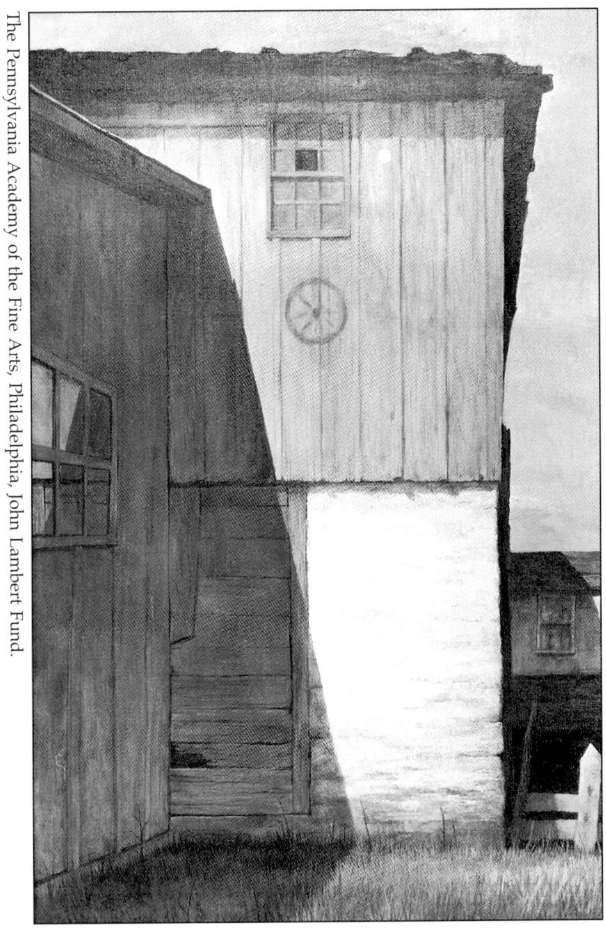
The Pennsylvania Academy of the Fine Arts, Philadelphia, John Lambert Fund.

I.1

Henry W. Peacock,
The Hex Sign, 1949.
Oil on canvas, 22" x 34".

painting reflected the profound influence of the academy on my work. To depart from these traditions and conventions was beyond me at that time.

I did not know then that earlier childhood patterns would in time prevail. When I was a child, the coast of Maine, with its vast stretches of rocks and sea, was indelibly inscribed in my memory. Each summer when I was very young, our family visited an island in Casco Bay. The children played on the rocks, swam in icy water, fished, and rowed punts and other small boats. I still can remember exploring the island alone, climbing fearlessly on the great salt-streaked rocks. It was a new and exciting visual world, full of wonder and far removed from the more familiar toy trucks and tractors in the flower bed at home.

The forms and patterns stamped into our subconsciousness are infinite and varied. The images we recall are important; they condition us and our individual responses. They are the essence of individual expression.

The Representation of Form

A child draws the everyday facts of his surroundings without fear or hesitation. They are simplified expressions of people, animals, houses, grass, trees, and suns. This is the child's captivating, personal world derived from his immediate experience of the real world. Children's drawings magically hold together. They have a remarkable consistency. The forms are distorted naturally because the child has little visual knowledge and does not care about proportions.

The difference between art made by children and great works of art is that children create art with purely emotional responses to form, guided by intuition, while artists embody an awareness of their total and continually expanding experience through their work. If artists are truly creative, their work will develop constantly as a result of their objective and subjective experiences.

As children grow older, it is logical and natural for them to try to portray form as accurately as possible. Usually, the more realistic a drawing or painting appears, the more it is praised by an artist's peers; after all, the artwork is conforming to recognized standards. Regardless of influences, the realistic portrayal of form becomes indispensable to expressing the appearance of the world.

The New Yorker Magazine reported what happened when a fifty-year-old man regained his eyesight after forty-five years:

> When the bandages were removed he heard a voice coming from in front of him and to one side: he turned to the source of the sound, and saw a "blur." He real-

> ized that this must be a face. He seemed to think that he would not have known that this was a face if he had not previously heard the voice and known that voices came from faces.
>
> The rest of us . . . create a sight world from the start, a world of visual objects and concepts and meanings. When we open our eyes each morning, it is upon a world we have spent a lifetime *learning* to see. We are not given the world: we make our world through incessant experience, categorization, memory, reconnection. But when . . . after being blind for forty-five years—having had little more than an infant's visual experience, and this long forgotten—there were no visual memories to support a perception, there was no world of experience and meaning awaiting him. He saw, but what he saw had no coherence. His retina and optic nerve were active, transmitting impulses, but his brain could make no sense of them . . . [1]

This account provides an understanding of how we all learn how to see, how we absorb and relate all of our visual experiences from childhood and throughout our lifetime.

Most people are attracted to representational drawing and painting because of their familiarity with form. It is a simple, conditioned response based on experience. All the forms in nature, our common space—animal, vegetable, and mineral—are accepted with a visual trust. Conversely, it is just as natural to mistrust the unknown.

Reality, however, varies among people according to their curiosity and perception. A creative person will look beneath the surface of form and beyond a factual summation of experience. One of the greatest challenges in teaching art is finding a way to overcome the student's conditioned response to form. For the student, it involves stripping off an outer layer of conditioned conformity to discover the inner self.

I used to collect beach stones, each one selected for its unique beauty from the endless variety of rocky strata below the high-tide mark in the Gulf of Maine. One appears as a

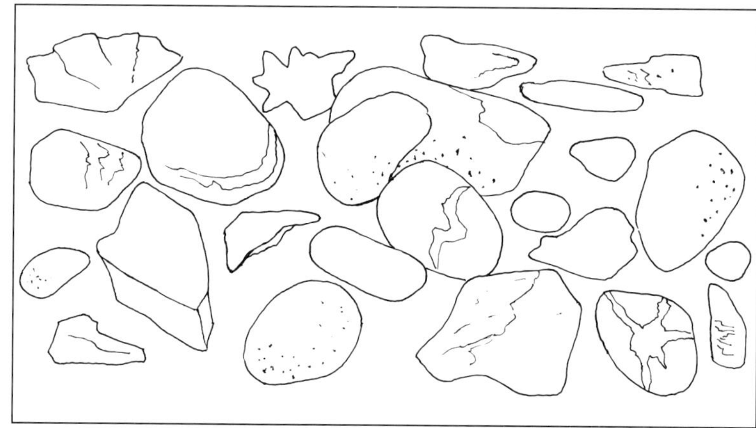

I.2 Author's Sketch of Beach Stones.

Color, texture, and uneven asymmetrical qualities all speak to the sensitive eye, imparting a curious yet related continuity.

large goose egg, deeply textured, an imperfect, off-white ovoid. Another is a warm, medium gray with bold, white calligraphic markings, and contrasts with one of iron red oxide. Others are salt and pepper granite and a few are the deepest charcoal gray. Color, texture, and asymmetrical qualities all speak to the sensitive eye, imparting a curious yet related continuity. When were these stones formed? How many millions of waves battered and rolled them into their uneven spherical perfection? The qualities in these stones are universal, yet their forms have been shaped and tempered individually.

Form is defined as the contour and structure of something as distinguished from its substance. Each fragment of our universe has it own structure and its visual extremities are related to its journey in time and space. To see any form wholly requires attention to its internal force first, and then to the relationship of this energy to its spatial environment.

Our own existence must be seen not as part of our immediate society, but in the larger context of humans as part of nature and evolution. We are nature; we breathe and exist in a common, unifying space. Biology and art are brothers. We tend to ignore the basics; we forget gravity is an essential force and we take for granted space and the common air we breathe.

Reality, then, should not be confined to surface appearance. It is subject to human interpretation. This means that we must rely on a deeper, subjective response to all form. The fundamentals of our existence provide the basis for our objectivity.

> Turning to the dominant world view of classical China, we begin not from a two-world theory, but from the assumption that there is only the one continuous concrete world that is the source and locus of all of our experience. Order within the classical Chinese world view is "immanental"—indwelling in things themselves—like the grain in the wood, like striations in stone, like the cadence of the surf, like the veins in a leaf. The classical Chinese believed that the power of creativity resides in the world itself, and that the order and regularity this world evidences is not derived from or imposed upon it by some independent, activating power, but inheres in the world. Change and continuity are equally "real."[2]

The Nature of Space

> . . . the wise man looks into space and does not regard the small as too little, nor the great as too big; for he knows that there is no limit to dimensions.
>
> —LAO-TSE, *The Family of Man*[3]

Many people fail at making art because they take space for granted both in nature and in their drawing and painting. They do not realize that space is the basic medium for perception. A more comprehensive understanding of space is fundamental to increasing one's visual perception.

Perception is a process by which we distinguish one thing from another. It is difficult for psychologists to determine the relationship between sensation and perception because adults have had so many experiences. Generally, sensation and impression appear at the same moment and cannot be separated. Creativity and intelligence are instrumental in developing acute perceptive abilities. The expansion of one's perception involves looking again and again to explore relationships and meanings that one would not ordinarily see. Artists must learn how to see differently than others. They learn to question everything they see to perceive the relativity of form, space, and color.

On some days, when I look at the vast panorama of the Bay, I can see the horizon, standing up like a dark wall, advancing in my vision; on other days it recedes. I have become sensitive to the light conditions that create these differences. The way I look at nature is always in terms of proportional interchange, tonal differences, and color changes. It is the way I see painting. My eyes have learned to assess relationships. Creative drawing and painting are problem-solving processes. The first step is to obtain as much visual information as possible. Artists use a systematically curious and searching mode of observation to expand their perception.

A structure is something that is built, or composed of parts arranged together as they are defined by their coexisting space, and includes the manner of building, or the way that the parts are made and hold together. A structure may also be an association of related parts that are the basis for formulating ideas, methods, and further developing reality.

Albert Einstein believed that time and space cannot be considered apart from one another. Time is a measurement of the extent of space. A Beethoven symphony is an auditory structure that occupies space and takes place over time. Both space and time measure the relative breadth and length of each note; this defines the note's interrelationship with the whole. A trumpet's blast pierces the air and has a greater amount of energy than a softer note on the piano. Each sound displaces a specific amount of space by means of three-dimensional vibrations. Because of their differences (proportional interchange), these sounds are distinctive and alive. They each have a relative amount of energy that shapes an equally alive corresponding space.

Although Beethoven was deaf in later life, he was able to hear the beginning, the breadth, the length, and the ending of his symphonies. His grasp of the whole was only possible through an intuitive awareness of spatial limitations. Each note must be indispensable to the whole. Too little is too little, and too much becomes gibberish.

Regardless of the medium, be it music, creative writing, drawing, painting, sculpture, or another creative endeavor, making art requires an instinctive control of the proportional interchanges between all of the parts and of their relationships to the whole. For example, in his novels, James Joyce's stream of consciousness is like the sweeping flow of innovative tones in progressive jazz. Both writer and composer are controlling their expressions by shaping form in space.

Time, according to Einstein, is a moving point of reference. It is the clock ticking, second by second, in progression. Each second is a point of reference. Each second is also linked to immediate experience. Time cannot be touched or seen or heard, but it is a fourth dimension that is always present and that consequently is inseparable from three-dimensional vision. One's perception of form is also based on immediate experience and is formed over time. Because any perception of form depends on an accompanying perception of its coexisting space, time and space are linked together and can be thought of as the medium in which all form exists.

In drawing and painting, it is the relationship between the parts that gives meaning to each and to the whole. As an example, take a blank sheet of white paper and draw two black lines on it. Make one thick and one thin and vary their directions. As you draw, think of the sheet of paper as a spatial field. As the lines are drawn, the space they occupy is displaced. The leftover space created by the shape of the lines is a negative impression of their form. Both the lines and their coexisting space should be recognized as equally important. Their interrelationship is the simplest kind of visual structure.

To simplify perception further, think of the lines as relative weights. This is easy. Weight is perceived instinctively by means of comparison. The thick line appears heavier than the thin line and both are heavier than their coexisting space. The heavy line attracts the eye first and is referred to as positive. The lighter line is seen to be further away from the eye and is relatively negative. The spatial field in which they exist is the picture plane, and is negative. The picture plane is defined by its size and proportions and by its horizontal and vertical dimensions.

I.3 Lines Seen as Relative Weight.

Perceptions of the qualities of these lines are made by comparison to each other and to their coexisting space. The arrows show how the eye measures the proportions of form and space.

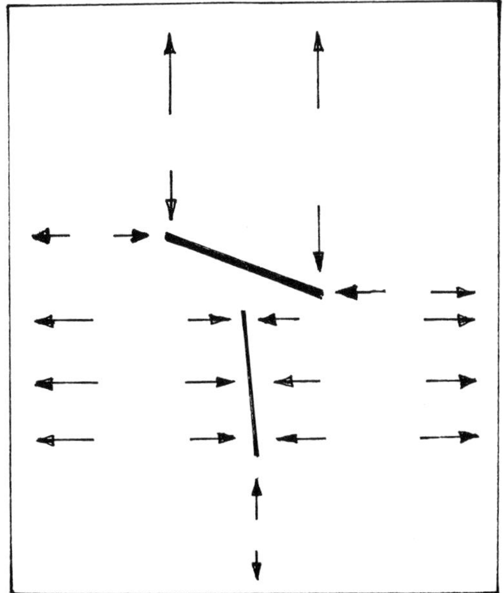

Gravitational Base

The heavy line advances in the picture plane, whereas the lighter line recedes from the observer's eye.

In traditional painting, the picture plane can be perceived as an open box. The depth of the box is relative to the amount of depth (illusion) portrayed in the painting.

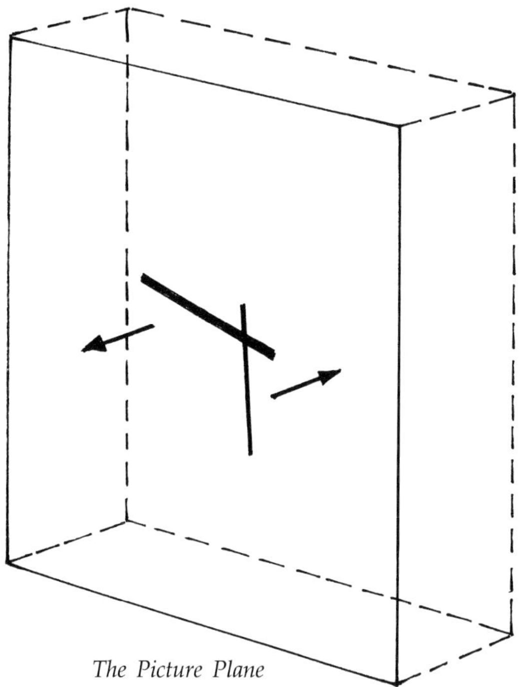

The Picture Plane

Two kinds of movements can be seen in this simple drawing: first, movements created by the direction and shape of the lines on the surface of the paper are seen by comparison to the horizontal and vertical edges of the picture plane; second, movements in space are seen as forms that appear to advance to, or recede from, the eye.

The relative depth of these lines is not seen on the flat, two-dimensional surface of the picture plane as an illusion, but is an optical, plastic reality. When the heavy line is thickened, it is seen immediately as closer to the eye, and the thinner line and coexisting spatial field are seen to be further away from the eye. As one dimension is changed, there is a reciprocal change in all the other dimensions in the composition. Hence, each line has a degree of innate energy relative to the others. In turn, the coexisting space is seen as an active participant or as a field with related energy.

The simple structure of the two lines within the limitations of the picture plane can be evaluated objectively by an experienced eye in terms of visual interest, movement, placement, and balance. The complex visual structure of a painting takes more time to evaluate, but the visual process is the same. Each element, as it is shaped, is seen as positive or negative in relation to the whole field of play.

Leonardo da Vinci often made pencil sketches of the human figure, varying his approach as he drew. In some places, his line was like a whisper, barely seen, receding from the eye; in other places it was dark and heavy, advancing to the eye. His line skipped over, was interrupted by, and fused into the space of the paper. He was extremely conscious of his white paper as a spatial field.

Movement

> Life does not exist without movement and movement does not exist without life. All movements are of a spatial nature. The continuation of movement throughout space is rhythm. Thereby rhythm is the expression of life in space.[4]
>
> —Hans Hofmann

I.4 Movement.

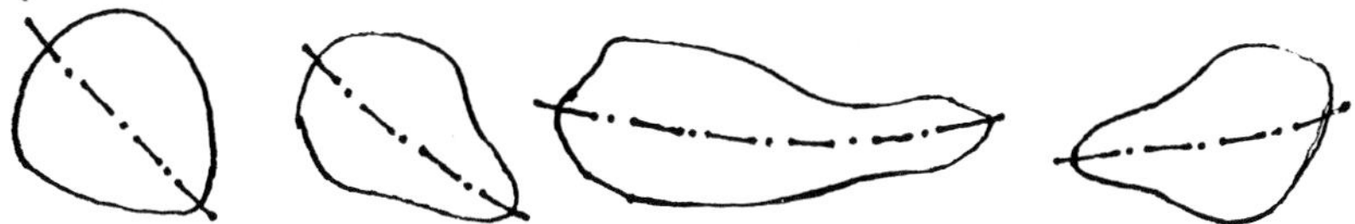

All forms have a major axis that subdivides equally their volume.

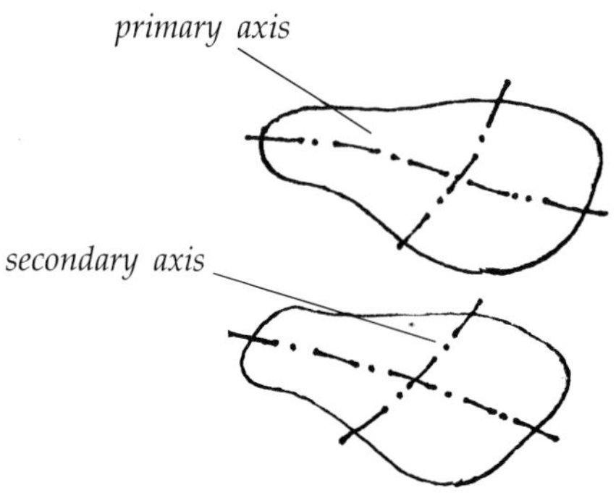

primary axis

secondary axis

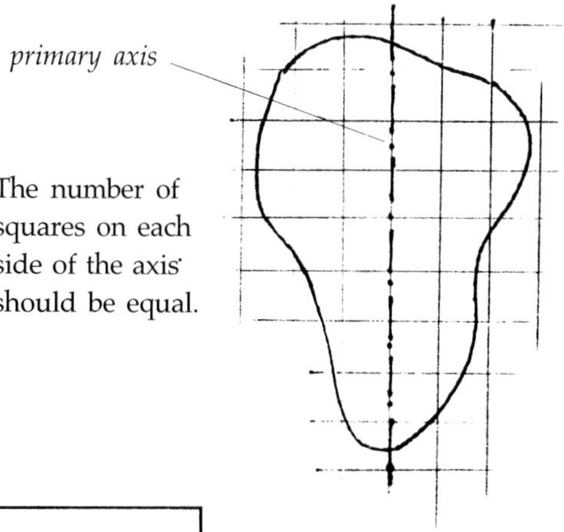

primary axis

The number of squares on each side of the axis should be equal.

As this form is limited by the confines of the picture plane, its coexisting space has a relative amount of energy. The small arrows illustrate where the space is compressed and has greater energy than that seen in the larger areas of space.

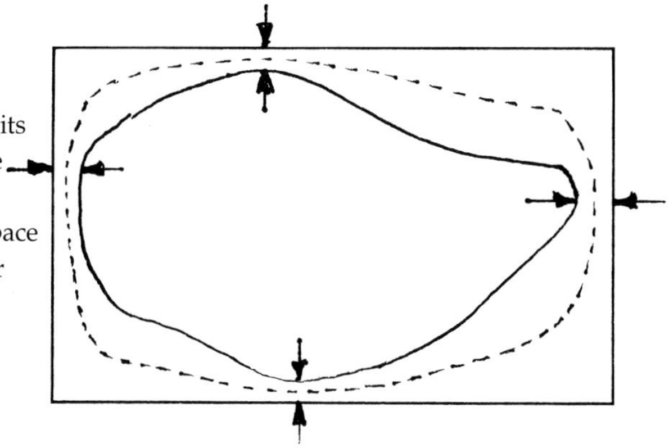

The dotted line shows the thrust line, or axis, of the surrounding space.

As any form is activated and perceived as energetic, the space that surrounds the form is also activated.

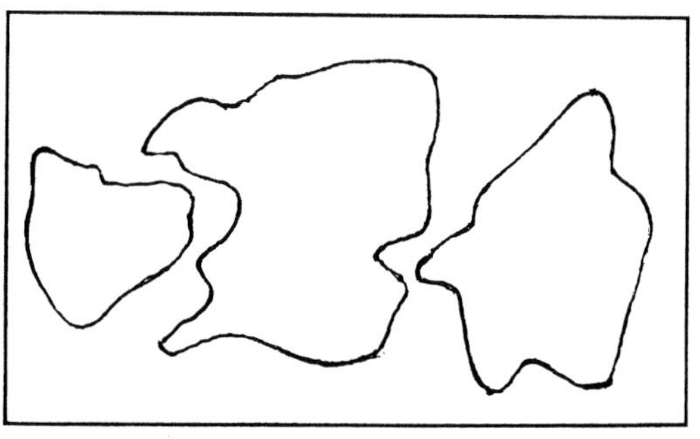

I.5 Axes in Organic Form.

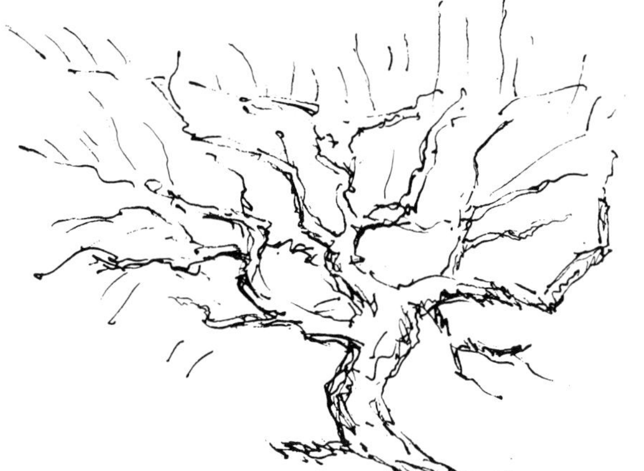

The thrust lines seen in this fruit tree follow the trunk and major branches.

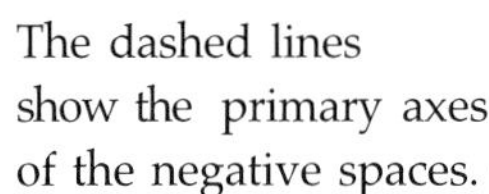

The dashed lines show the primary axes of the negative spaces.

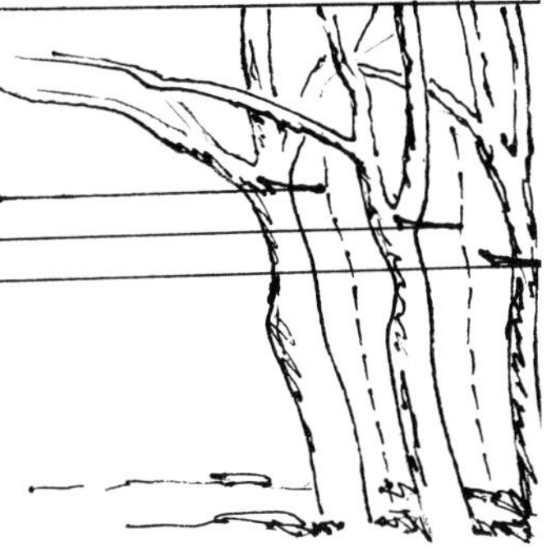

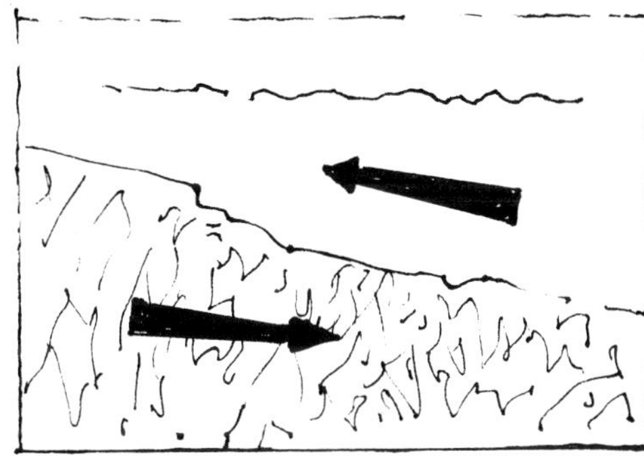

The large arrows show the inherent movement of these basic forms.

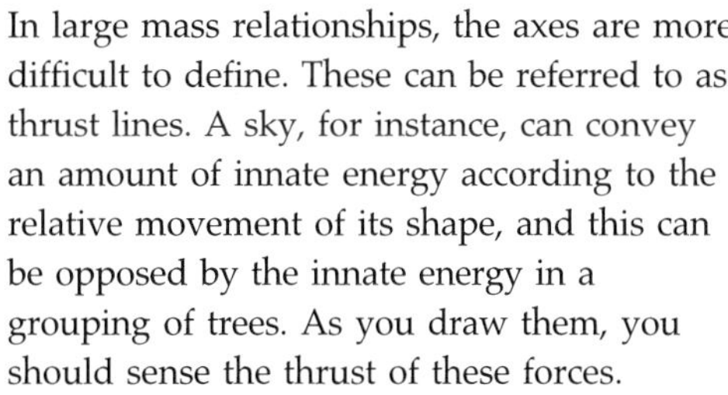

In large mass relationships, the axes are more difficult to define. These can be referred to as thrust lines. A sky, for instance, can convey an amount of innate energy according to the relative movement of its shape, and this can be opposed by the innate energy in a grouping of trees. As you draw them, you should sense the thrust of these forces.

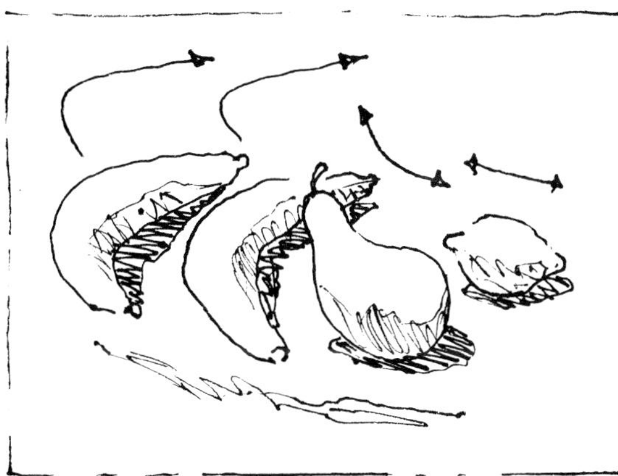

The curvilinear axes of the bananas on the left push to the right and are opposed by the axes of the pear and lemon.

I.6 Depth Characteristics.

The near shape, #1, is in front of #2 and #2 is in front of #3. The negative space, #4, is seen last. As the planes are shaded, the illusion of depth is increased. This is a principle used in cubist painting.

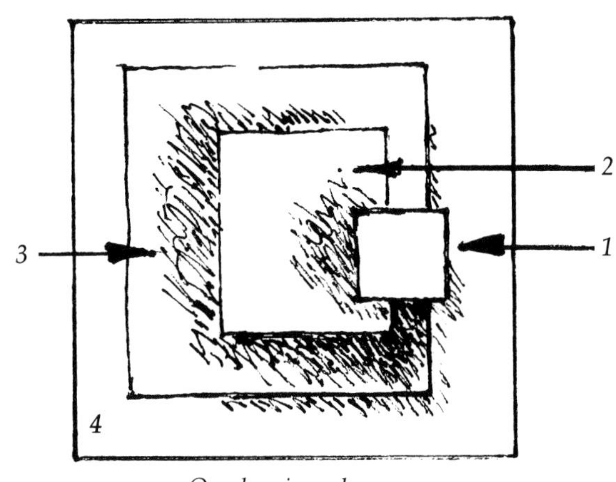

Overlapping planes

The drawing of the cylinder creates the illusion of volume, with its own inherent movement.

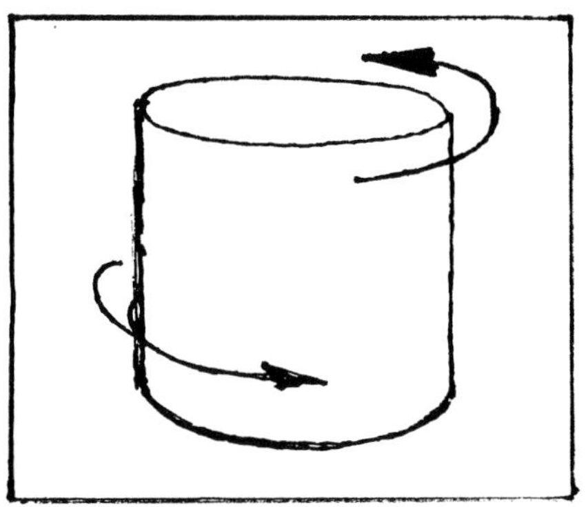

Form seen as volume

As the cylinder is shaded, using gradations from light to dark, the sense of its volume is increased. The negative space, in contrast, appears to be deeper.

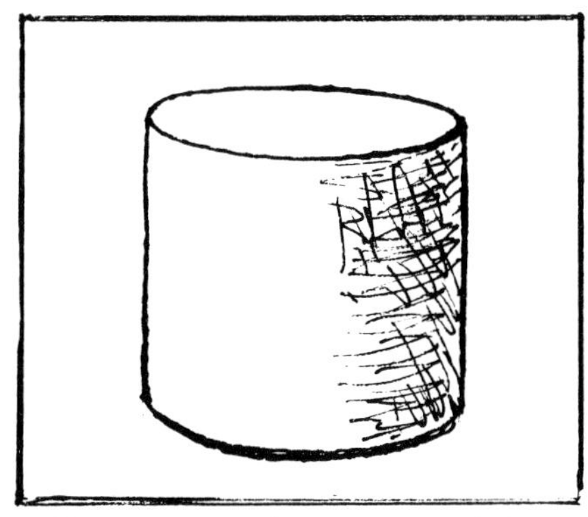

Form seen as volume using gradations

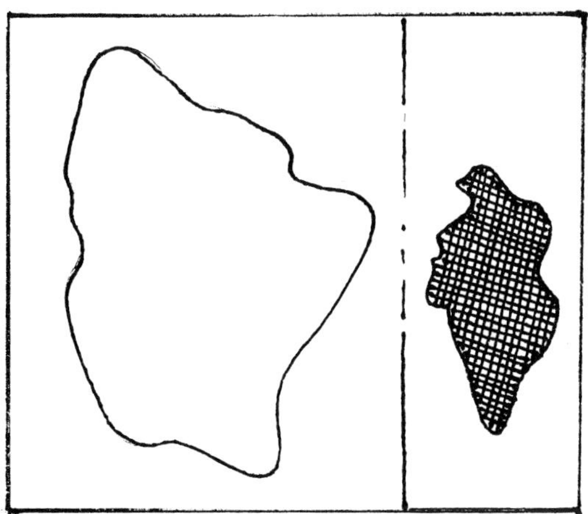

Contrasting size and shape

I.6 *continued.*

The smaller shape is seen first and is the primary positive. Because of its weight and startling contrast, it has greater energy and advances toward the eye. The large form is seen second and the space last. The principal movement in both the forms directs the eye toward the line that separates the background areas.

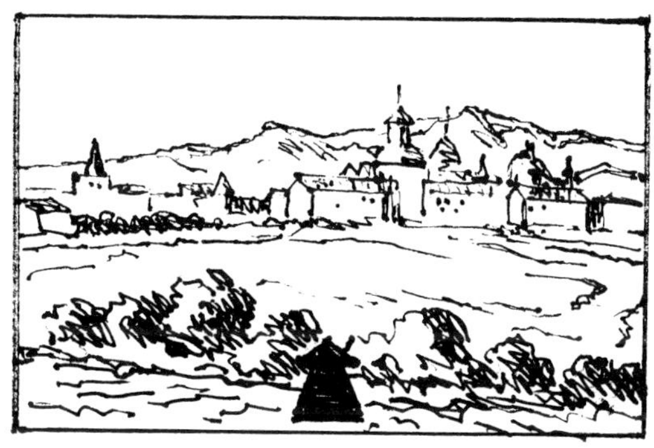

Aerial perspective

The eye enters the picture at the broad gravitational base and then moves to the lighter lines used in the distant buildings and mountains. Moisture and dust in the air tend to obscure distant objects. The foreground is heavier and in focus.

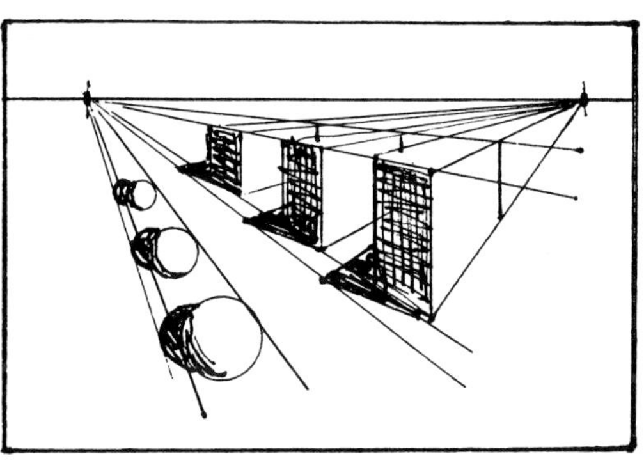

True perspective

An object gets smaller as the distance between it and the eye increases. The planes, or flat surfaces, have two dimensions—length and width—creating a sense of depth. The shadows in both the cubes and spheres increase the sense of volume.

Since our spatial intuitions embody a sense of gravity and the related criteria of balance, the eye is able to distinguish movement in any form by means of comparison, always toward or away from the vertical and horizontal.

Every form has a primary axis that is its structural backbone. This is the centerline of its volume. The relative movement of this axis establishes the innate life in the form. These axes are easy to define in linear forms such as tree trunks, branches, narrow clouds, and so forth. The major axis in a pine tree, for instance, is its trunk, which is seen as a long, vertical movement. The axis in an apple tree is shorter and markedly twisted, conveying greater innate energy.

Forms also have secondary axes or thrust lines. The secondary axis in a simple, oval-shaped volume, such as an egg, is the centerline through the width of the volume. The large branches in a tree can be seen as secondary axes growing out of the primary axis of the trunk.

A classic figure pose that is often used in life drawing is referred to as counterposture—a standing figure, twisted, so that the planes of the shoulders and hips are seen at divergent angles. In this pose, the primary axis can be perceived as the changing vertical centerline of the torso, and the two angles through the shoulders and hips are the secondary axes. The direction of any axis can always be doublechecked by using a stick of charcoal or a brush handle as a sighting device aligned with the axis of the form and then transferred to the paper, making sure that the alignment is retained.

In many of Matisse's quick sketches and drawings, there are unerased guidelines. He drew the large primary shapes first, very freely. He said, "The hand is but an extension of sensitivity and intelligence. The more it is supple,the more it is obedient. Never should the servant girl become the mistress."[5]

Here is a simple finger-tracing exercise to evaluate relative movement. With your index finger, trace the contours of all the major forms in your drawing or painting, using, as much as possible, a constant rate of speed. You will discover that the rate of speed will vary according to the relative simplicity or complexity of the forms. Long, straight, or gradually curved contours will increase the speed of the

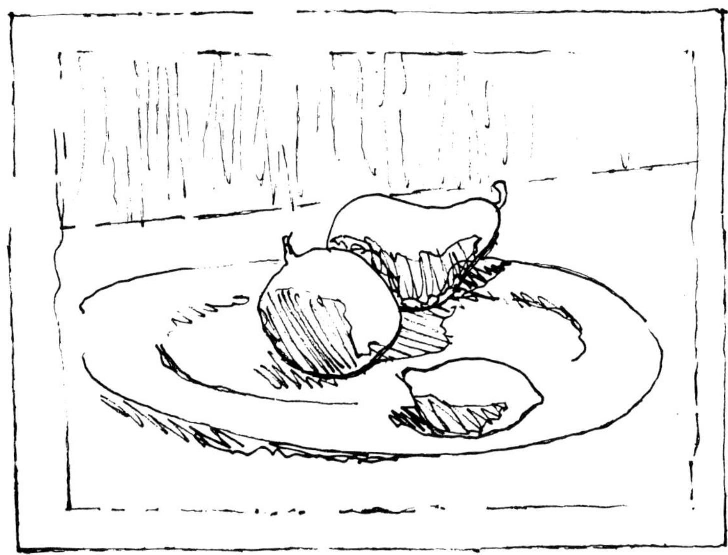

I.7 Three Kinds of Movement.

Three kinds of movement are seen in this sketch:

1. Pictorial depth is created by overlapping planes. The fruit is on top of the plate and the plate is on top of the table. The lemon is in front of the apple and the apple is in front of the pear. The tabletop is in front of the background.

2. Pictorial depth is also created by shading, or gradating tonal values to increase the sense of volume in the forms.

3. Surface movement is created by the direction of all the forms as they are perceived on the surface of the picture plane. Each line has its own related energy and is seen by comparison with all the other lines and their juxtaposition to the horizontal and vertical perimeters of the picture plane. Negative space, seen as the white paper, feeds in and out between the interrupted lines.

The eye must intuitively assess the axes of the three pieces of fruit, the plate, the tabletop, and the background.

I.8

Paul Cézanne, *La Montagne Sainte-Victoire,* 1886–88, oil on canvas, 66.8cm. x 92.3cm.

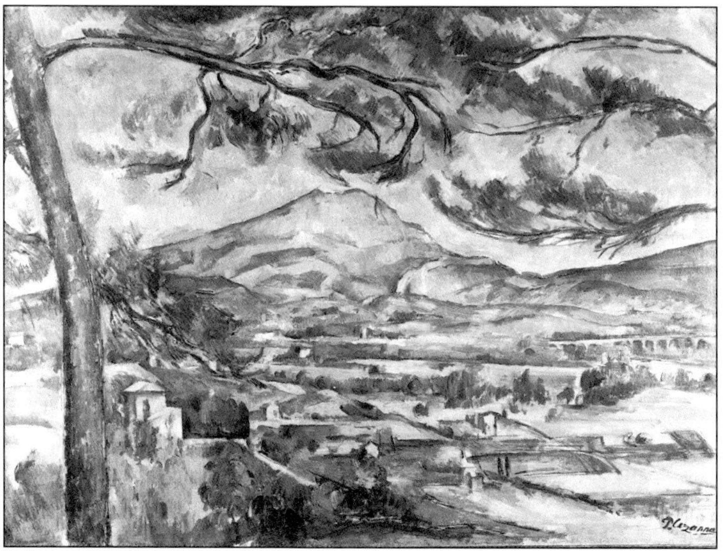

The Courtauld Institute of Art, University of London.

Cézanne leads the observer's eye in a movement sequence by his placement of planes, lines, and color, beginning with the tree trunk in the lower left, then upward, following the branches into the painting. The tree branches in the upper right effectively counter these movements by directing the eye into the painting and pushing it rhythmically through contour and mass relationships to the apex of the mountain, which can be seen as the primary focal point in the painting. In effect, all the movements in the painting are informally directed toward this point.

I.9

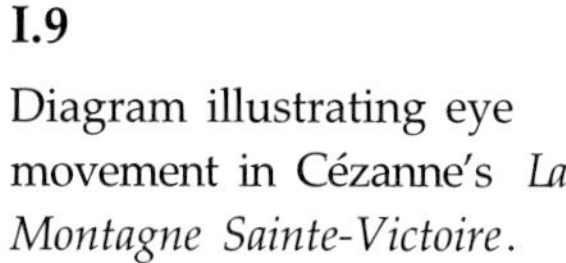

Diagram illustrating eye movement in Cézanne's *La Montagne Sainte-Victoire*.

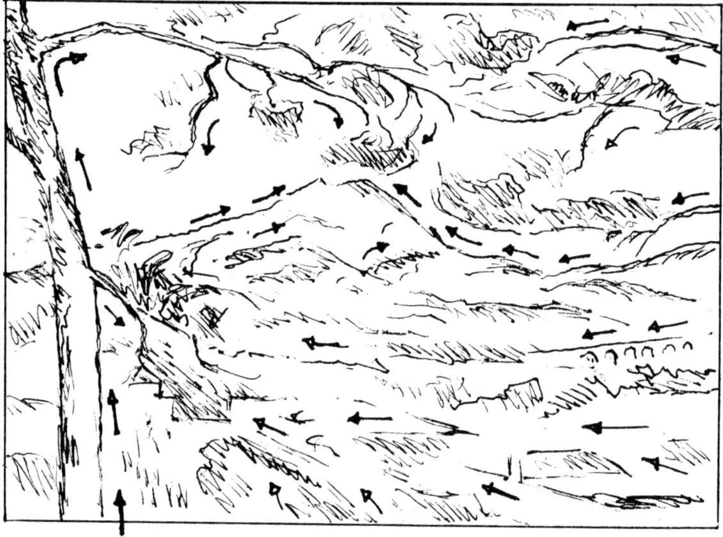

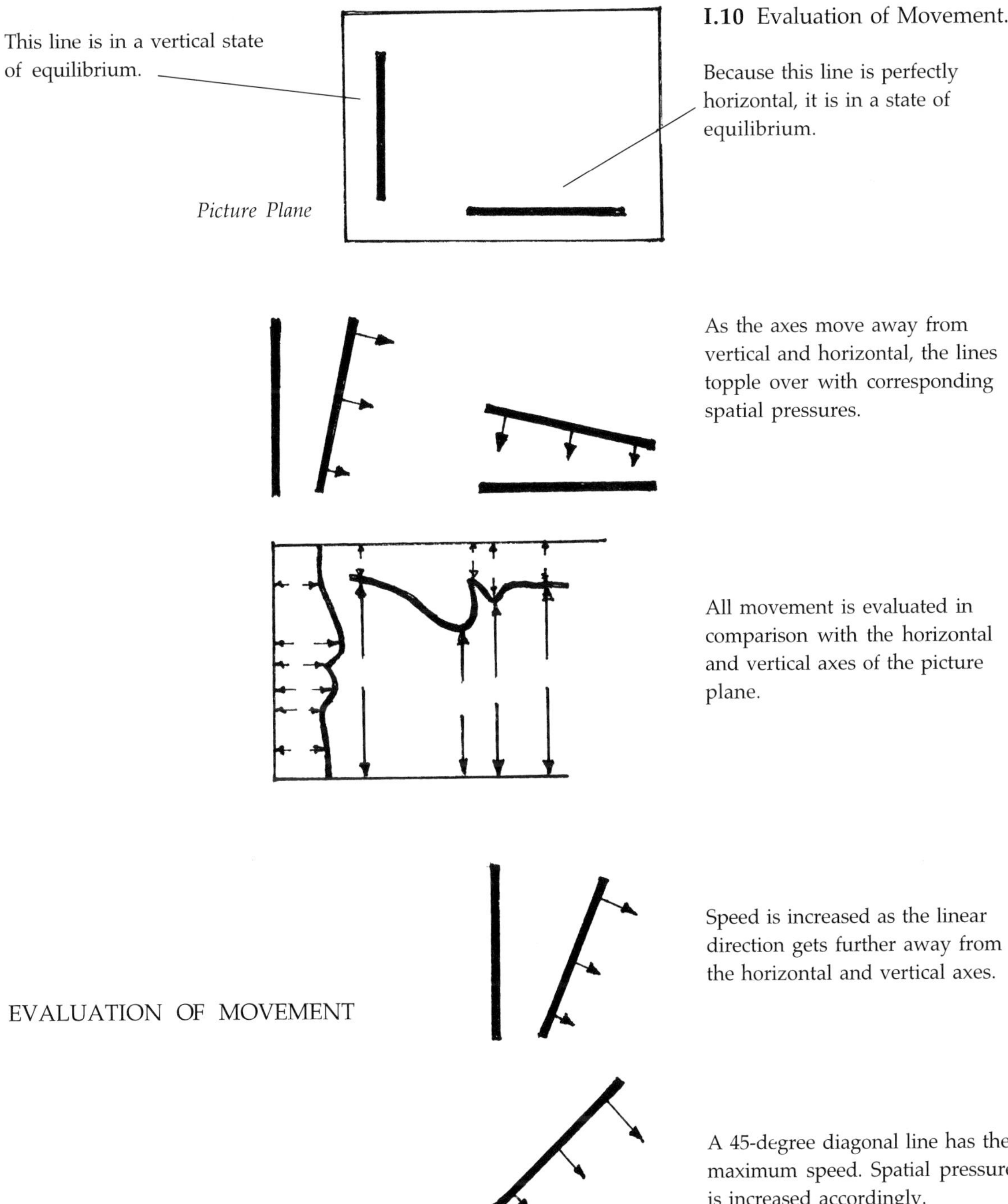

I.10 Evaluation of Movement.

Because this line is perfectly horizontal, it is in a state of equilibrium.

As the axes move away from vertical and horizontal, the lines topple over with corresponding spatial pressures.

All movement is evaluated in comparison with the horizontal and vertical axes of the picture plane.

Speed is increased as the linear direction gets further away from the horizontal and vertical axes.

A 45-degree diagonal line has the maximum speed. Spatial pressure is increased accordingly.

I.10 *continued.*

A curve has speeds that vary according to its spatial relationship to gravity as well as to its degree of simplicity or complexity.

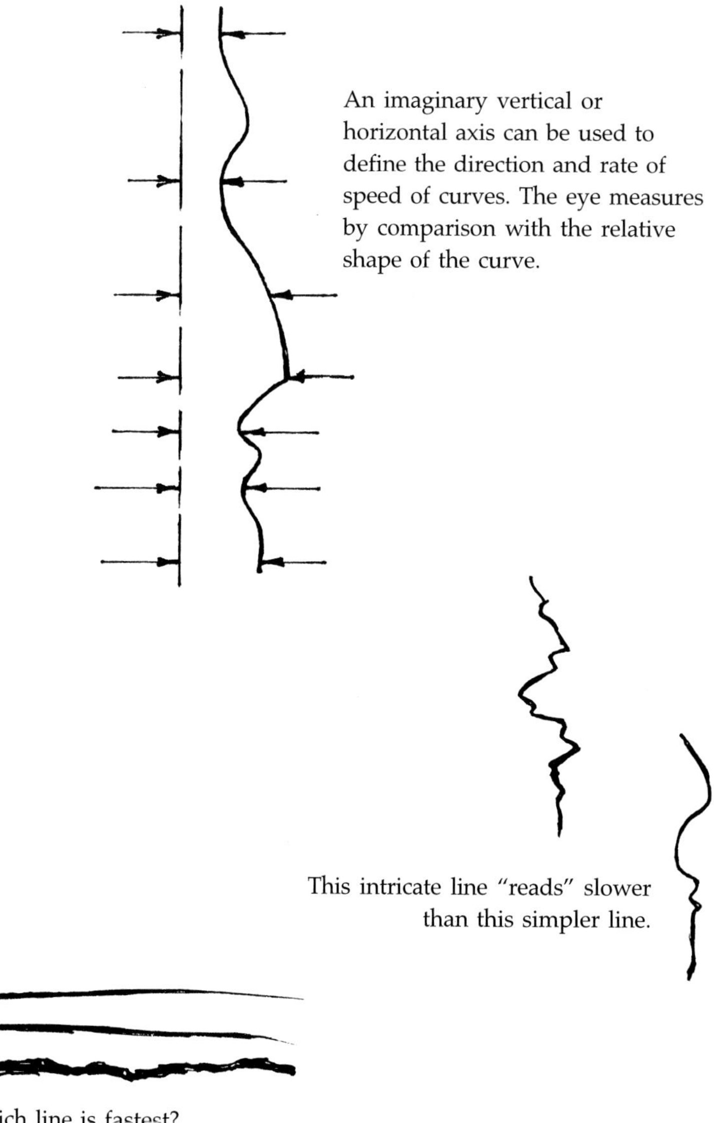

An imaginary vertical or horizontal axis can be used to define the direction and rate of speed of curves. The eye measures by comparison with the relative shape of the curve.

This intricate line "reads" slower than this simpler line.

Which line is fastest?
Which line is slowest?

Because of the complexity of proportional interchange between different kinds of movement and different rates of speed, the measurements of these differences are made by intuitive comparisons based on one's sense of gravity.

The artist who has mastered drawing is, in fact, controlling the observer's eye with various rates of speed in all the elements of the work.

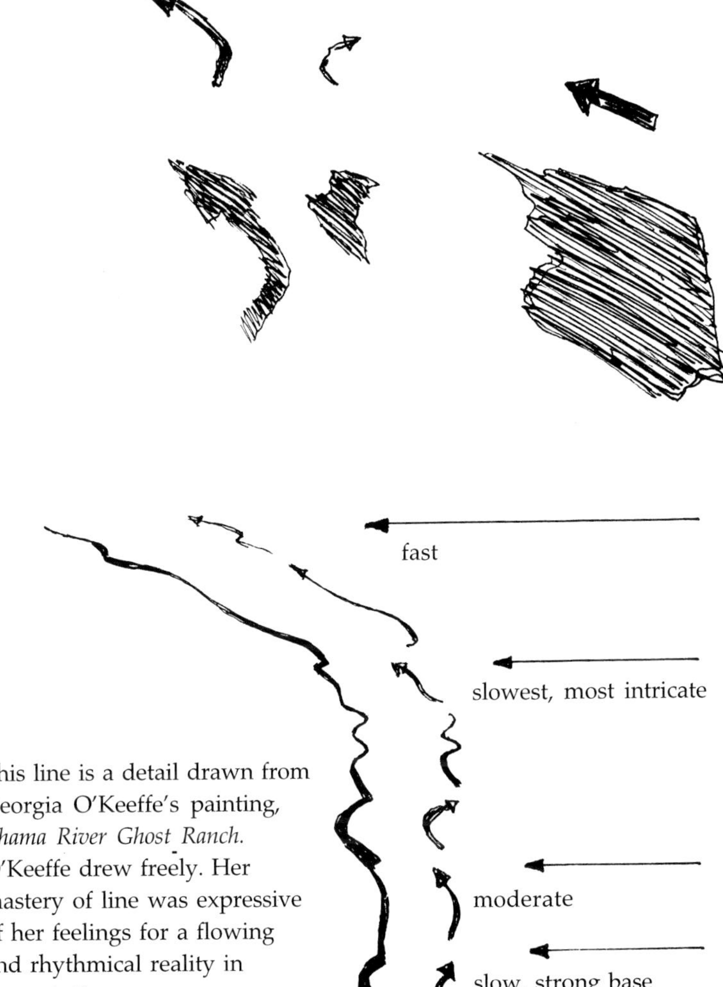

I.10 *continued.*

The arrows show the movements of these massive, energetic forms. They are copied from John Marin's painting, *Movement: The Sea and Pertaining Thereto.*

The arrows show how the movement of the line varies in its different directions.

Gravity is an essential factor in shaping line as it pertains both to controlling eye movement and to an innate response to the internal force of line. The eye is attracted first to the heavy bottom of the line and then moves to the top.

This line is a detail drawn from Georgia O'Keeffe's painting, *Chama River Ghost Ranch.* O'Keeffe drew freely. Her mastery of line was expressive of her feelings for a flowing and rhythmical reality in her painting.

I.11

Henri Matisse, drawing from *Cahiers d'Art*, 1935.

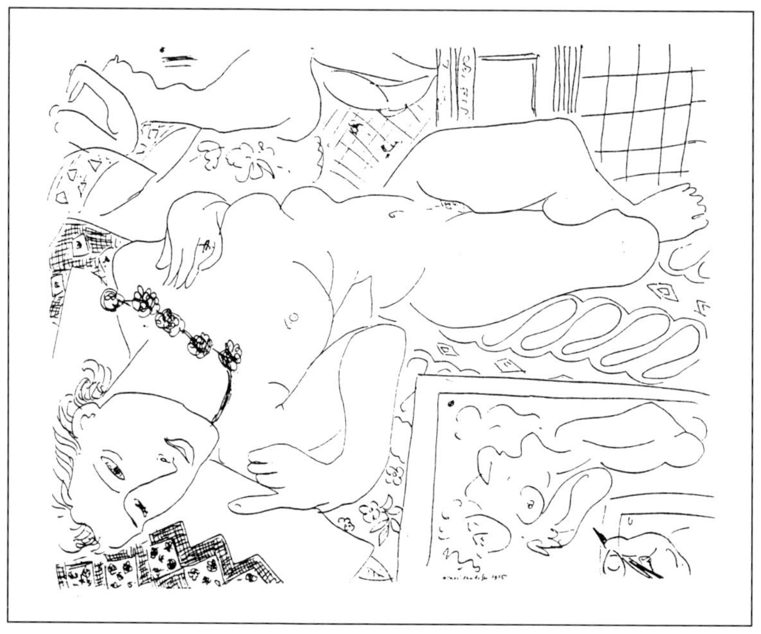

"In determining the vertical direction, the plumb line along with its opposite, the horizontal, forms the compass of the draftsman. Ingres used plumb lines; in his studies of standing figures note the unerased line that passes through the sternum and the internal anklebone of the leg that bears the weight.

Around this fictive line 'the arabesque' evolves. I have derived a constant benefit from my use of the plumb line. The vertical is my spirit. It helps me to define precisely the direction of lines, and in quick sketches I never indicate a curve, that of a branch in a landscape, for example, without being aware of its relationship to the vertical. My curves are not mad."[6]

—Henri Matisse

movement, whereas highly intricate contours slow down the rate of speed. These relative speeds are correlated to the way that the eye perceives movement in the composition. Ideally, there should be a continuity in the rate of speed, that is, a harmonic balance between all of the movements in the painting. Disparities in a composition are revealed by distinct differences in the rate of speed. Corrections can be made by simplifying overly complex forms that take the eye out of an overall rhythmic flow.

Balance and Its Significance

We know that a material object has weight. Its comparative lightness or heaviness is a judgment that we can instinctively approximate according to our knowledge of the material, i.e., space is airy and light, salt water weighs 64 pounds per cubic foot, and lead, one of the heaviest materi-

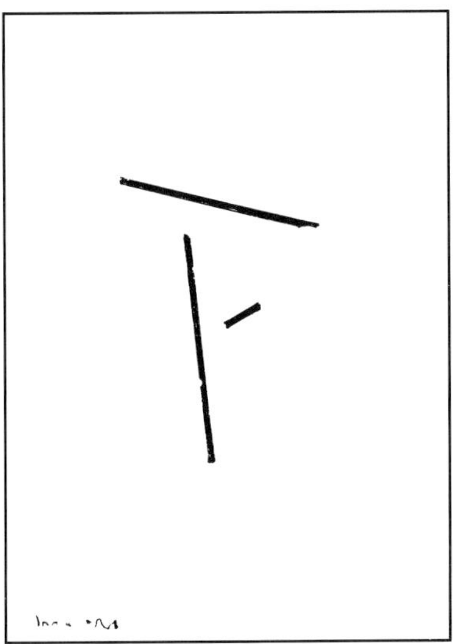

I.12 Fundamentals of Balance.

The eye must account for proportions of the lines and how they are shaped, the corresponding proportions of the negative space, and movement of the line, including both surface and depth characteristics. The signature in the lower left corner is used as a counterbalance. Because the top line is slightly diagonal, it demands counterbalancing with diagonal lines.

als, weighs 700 pounds per cubic foot. All objects have an innate amount of energy that is inherent to their size, shape, and weight, and to their position in space. Very simply, this is true because weight is the measure of the force with which an object is pulled toward the center of the earth by gravity. If gravitation were suddenly turned off like an electric light, the universe would fall apart. Our sense of gravity is constantly at work and our equilibrium depends on it.

In picture making, balance is equally important. Without balancing all of the elements that make up the whole, the work appears chaotic and its meaning is diminished. Balance is the means to control the relativity of form and space, to weigh their proportions by comparison, to establish an equilibrium that is essential for a conclusive and harmonious result.

Try a simple experiment to demonstrate the basic principles of visual balance. Place an eighteen-by-twenty-four-inch sheet of newspad on your easel in an upright, absolutely vertical position. Draw a straight line with charcoal, no more than ten inches long, in any direction anywhere you like in the picture plane. Close your eyes and draw a second straight line on the newspad—anywhere, but do not cross over the first line. Stand back from the easel ten feet or

I.13 Diagrams of balance.

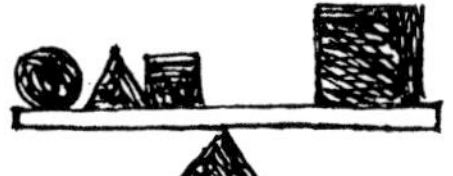

The seesaw equation Balance is instinctive Gravity is always a factor	=	The eye weighs forms and makes judgments by comparison

Awareness of space is essential.

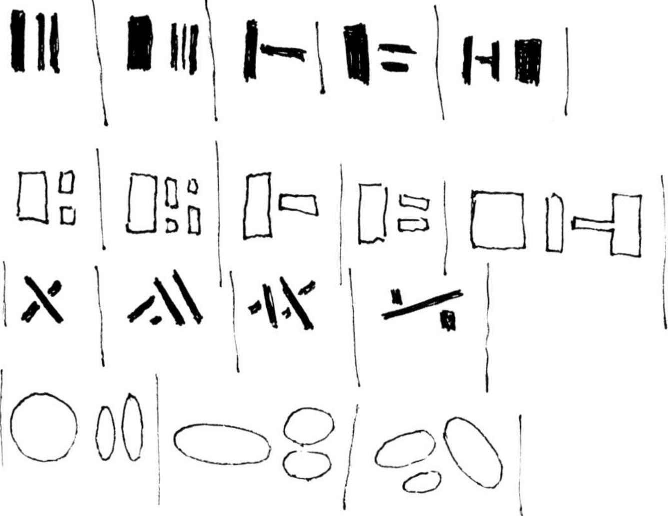

The simplest kinds of oppositions

The principles are the same.

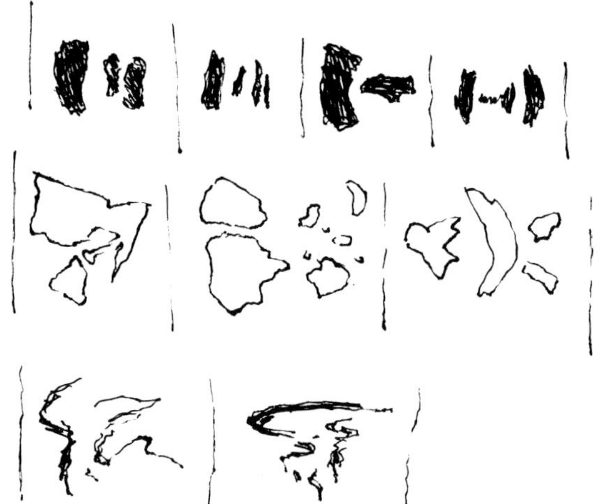

Translated into organic forms

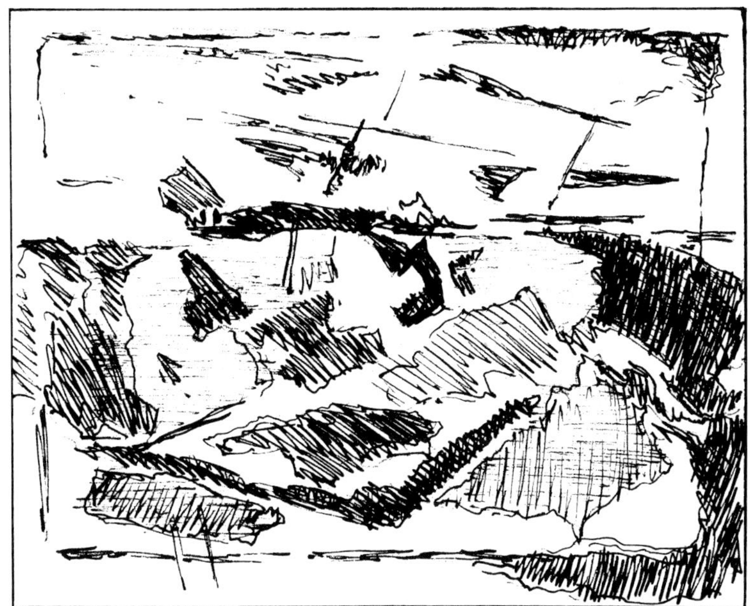

A sketch of John Marin's painting, *Movement: The Sea and Pertaining Thereto,* to show the basic forms.

I.14

As he painted, Marin suggested the essence of each form in an imaginative and simplified way. He often used lines as a way to counterbalance the internal forces in forms as well as to suggest varying planes, breaking up the larger shapes of sky and water. Clouds, water, rocks, and trees are seen as geometric wedges, blurs, and squiggles to satisfy his expressive needs in each painting.

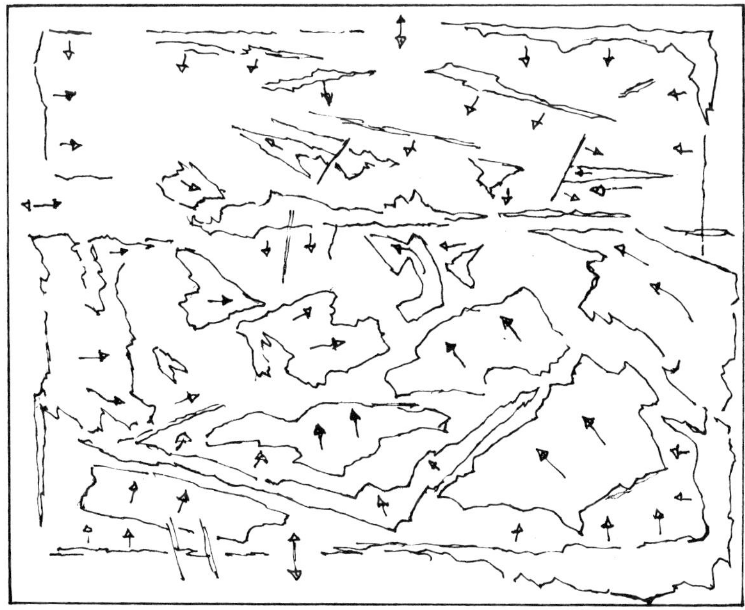

The arrows in this sketch show how Marin balanced his energetic forms with opposing forms; in his words, "great forces are at play." He regarded the picture plane as a spatial environment within which all the elements in his composition could be charged with varying degrees of rest and unrest. As he painted, he thought of space as a viable form that had its own indigenous energy.

Note how the larger, heavier forms toward the bottom of the picture push upward opposing the forces of gravity.

I.15 Seeing Forms In Tension.

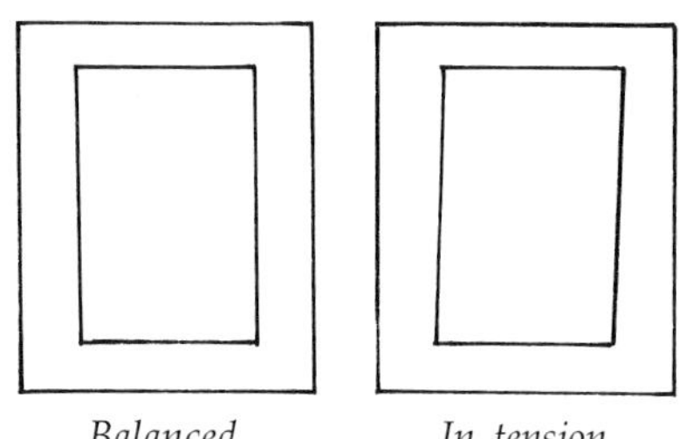

The left-hand form is perfectly centered (static). The right-hand form leans toward the right side, increasing visual interest.

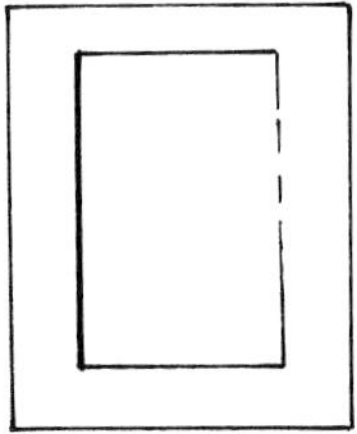

This form is perfectly centered, but a heavier line is used on the left side.

more and study briefly the relationship of the lines and how they are positioned in the negative space of the picture plane. Now, quickly, without thinking, draw a third line in the picture, counterbalancing the first two lines. This line must be drawn intuitively, because any kind of conscious evaluation as to its placement will negate a perfect balance of all three lines in the spatial field. What you will discover, regardless of your experience, is that as long as you think of the lines as weight relationships in space, you will balance them with an immediate, intuitive response.

Tension

A drawing or painting that is slightly out of balance can be described as being in a state of tension. Because the eye naturally seeks an equilibrium between all elements in the work, there is a sense of the composition being tilted one way or another that gives a sense of unrest to the eye. The result often magnifies the feeling of inner life in the work.

Creative tension requires a perceptive response to the structure of the composition and the inherent demands of all its elements seen as weight relationships and opposing directional forces. Effective tension, of course, should not be confused with the instability in the work of some artists who inadvertently upset the balance and unity of their composition.

Chinese calligraphers were concerned with many qualities as they developed their figures, including light and heavy, condensed and dispersed, strong and weak, dry and wet, fast and slow, sparse and crowded, fat and lean, thick and thin, and connected and disconnected. These may also be interpreted in terms of balance, symmetry, tension, contrast, harmony, proportion, confrontation, and yielding.[7]

Static and Organic Forms

A static form is a symmetrical, manmade form devoid of inner life. Circles, squares, and equilateral triangles are static forms. In contrast, an organic form has a sense of

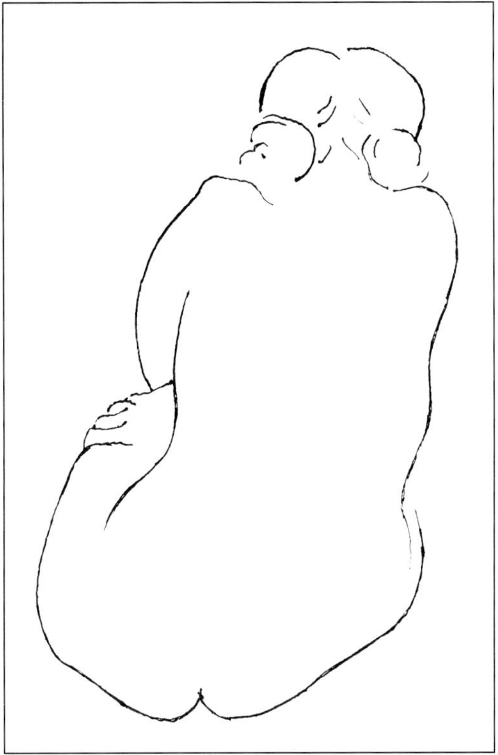

I.16
Sketch of Henri Matisse's *Seated Nude, Back Turned*, 1914. Lithograph (stone), 19¾" x 13".

Matisse increased visual interest by drawing the nude overbalanced toward the upper right (in tension).

inner life and is asymmetrical. All the forms seen in nature are organic forms. There are no perfectly straight lines seen in nature, or perfect circles or squares.

Any static form can be evaluated by comparing one side to the other by drawing a ghost line through the center of its shape. When the eye is attracted to each side simultaneously, the form appears uninteresting.

Any change on one side of the shape produces asymmetry in the whole form. The form, then, is easier to perceive as a whole and gains a sense of inner life. It has become an organic form. A ghost line can be used to evaluate symmetrical qualities in both the positive form and the form of negative space.

Any kind of alteration in a drawing that deviates from static, manmade qualities can be seen as a proportional

I.17

Diagram of Andrew Wyeth's *Watch Dog*, 1970.

The dog is the primary focal point and attracts the eye first, creating a strong opposition to the geometric pattern of the open window first, and walls and floor, second.

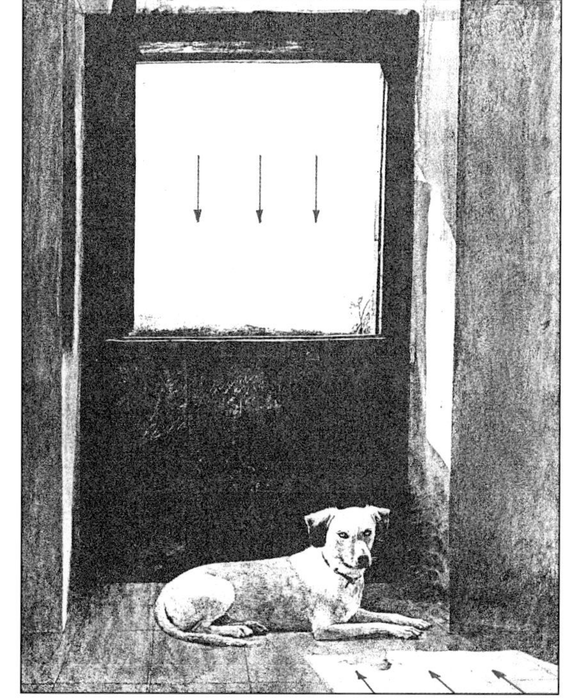

The painting pulls slightly to the lower left and is in tension.

Thrust line used as counterbalance to triangles.

Diagram of Richard Diebenkorn's *Interior with View of Ocean*, 1957.

The large triangles of light on the tabletop and floor are counterbalanced by the large windows. The curvilinear forms of the chairs can be seen as focal points that provide interest and help balance the composition.

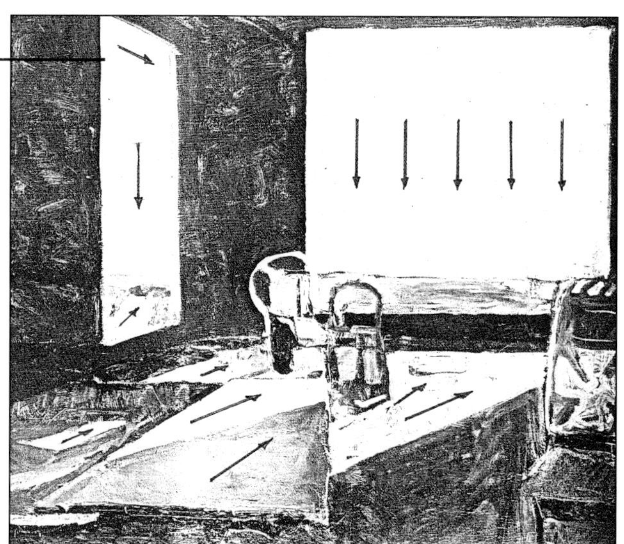

This painting pulls to the right and is slightly out of balance and is in tension.

Focal points can be used for balance. (Note the similarity between these two compositions.)

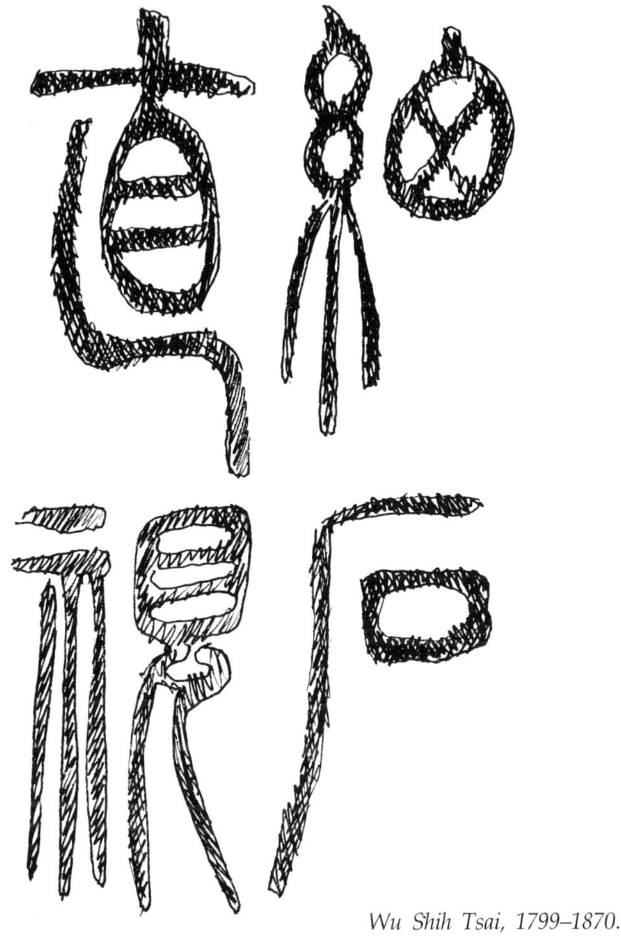

Wu Shih Tsai, 1799–1870.

I.18

This figure opposes the figure; it reads from left to right (left side is heavy), and is in tension.

This figure opposes the figure. This figure needs a stop. It reads left to right. It is out of balance because the lower right is in tension.

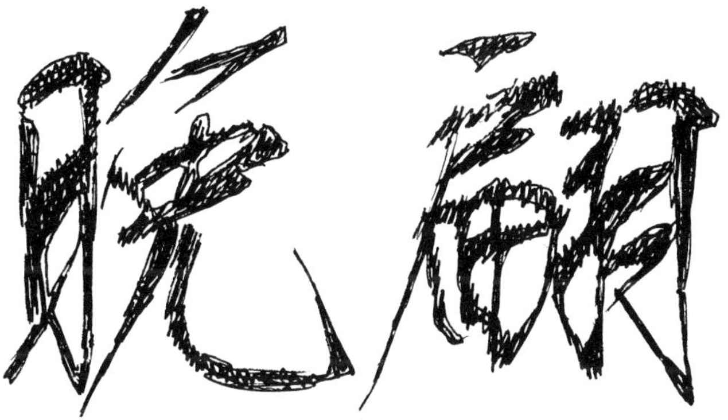

These figures are in tension. The left-hand figure opposes the right; it reads toward the left. The right-hand figure is slightly heavier.

Emperor Hui Tsung, Sung Dynasty, 1002–1135. His calligraphy is completely personal.

change that has intrinsic value to the whole form. A perfect curve, for example, is a static shape and the slightest change toward flatness or to a reverse curve or to a tighter arc produces innate life in its shape as well as in its accompanying space. The slightest nuance of thinness or thickness in a line produces life in both the line and its accompanying space.

Flat surfaces are static. Almost flat surfaces that have a subtle interchange of tonal values have an inner life because they breathe, or create an illusion of varying depths to the eye.

Negative space is activated visually by the innate energy in an organic form and conversely has less energy when seen next to a quieter, geometric form.

I.19 Organic Stone and Leaf Forms.

The most subtle interchange of proportions produces a liveliness in each form and its accompanying space.

I.20 An Analysis of Organic Forms.

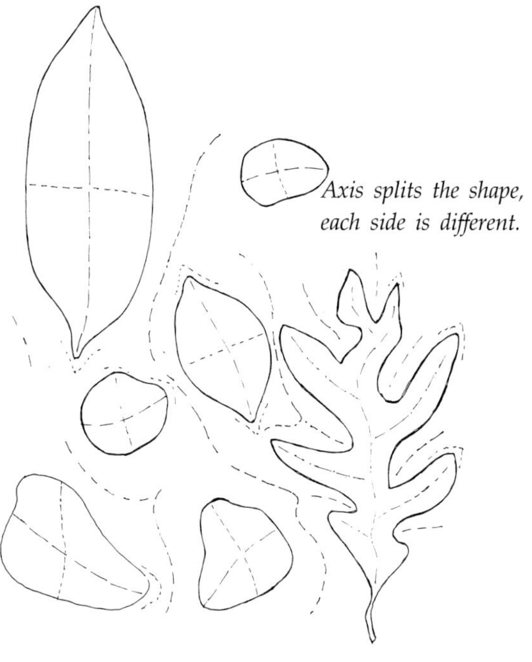

KEY
_ _ _ _ primary axis
---------secondary axis

I.21 Nature is Our Teacher.

There are no static forms in nature. Each kind of form has its own distinctive shape that is expressive of its function. The disparate qualities in each form impart both uniqueness and beauty.

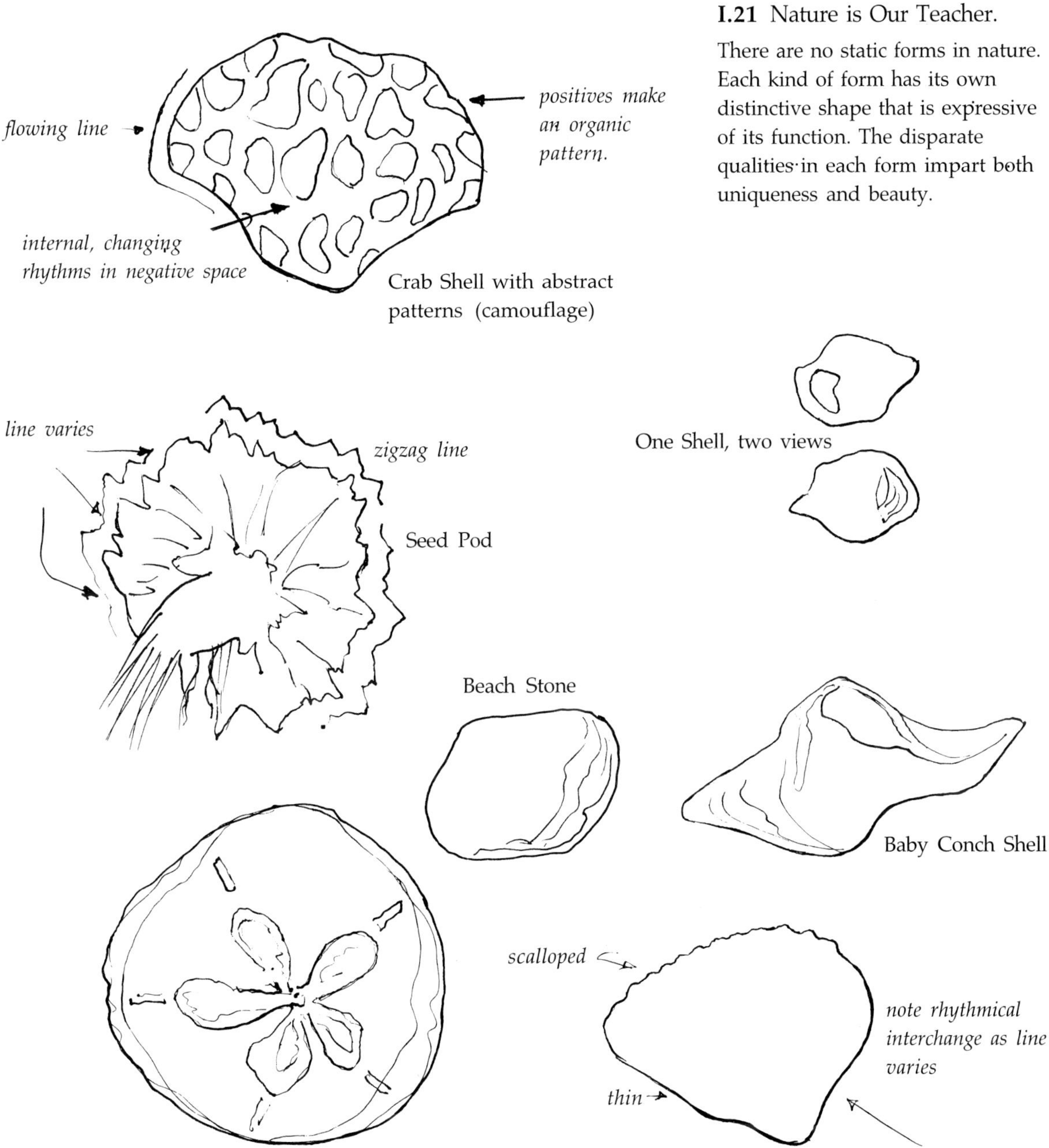

Sand Dollar, reverse side

Baby Scallop Shell

I.22

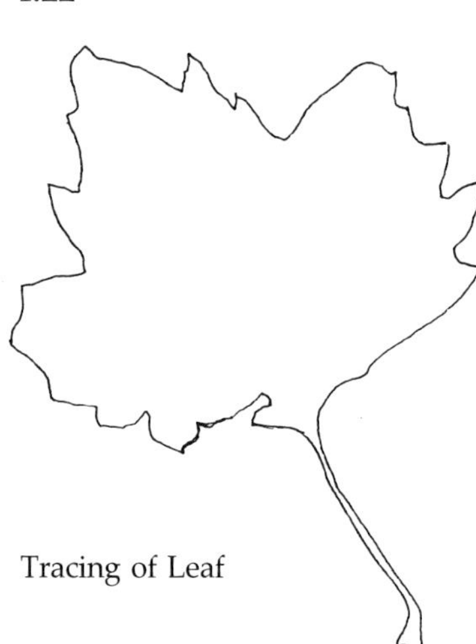

Tracing of Leaf

A stunning organic shape. Note how right side is completely different from the left side.

To demonstrate the relationship between positive form and negative space, trace the outline of various forms found in nature, such as a few different kinds of leaves and shells, on a sheet of paper. As you trace a leaf, you will discover how one side differs from the other side. There will be a number of small differences in angles and curves, and the veins in the leaf, which denote the principal axes in its form, seen as subdivisions, also vary.

One principle to remember in drawing is that the slightest variation in a positive produces a proportional interchange in the negative; the changes from one side to the other permit seeing the leaf as an organic whole form and the space surrounding the form is equally alive. The primary axis in the leaf is its major vein or backbone, which is the thrust line for the placement or basic movement of the leaf within the picture plane; the smaller veins are seen as minor axes. In the same respect, the smaller shapes are seen as details that articulate the overall mass shape of the leaf.

Perception and Vision: How to Look at Form

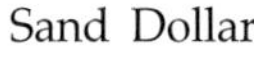

Sand Dollar

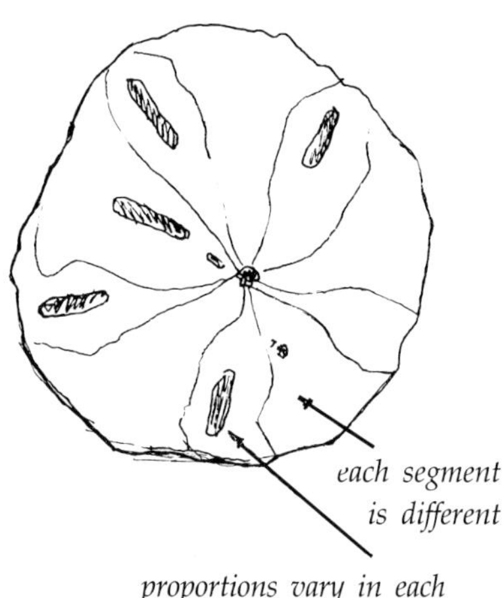

Aerial perspective is a result of the fact that objects seen at a distance are affected by the atmosphere, and are out of focus to the eye. They appear blurred and are generally lighter in tone and cooler in hue (bluer) than objects near to the observer's eye, which in turn appear sharper, in focus, with brighter, warmer colors.

Squinting, with one eye closed and the dominant eye almost closed, rules out reflected light and greatly simplifies seeing form in its entirety. To find your dominant eye, hold a pencil vertically in front of you at eye level. With both eyes open, line up the tip of the pencil with a distant object. Close one eye at a time. Whichever eye is open when the pencil remains lined up with the object is your dominant eye.

Stereoscopic vision is the ability to judge depth produced by the slight differences between the images seen by the right and the left eye. Each half of the brain receives an image from each eye and the brain forms a single image from the four images received. When looking at a distant object, the axes of the eyes are almost parallel; when looking at an object close at hand, the eyes turn toward each other. With a conscious effort, it is possible, when looking at a distant view, to shift your eyes from a natural focus to an out-of-focus mode. Images appear less distinct. At first this seems unnatural because the normal way of seeing is to focus on specifics. The out-of-focus mode is referred to as parallel vision and it enables us to see the relationship of movements, colors, and shapes in context of the whole field of play without any one thing being more important than the next. It is a form of "squinting," which makes the picture whole without reducing the light, as occurs when one is squinting.

Neil Welliver, the contemporary Maine landscape painter, described parallel vision as "the act of looking at the other person's right ear with your left eye and their left ear with your right eye." Welliver relies on parallel vision ninety percent of the time as he paints, and the other ten percent on focusing his eyes to specific parts of his painting. He has said that he literally needs an hour or so to come back to a normal focus after a day in the studio.[8]

Line Drawing

Any line drawing has its own indigenous characteristics. The lines can be thick or thin, dark or light, hard or soft, blurred or lost. Lines can be angled, curved, fast or slow, scribbled, corkscrewed, or rhythmical. Each line as it is drawn should be seen distinctly in its relationship to its accompanying space.

Each approach to drawing should be regarded as having its own distinct limitations. A neutral line drawing, for example, can be distinctive because the artist limits himself to a specific structure, or the artist chooses to work with a lost and found line, or possibly with thick and thin, interrupted lines. This does not mean that one cannot mix one style of drawing with another—far from it—for there are no distinct rules; but by recognizing and limiting one's choices in a specific drawing, as well as intuitively understanding its limitations, the finished drawing will have

I.23 Analysis of Line.

A straight line, drawn with a ruler, that has no variance in its thickness can be called a neutral line; it is geometric, manmade, and continuous or unbroken.

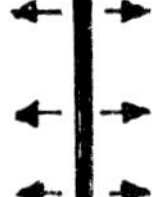

The energy in its surrounding space is uniform, which means spatial pressure is evenly distributed. This produces a static relationship between the positive and negative spaces.

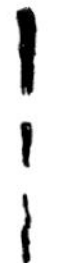

When a straight line varies in thickness, the energy distribution in both positive and negative space varies accordingly. When seen as a weight, the heavier part of the line advances to the eye. There is a corresponding visual push and pull in this line because it is an organic form.

A thin line appears as a light weight, which means it is seen spatially as a relatively weak form of energy or one that barely projects from the surface of the paper.

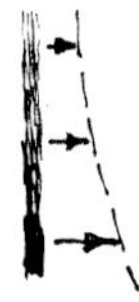

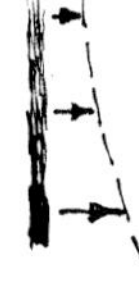

In contrast, a broad, massive line that is drawn from very light to very dark produces an energy curve. The darkest part is the heaviest and most active. This is an organic line.

A broken line is interrupted by space. If this kind of line is used to illustrate a contour of a form, the eye can move into space from the form. Broken lines can be used effectively to produce organic qualities, to slow the viewer's eye movement, and to unite the positive form with its surrounding negative space.

greater expressive force than a drawing that is indiscriminately handled.

Drawing any kind of form well makes the line come alive in its relation to space. Inadvertent repetition of contours, or of any of the proportional interchange that shapes the whole, creates static, lifeless forms. The development of an ability to perceive fully integrated, organic relationships is more important than developing your ability to copy form.

One of the problems of drawing well is to find your own pace—fast and spontaneous, yet slow enough so that your eyes can perceive each line in context to the whole.

Generally, the way you draw from a subject should be intuitive. The entire process of drawing is based on seeing the form wholly and with emotion. The line is shaped because of a dual concentration on the subject and the paper, without any conscious thought or planning. Lines, then, as they are drawn, are not a result of any form of intellectual design that would constrict one's personal feeling for the subject.

The artist's specific approach to drawing (such as using a neutral line), however, is prescribed in one's mind; it is, in fact, a distinct way of seeing. From this perception, the work of creative drawing begins, with feelings of one's vision based on intuitive response.

Tonal Drawing

Tonal values are simplified in two ways. They are perceived as weight relationships where each tone has a relative weight according to its relative lightness or darkness as well as to its size. A brilliant white leaps forward from a black background, or similarly a black advances to the eye when seen against a white background. Tones are seen as positive or negative. Furthermore, tones are simplified by squinting at them. This process is used over and over again in order to see form in its essence.

All forms in nature have relative densities that are indigenous to their tonal characteristics. Light either is refracted back to the eye or it is absorbed in the substance.

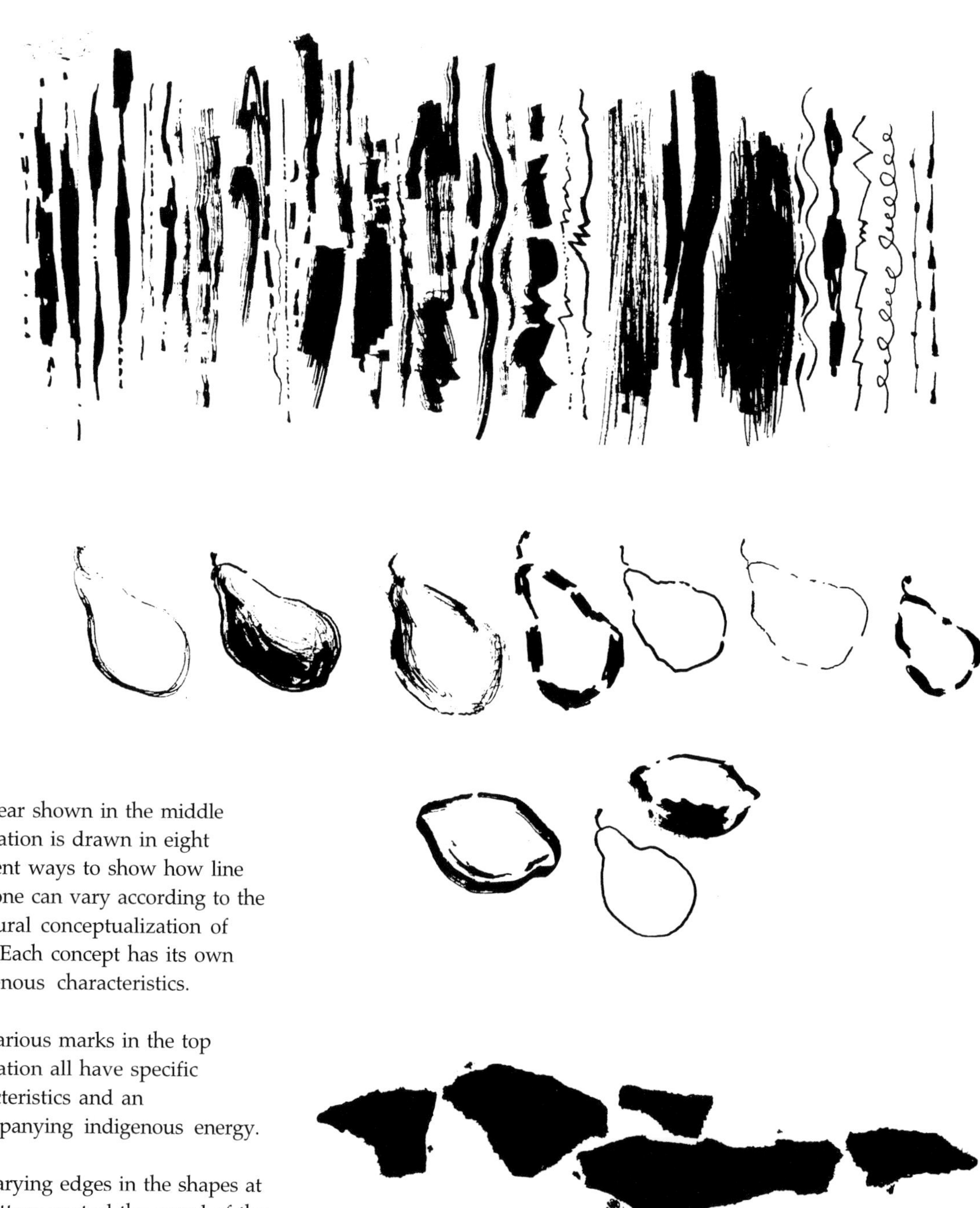

I.24

The pear shown in the middle illustration is drawn in eight different ways to show how line and tone can vary according to the structural conceptualization of form. Each concept has its own indigenous characteristics.

The various marks in the top illustration all have specific characteristics and an accompanying indigenous energy.

The varying edges in the shapes at the bottom control the speed of the observer's eye.

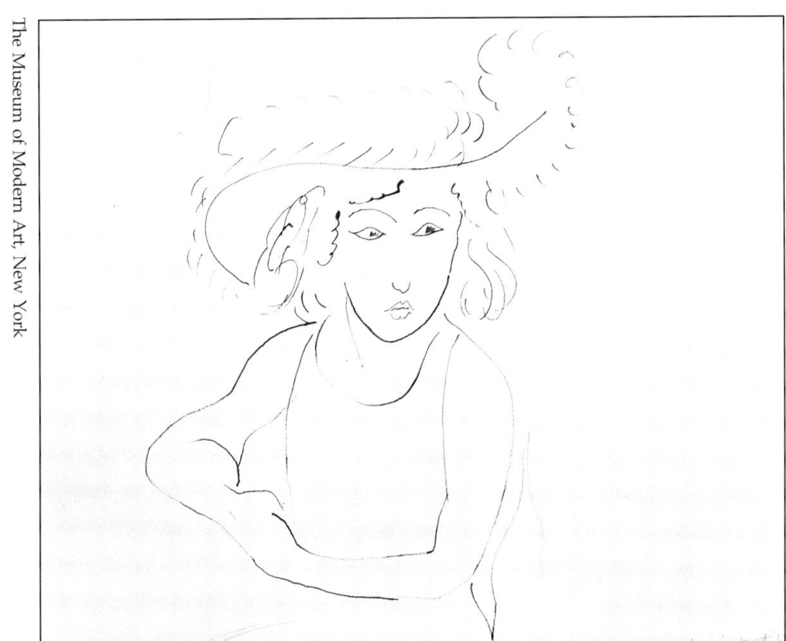

A deliberately simplified neutral line drawing by Matisse.

I.25

Henri Matisse, *The Plumed Hat,* Nice, 1919. Ink, 14¾" x 12½".

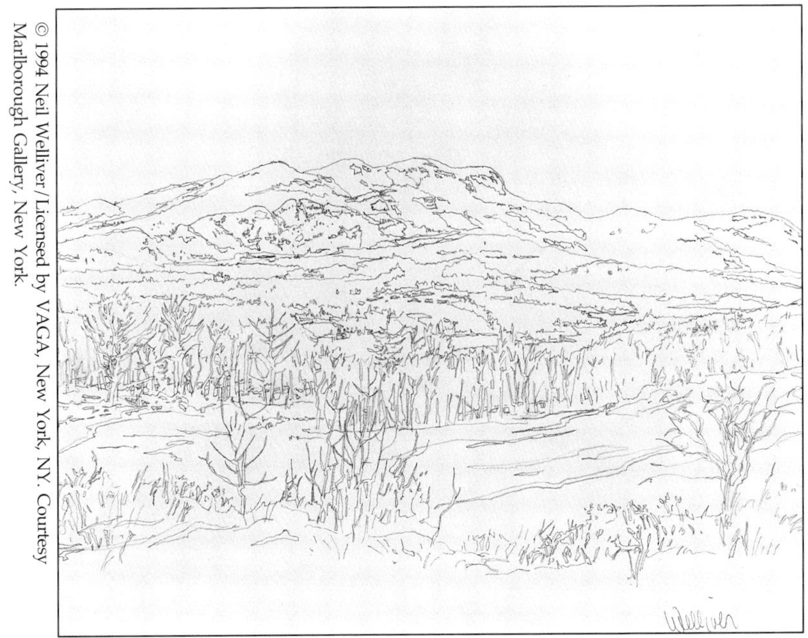

Neil Welliver, Study for *Megunticook Mountain,* 1983. Pencil on paper, 14" x 16½".

I.26

Neil Welliver's pencil drawing has a subtle transference of lost to found in the linear relationships (unlike the neutral line drawing by Matisse). Welliver establishes a deliberate reciprocal push and pull with varying weights of line in the related parts, taking the eye to the ridge of the mountain, for example, in the upper left, with the upper-right ridge seen as out of focus and in the distance. A river meanders through the right middle of the picture and is strengthened as a focal point by a contrasting use of heavier line. In the immediate foreground, some of the forms are almost completely lost. All the forms are drawn within a perceptual framework of the whole.

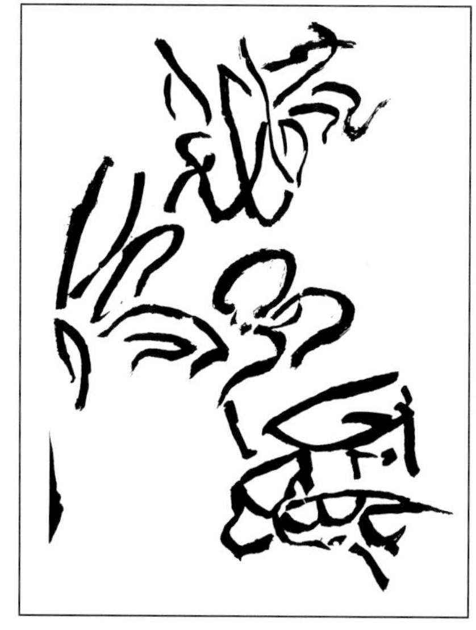

I.27 Line drawing of graffiti by author.

The heavy line was drawn with a brush so that the weight of the line could be varied. The proportions of the negative space are just as important as those of the line. In fact, each shaped the other.

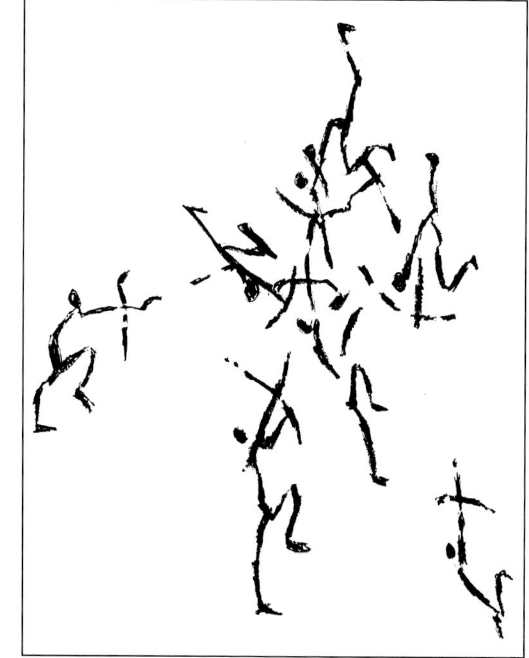

I.28

Author's sketch of *Archers Fighting*, cave painting, width 15¾".

Late Magdalenian period, Morella la Vella, Spain. From Roland, Benjamin, Jr.; *Drawings of the Masters—Cave to Renaissance*, 1965.

The artist was aware of the changing intervals in the spatial proportions between the rhythmical unity of the lines. Because of the dissolution of illusionary qualities in the figures, the lines and their shapes and movements are seen as objective reality. The simplistic, almost childlike handling of form is imaginative and appealing, as well as in keeping with the contemporary ideology that "less is more." Organic relationships are more important than developing the ability to copy form.

Blackness is the total absorption of light; whiteness is maximum light. In any visible form, there is always a lightest tone and a darkest tone. A middle tone is in between these extremes. If I look at a white stone, the white can be seen as its highlight, the point closest to the real light. The middle tone is a very pale gray and the darkest tone a slightly deeper gray. Every object in a given light has a base tone and this is its principal tonal characteristic. A dark gray stone has a base tone of dark gray, a highlight of a paler gray, and black in its shadow.

Any equilibrium between the tones that produces a simultaneous visual attraction creates a static relationship. Each tone, because of its relative size, has a similar amount of energy.

It is always easier to see tonal relationships when the forms in the subject matter are relatively colorless. A pair of steel scissors seen on my white-surfaced drawing table stand out as a simplified shape. I must squint at them to determine the base tone and this permits seeing the form as a fairly solid dark against the brilliant white surface. The deepest darks are found in the angled steel away from the light while the lightest lights are still considerably darker than the white background. In order to make a good, strong drawing of this subject, I would probably limit it to four tonal values, beginning with white through to almost black.

If these same scissors had bright orange handles and were seen as color, the drawing would be more difficult. The orange would have to be translated as a specific tonal value or a certain shade of gray. Again, this choice is relative to the tone of orange as it is seen against the white background. The same scissors seen against a dark background appear quite differently. The darks are perceived as darker and the highlights in the metal are brighter.

Each color as it is seen in a subject is translated as a relative weight that has a specific tonal value. The base tone of a dark green is a deep charcoal gray . . . of a bright red, a medium gray . . . of a pale yellow, a very pale gray.

To further simplify a tonal drawing, to gain freshness, expressive strength, and a clarity of execution, it is good practice to limit the number of tones to five, regardless of

I.29

Henry W. Peacock, *Afro-American Model*.

Lithograph pencil drawing of Afro-American model by author done in life class at The Pennsylvania Academy of the Fine Arts about 1948. There is good tonal range and a sense of solidity in the form, but the background (negative space) was not considered important and can be seen as nothing more than a by-product of the fully developed positive form. My principal objective was to develop a good likeness of the model. This drawing was developed from light to dark.

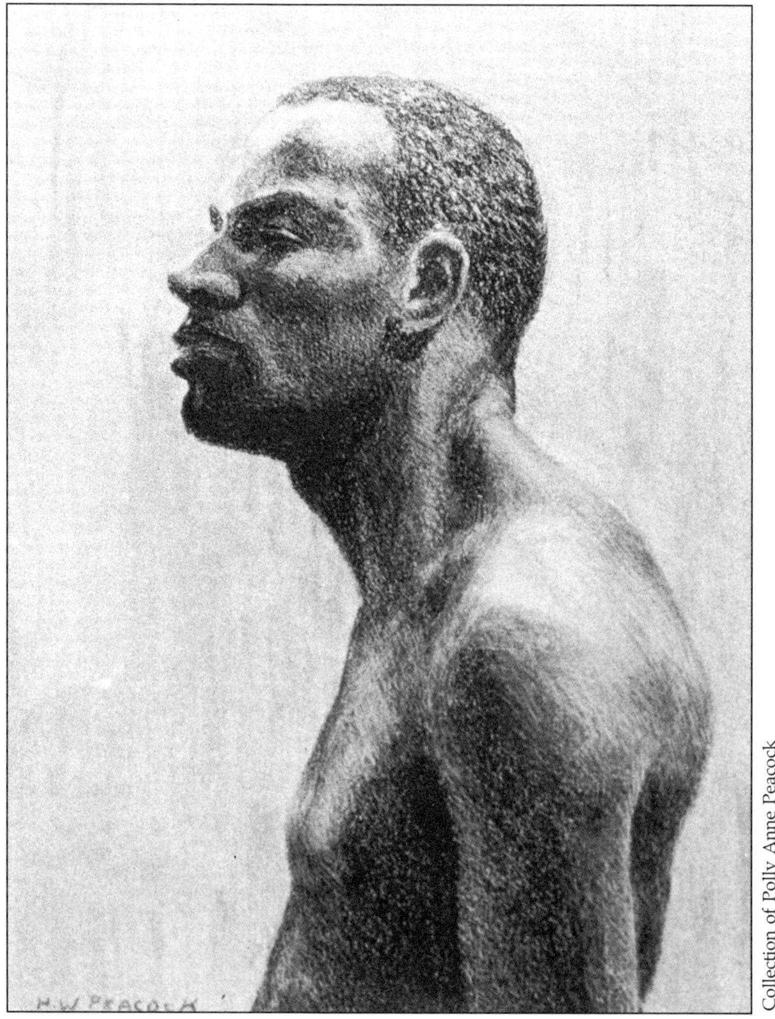

Collection of Polly Anne Peacock

the complexity of the subject. These should include white (or the white paper), a middle tone, and a dark tone, with two intermediate tones in between.

Tones should be balanced according to their mass/weight relationship. The eye can instinctively measure, by means of comparison, the weight of each form. Each tone should contrast with an adjacent tone so that they are all seen distinctly. Learning to evaluate tones in the subject and then transpose them directly onto the paper is fundamental

I.30 The Perception of Tonal Values as Weight Energy in Space.

White
maximum brilliance
total light refraction

Gray
middle tone
one-half in light
50% refraction

Black
deepest tone
complete darkness
no light refraction

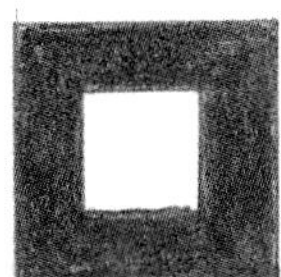

Light is increased
surrounded by black

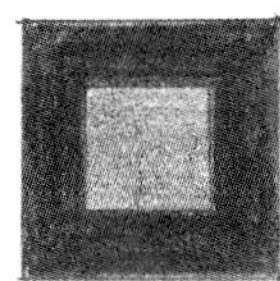

Gray is lightened
surrounded by black

Black is increased
surrounded by
white

Which Is Positive and Which Is Negative?

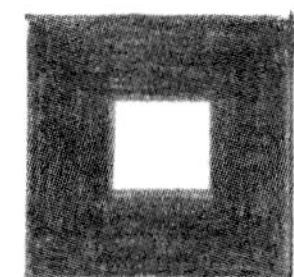

Black is positive
White is negative

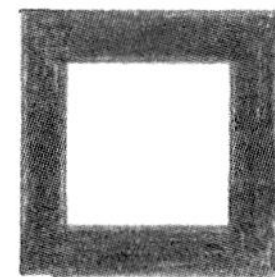

White is positive
Black is negative

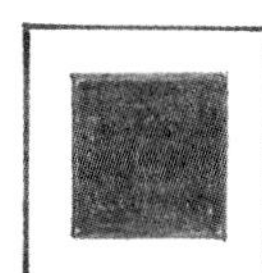

Black is positive
White is negative

Any equilibrium between the tones that produces a simultaneous visual attraction creates a static relationship. Each tone, because of its relative size, has a similar amount of energy.

to good drawing. As one progresses to more complex tonal problems, the ability to discriminate between tonal variations is similar to learning the keyboard on the piano.

The Importance of Drawing Freely

Using your intuition is a creative mode that you slide into without being aware of the transition from the conscious to the subconscious. It is a giving-in to the problem at hand with oneness and receptivity.

I emphasize drawing freely, particularly in the early stages of your development, to overcome any kind of regimentation and to loosen your attitude toward drawing. If, from the beginning, you draw in a tight and restricted style, your work will reveal a determined attitude that is usually based on predetermined ideas of quality. You can work and rework your drawing to make it better, but as you do so, you will be impeding your natural intuitive responses to form.

From an analytical point of view, any act of drawing makes a visual equation with self-imposed, inherent problems that must be solved in order to reach a meaningful conclusion. A creative approach to solving the problems in drawing is flexible, open-ended, and explorative. What happens if the line moves this way in a rhythmical flow, or what happens if this tone is darker, opposing a lighter tone? A searching, receptive attitude of not knowing a precise solution to the evolving problems should replace any stultifying, restricted attitude that demands quality. The resulting form, as it is drawn, is freed from its conventional confines. The end result is a conclusion based on a series of perceptions during the process of drawing that were generated by inner responses to the form.

Creative drawing demands a more abstract mode of perception. In a sense, the drawing becomes unconscious as the mind searches in and out and back and forth at lightning speed. This is the wonder of the mind and its interaction through the nerves from the eyes to the hand. My principal thought is that this is an innate capacity that we all more or less share, for we are all, at least to some extent, creative. Try to break the shackles that impede your natural growth, for they are the unrecognized fears that result from the herd instinct for conformity and approval.

Your drawing, at each stage of your development, is a mirror of your ideas about form as well as of your relative creative growth. Some students' work is halting, uncertain, and timid. A contour drawn on the paper from the figure may appear undecided as it is traced over numerous times because of lack of confidence. Other students' works are overly aggressive (this is rare) and are drawn so fast and furiously that the eye does not have time to catch up and measure proportions. This drawing often is full of feeling but, because it is out of control, the results are uneven at best.

True confidence can only be gained through expanding one's perceptions by drawing constantly. Learning to draw is how one begins to learn a visual language. There is no single magic moment when you think that you have gained sufficient knowledge and technical know-how to create masterpieces. Each completed drawing represents a small step in an ongoing creative process. You must adopt goals to exceed your given talent and you must mistrust any kind of facile, superficial handling of form.

Learning to draw well can be thought of as a process, whereas taking delight in drawing can be an end in itself. In the broadest sense, drawing can be considered the key to discovering a new visual world. From the beginning, and throughout your life, your drawing should be thought of as a natural extension of self. It will change as you grow.

Save your best earliest drawings and sketchbooks. A common mistake is to devalue your early work. Sign and date them and put them away carefully. All of your work is a record of your creative journey. I believe the real measure of anyone's life is how far one has progressed beyond one's beginnings.

On various occasions in my life drawing classes, I have closed my eyes and listened to the twenty or so students drawing quick action sketches. I could always tell which students were doing the best work by the sound of the soft charcoal on the newspad—long, swinging strokes, some very fast, balanced by the more staccato sound of short strokes. The total effect was a continuous and rhythmical

I.31

These drawings by Edward Hopper show that his interest was directed toward drawing freely the whole form. This is a developed discipline that is fundamental to making art.

Edward Hopper, *Standing Nude with Raised Arm*, c. 1920. Conte on paper, 18" x 11½".

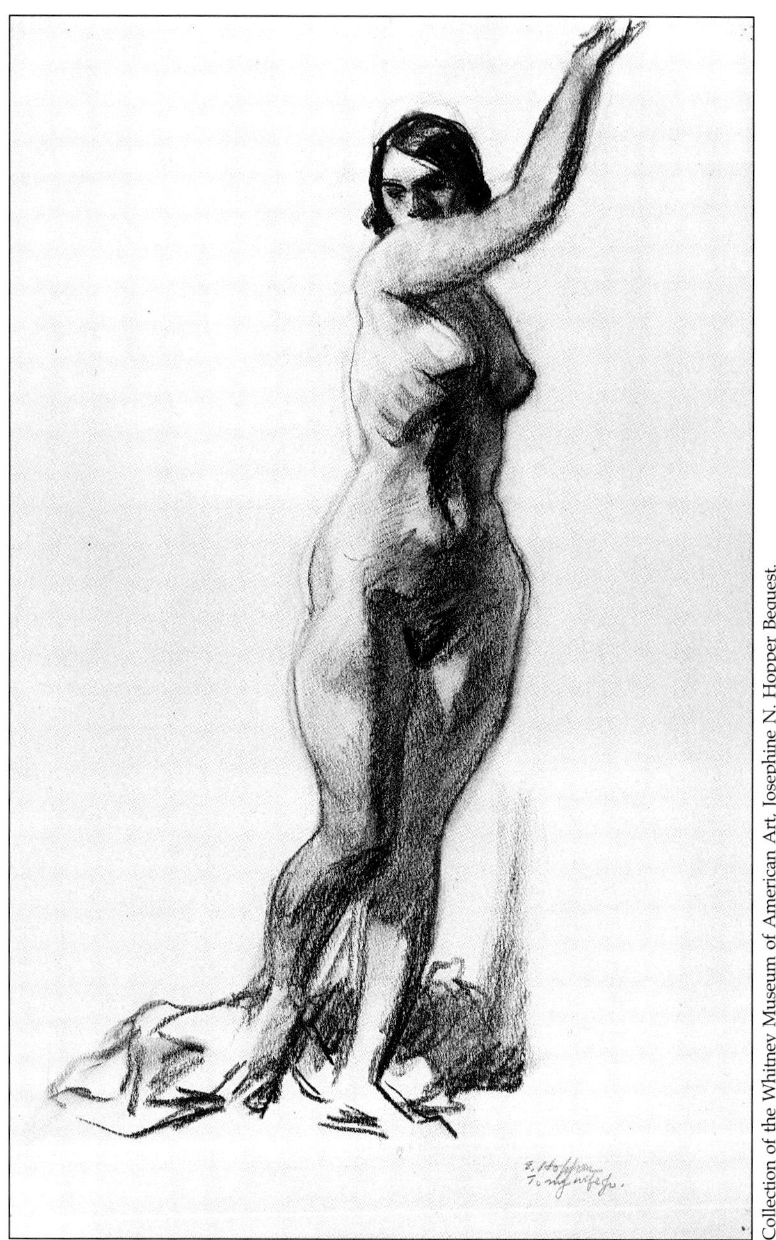

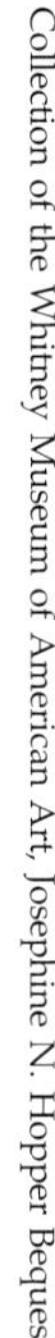

Collection of the Whitney Museum of American Art, Josephine N. Hopper Bequest.

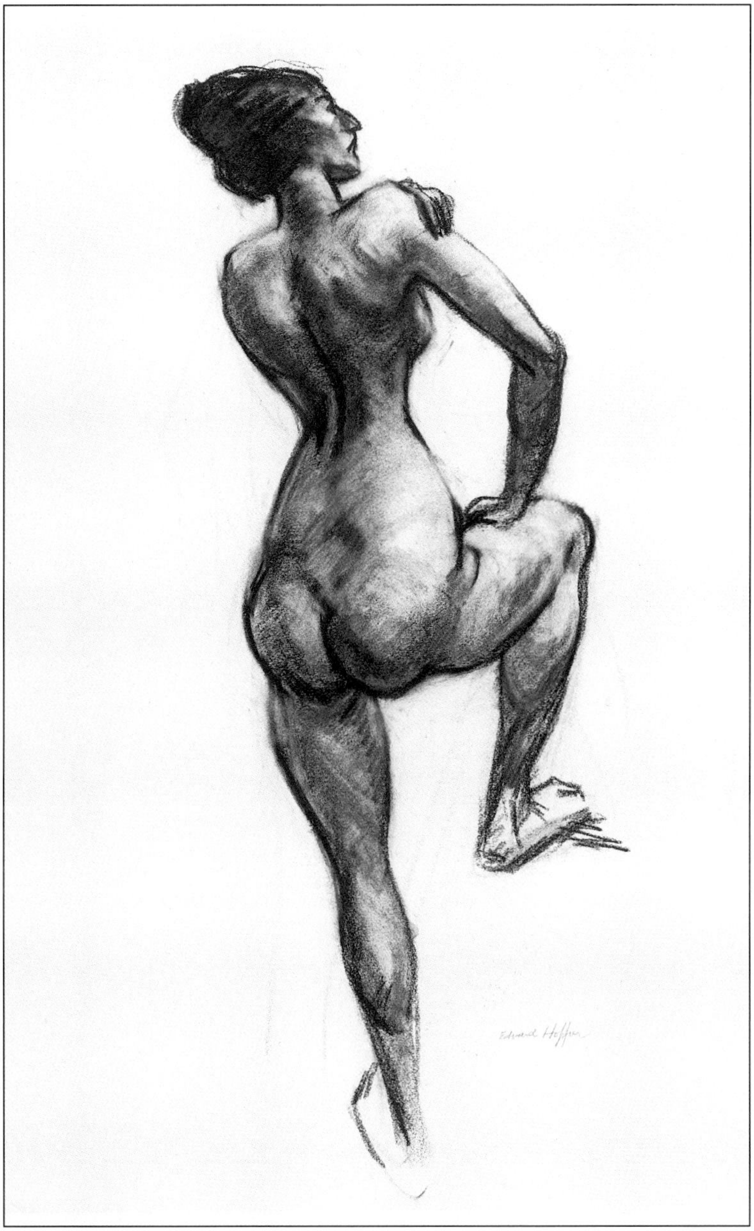

I.31 *continued.*

Edward Hopper, *Standing Nude*, c. 1920. Conte and charcoal on paper, 22 $\frac{1}{16}$" x 15".

interchange. The sounds of the charcoal in the weaker drawings were more tentative, hesitant, interrupted. Invariably, the weaker student was not confident of his innate drawing abilities. Remember, most children draw intuitively and without fear.

Rembrandt, perhaps the greatest master of traditional drawing, often drew very quickly using reed and quill pens and ink. His drawings were often sketchy and unfinished in appearance. He commonly used loose lost and found lines, directing the eye in and out of space, suggesting folds in cloth or a hand. Because of their speed in execution, the lines were seen as flowing, abstract relationships, holding together rhythmically as if an inner force shaped them into highly contemporary positive and negative patterns. Rembrandt's drawing was obviously intuitive. He learned that when you draw with speed, quality is a byproduct of direct expression, for there is no time to calculate and predetermine relationships.

> In Japanese painting the power intent was suggested by conceiving a stroke outside the paper, continuing through the drawing space to project beyond, so that the included part possessed both power origin and projection. Even accident—which is never accidental, but intuitive fortune—was explained. If drops fall, they become acts of providence. If the brush flows dry into hairmarks, such may be greater in energy. And that in the painting certain objects possessing force, the sentiment of strength must be evoked and felt [sic]. I do not cite these tenets to show that we are directly influenced by oriental art. The forces involved have occurred in art without declaration.[9]
>
> —David Smith

As an art student at Hunter College in New York, David Smith rebelled against the tight, regimented approaches that were taught in his figure drawing classes and started to draw on extra-large sheets of brown paper with large brushes. He discovered a new kind of freedom as he relied on his own inner rhythms, releasing his strong visual emotions.

Form In Its Essence Is Abstract

When is a cloud not a cloud? The mind obviously has the capacity to recognize a cloud as a part of nature with its own reality, regardless of how it changes in its own formation as it is pushed by the wind or gets wispier or as light constantly changes its appearance. A cloud is a cloud because of prior knowledge of clouds. The word cloud is associated with its appearance. A cloud is also an amorphous shape. It comprises various planes and tones. A cloud is an organic shape. It moves, expands, and contracts. It has a generative thrust line.

Hopper simplified the forms he observed in nature. He said it had taken him years to bring himself into the painting of a cloud. As he progressed, he developed the ability to see the interrelationship of positive form to negative space.

A cloud is no longer a cloud when it is seen as a kind of specific, yet generalized, form that is adaptable to the needs of picture making. The form that was a cloud has become part of a creative process. The mind-set has shifted. Its form is a wedgelike shape, or towering like a huge anvil, or part of a linear rhythmical grouping. In essence, the cloud is seen as abstract; it has become a malleable shape to fit the needs of personal expression.

I pick up various pieces of bark from the ground beneath a sycamore tree and bring them back to my studio as subject matter for drawing. I select, I arrange, and I discover as I draw how each shape is interrelated in a common space. The differences in all of these shapes stir my curiosity and rouse visual interest. Each shape has its own identity. Yet, because they all are composed of long, sweeping curves, angles, and interior whorls, they have a remarkable consistency.

In my mind, the bark no longer pertains to the reality of the tree as I draw, but instead as the line expresses my idea of the form, it has its own reality. And it is in this sense that the drawing is abstract. The line is thought of apart from the object of the tree. Any semblance to real tree bark is an illusion, portrayed on a flat, two-dimensional surface.

An important principle to understand is that any fine

work of art, regardless of how its subject is perceived and portrayed (either representational or nonrepresentational) is in its essence based on an abstract relationship of its qualities to the limitations of the paper or canvas.

Edward Hopper drew railroad locomotives, highways, gas stations, hotels, Victorian houses, lighthouses, and trees. He fashioned clouds and shadows into long, wedgelike shapes that were both fluid and consistent with the demands of the adjoining negative space. He was always concerned with a direct use of light to reveal monumental power in his forms. Hopper's genius lay in his ability to organize pictorially the mass interrelationships found in related parts of structure. He organized form in the most abstract way and was conscious of each detail as a selective choice that enhanced his massive primary forms.

The Significance of Distortion

There is nothing worse than a lifeless facsimile of subject matter. A lifeless drawing or painting is devoid of emotion because its creator's purpose was an attempt to "recreate" beauty. This is a self-defeating approach. When making art, the process is all important. It is not a question of painting in a representational way, but rather a question of how the reality of form is represented. Copying form is both a relatively easy process and a limited process, because the eye concentrates on an exact replica of contours as well as on a preestablished proportional interchange. Creativity is suppressed; the process prohibits an original composition of form.

Frank Lloyd Wright once said, "It is better to tell a poor truth than it is to tell a good lie." A poor truth in drawing or painting may be crude in its technique, but it is original and expressive of the artist's inner feelings. On the other hand, a good lie most often is technically well-executed, because the artwork conforms to another artist's idea of painting as well as to the technique used to convey that idea. It is a form of copying or influence that allows for minimum originality.

Fully realized composition requires some distortions of forms to place subject matter selectively in the picture plane. One's empathy can be used to sense qualities in form, color, and space, which can be transformed in an expressive way to the two-dimensional surface of the picture plane.

In realistic drawing and painting, the simplest kinds of distortions can make the work more cohesive. This is sometimes referred to as "artistic license," or portraying form in a personal way. In landscape painting, a tree can be moved from its natural location or it can be enlarged, or numerous details can be left out to simplify the composition. Generally, most distortions of subject matter are made without any realization of their significance; that is, they are a result of a natural response to the motif that produces inner life in the developing work. More weight, for instance, can be tacked on a heavy figure to make it appear more massive and monumental; conversely, a slender figure can be elongated to further accentuate a tall, thin quality. Rhythms can be pronounced or angularity can be emphasized. As form is naturally distorted, it appears more convincing to the eyes of its creator and to its viewer.

By eliminating distortions, all the elements of a creative approach are ignored—originality, inventiveness, selectivity— and within the process expression is suppressed. Distortions in a work of art are the result of feelings, intuition, and harmony between the subject and the psyche.

Many representational artists believe that any kind of distortion takes away from the convincing qualities and subsequent "authenticity" of their pictures. This is because distortion is often thought of as deforming, contorting, twisting, or torturing form, often in context to the plight of human beings; distortion also takes away from the exact and undeviating interpretations of reality by misrepresenting the laws of true perspective and the materialization of form.

In 1901, Robert Henri told the students of the School of Design for Women in Philadelphia:

> I knew men who were students at the Académie Julien in Paris, where I studied this year and found some of the same students there, repeating the same exercises and doing work 'nearly' as good as they did thirteen years ago.

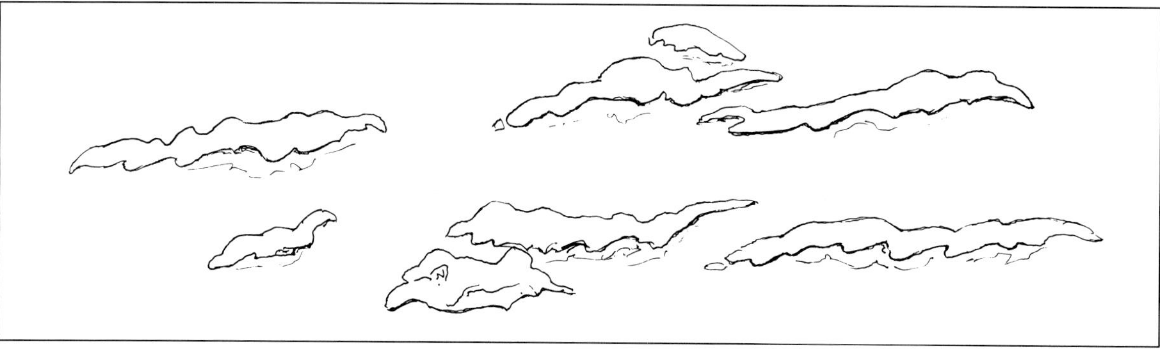

I.32

A copy of Neil Welliver's clouds.

The way a painter draws and paints clouds reveals the innate character of his work. Welliver works very directly. He is completely aware of the placement of each cloud and how it affects its corresponding negative space. Welliver's clouds are painted freely, expressively; they appear to belong to nature's internal rhythms and indescribable abstract qualities.

A detail copied from Neil Welliver's painting, *Winter Stream*, 1976.

Ice forms stacked on top of each other are a combination of geometric angular forms integrated with organic free forms. Although at first glance they appear as an abstract jumble, each movement and each shape is structurally integrated into his overall composition.

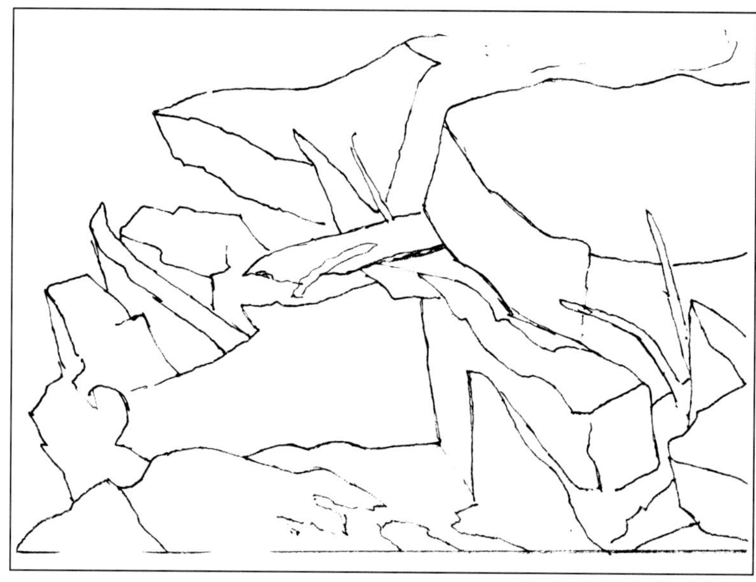

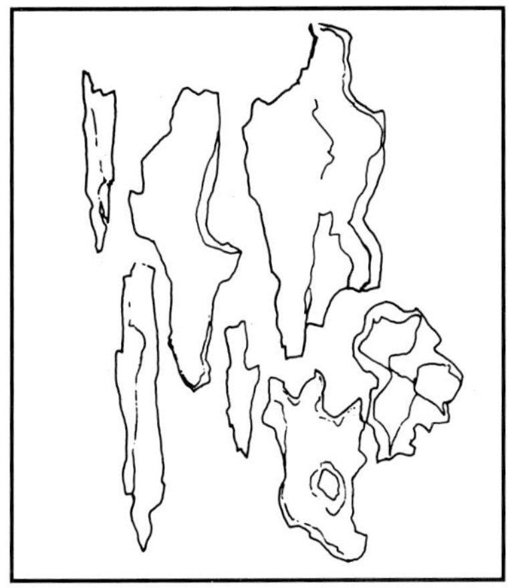
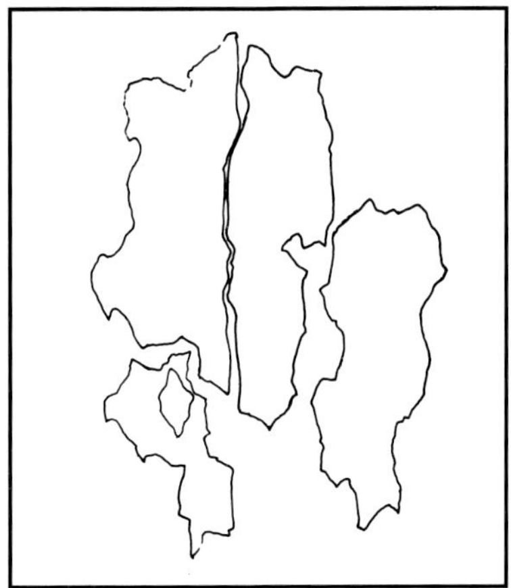
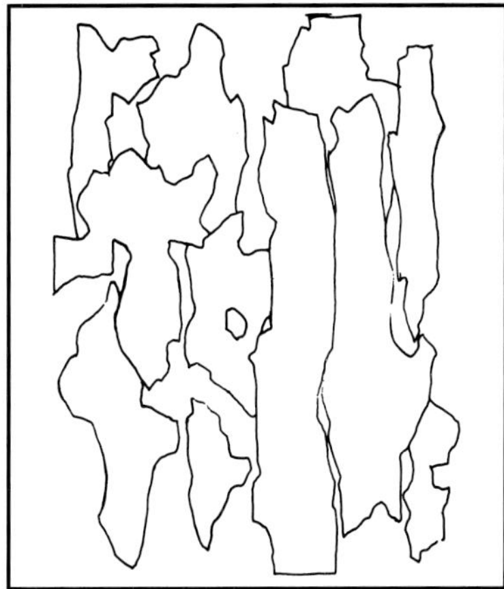

I.33 Tree bark.

These pen and ink drawings of tree bark illustrate the organic, abstract qualities that are so commonplace in nature. There is a rhythmical unity in these forms—the way the contours shape relatively intricate movements and longer sweeping flows defines varying proportions in both positive forms and negative spaces.

As I draw, the pen varies its pressures on the paper, creating a subtle lost and found life in the line. Ink is indelible. To draw directly with ink requires spontaneity and a certain boldness. You can't erase it as you can a pencil. Have you ever wished you could have a line back after you drew it? I have.

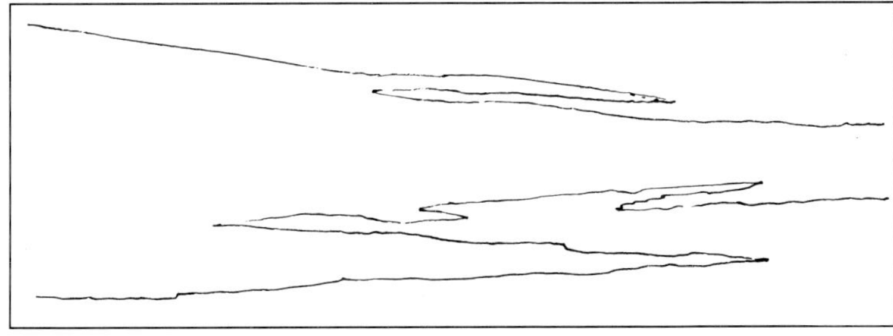

I.34

A simple cloud formation copied from Edward Hopper's watercolor, *Road and Houses, Cape Cod,* about 1940.

I.35

Markings, a sketch by the author, is a nonobjective interpretation of different kinds of organic form. Each mark has its own distinct qualities, yet they all, to a certain extent, belong to each other because they were drawn intuitively in a continuous flow with an awareness of space as a common denominator. The loose, scribbled pen line was used purposefully in a flexible way to show freely shaped mass relationships.

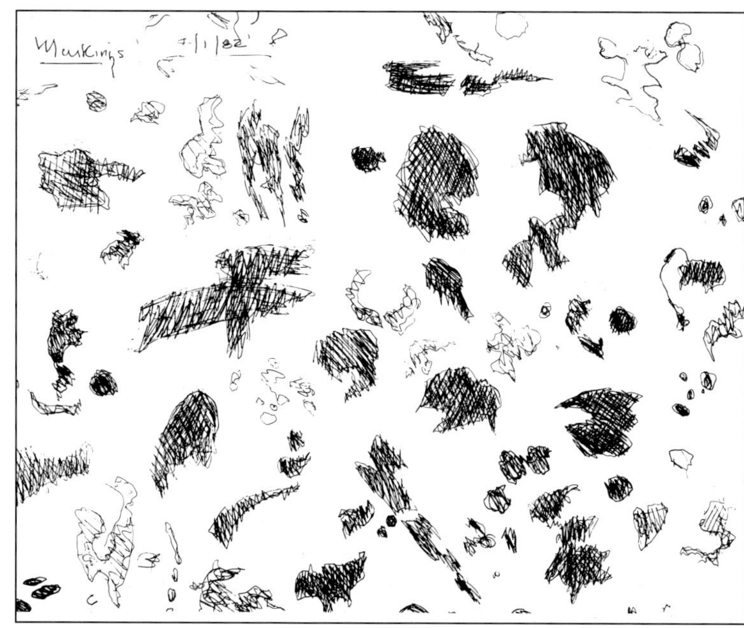

> At almost any time in those thirteen years they have had technical ability enough to produce masterpieces. Many of them are more facile in the trade of copying the literal drawing and proportion than are some of the greatest masters of art.
>
> These students have become masters of the trade of drawing, as many others have become masters of their grammars. And like so many of the latter, brilliant jugglers of words, having nothing worthwhile to say, they remain little else than clever jugglers of the brush.[10]

The process Robert Henri described at the Académie Julien in Paris can be found in many art schools, art centers, and painting workshops. The basic idea is to make art as realistic as possible by depending on one's perfection of techniques. When one copies a photograph, the composition is already established. The expressive response to the subject is subjugated to the choices made by the photographer. The

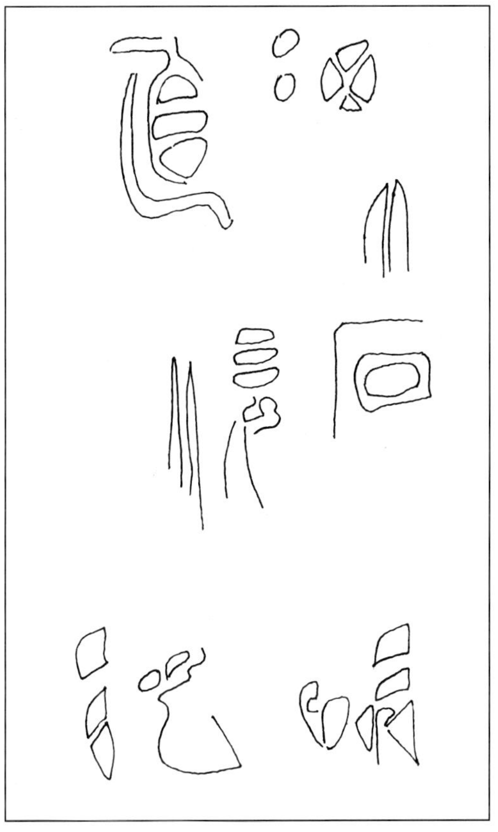

I.36 Negative Spaces.

Note the continuity in these negative shapes derived from the Chinese calligraphy in Illustration I.18. In each instance, the artist shaped the forms according to the reciprocal relationship of the positive form and negative space, paying attention to the proportions of each, as well as to pressure, balance, and tension. The organic qualities in these ancient forms are distant relatives of those in the sketches of tree bark.

world is seen through his eyes and his experience as an artist. Regardless of how realistically the subject with all of its detail is represented, the resulting image appears lifeless to the experienced eye.

An exacting comparison of any one of Paul Cézanne's landscape motifs to his interpretation of it shows many distortions of the subject to satisfy his demand for composition. He said, "To paint is not to copy . . . slavishly the object . . . it is to seize harmony between several correspondences, then to transpose them, following a new and original logic."[11]

In many ways, Edward Hopper's paintings are the antithesis of the work of the photo-realists. He selected his subject matter carefully and then naturally distorted it to fit a particular idea of composition. Hopper distilled form; he reduced it to more elemental qualities, shaping it in an abstract fashion so it flowed and was part of a rhythmical interplay. Sometimes he used it as counterpoint in the expressive beat of his composition. He wrote this statement about simplification: "I find in working, always the disturbing intrusion of elements not a part of my most interesting vision, and the inevitable obliteration and replacement of this vision by the work itself as it proceeds."[12]

Matisse said: "The simplest means are those which enable an artist to express himself best." For Matisse, this meant that he had to have a vision of his composition from the beginning. He sought the often subtle, melodious, and abstract patterns seen in nature—"a living harmony of tones, a harmony not unlike that of musical composition," as he described them.[13]

The Dual Responses to Form

Aesthetic response is a natural reaction to beauty as it is perceived in form, color, and space. The eye views an apple, for instance, as a pleasing shape made up of curves and colors. The proportions of the apple are revealed by its coexisting space.

Psychological response is a reaction to the basic identity of a form as affected by prior knowledge of it. The eye identifies the apple as a fruit.

All form has meaning. A triangle, circle, and square are perceived as the simplest kinds of geometric forms. We can respond aesthetically to these shapes. They convey a precise manmade, mathematical order. We also respond psychologically to them, because we have a prior knowledge of them as geometric shapes. Hence these forms evoke a dual response.

Dual responses to form are natural and unquestioned. Children instinctively use dual responses as they draw and paint. For example, when a house, grass, trees, and sky are painted by children, they freely arrange the shapes to please their inner sense of beauty while they simultaneously draw the house according to their knowledge of it. They see the house as boxy with a slanted roof. It has a chimney, door,

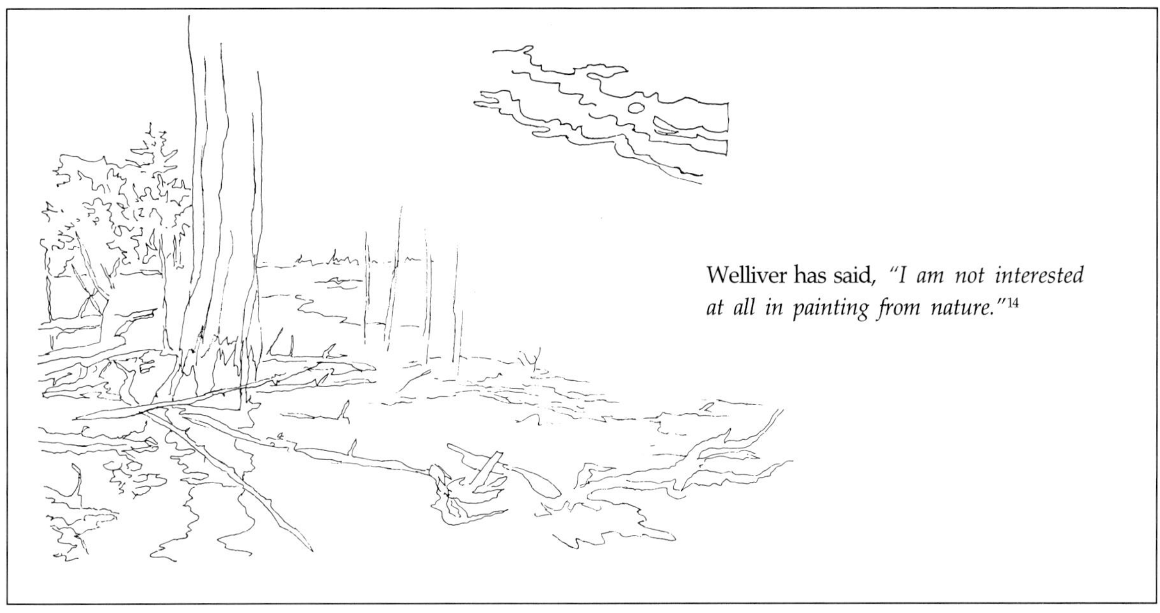

Welliver has said, *"I am not interested at all in painting from nature."*[14]

I.37

Pen and ink sketches of Neil Welliver's trees and wave patterns. Welliver distorts the forms in nature according both to his knowledge of them and to his idea of their relationships to the whole.

and windows. The tree is drawn according to their concept of a tree. It is painted green. The sky is painted blue. The two responses to form are interrelated and inseparable. As children paint, they convey their feelings about subject matter expressively, distorting forms freely in order to satisfy their idea of a picture.

One of the aspects of gaining maturity as an artist is the development of the ability to evaluate more clearly one's boundaries of expressions—that is, to express, at least intuitively, a more understandable guideline for personal direction. As artists progress with their own ideas of painting, they learn from the difficult task of originating quality in their work to rely on a stronger aesthetic response to color/form. They become more concerned with how their painting holds together. Why does a curve move this way or that way? Is it because of an inner rhythm that directs it? If so, is it also because of a persistent awareness of its directions in space; is it correlated to all the other curves?

A small number of my best students, as much as they tried, failed to master proportions in figure drawing. Heads, hands, and feet were often drawn too small or too large. Yet their distortions of the actual forms in the figure often produced powerful and rhythmical expressions of their feelings when comparisons were made to the more classic and conventional drawings made by other students. These same students invariably produced the most expressive paintings and went on to become successful, highly motivated, creative painters.

I have since concluded that it was their strong, almost obsessive aesthetic responses to form as they worked that blocked their ability to measure and interrelate proportions in conventional ways. Their work was immediately seen as more childlike and original than that of their peers, and, yet, because it was so creative, was always compelling to see and was strangely more sophisticated in its aesthetic qualities. Their particular mind-set prevented each of them from accurately producing form, or, conversely, their mind-set led them to distort form, each in his or her own way, according to an inner vision. This vision is not reasonable or decipherable. It spurns the illustrative side of realism.

The way form is distorted cannot be separated from a visual knowledge gained through creative experience. It is the quality of the curve, its roundness, or steepness, or subtle interchange with flatness, as well as its relativity to all the other forms in a composition, that direct the hand with the brush. The way that this curve is shaped is not entirely new to the eye. Distortions are a result of inner responses to form. They are not logical or conditioned.

An aesthetic response to form dominated Henri Matisse's painting:

> Expression to my way of thinking does not consist of the passion mirrored upon a human face or betrayed by a violent gesture. The whole arrangement of my picture is expressive. The place occupied by figures or objects, the empty spaces around them, the proportions, everything plays a part. Composition is the art of arranging in a decorative manner the various elements at the painter's disposal for the expression of his feelings. In a picture every part will play the role conferred upon it, be it principal, or secondary. All that is not useful in the picture is detrimental. A work of art must

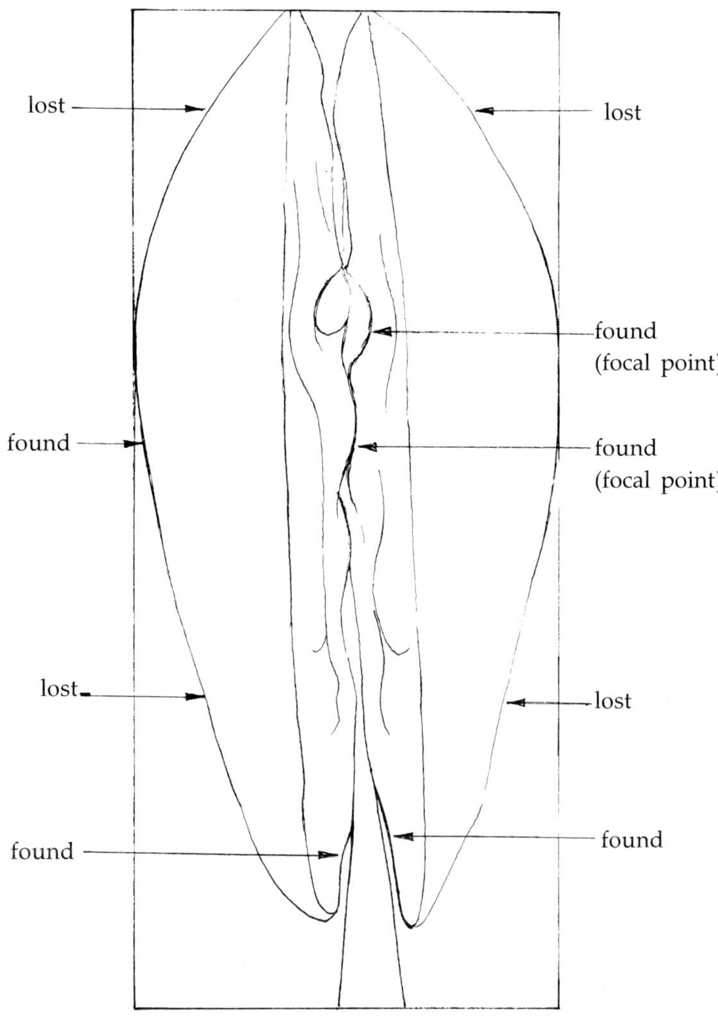

I.38 An Aesthetic Response to Form.

Pencil copy of painting, *Open Clam Shell*, by Georgia O'Keeffe, 1926, 20" x 9".

The clam shell is distorted to convey O'Keeffe's idea of an internal, rhythmical unity. The inner, almost parallel, straight edges of the shell (note that they converge slightly toward the top) oppose the subtle curvilinear interior and exterior of the shell. The shell is seen on an unstable diagonal, producing tension. The perceptive interplay of lost and found qualities in the painting are portrayed in this linear copy as darker lines, found, advancing to the eye and the lighter lines, lost, receding away from the eye.

be harmonious in its entirety, for superfluous details would, in the mind of the beholder, encroach upon the essential elements.[15]

Distortions can also be a result of an inner need to communicate deep-seated feelings about the time, events, and circumstances of the world we live in. But these kinds of responses must be integrated in concord with the demands of canvas, paint, and composition.

I.39 Aesthetic Responses to Form.

A comparison of the qualities in curvilinear forms. Picasso's emotions ranged from childlike curiosity to savage rage. In this instance, he expressed a rhythmic, harmonic flow with perfectly balanced forms.

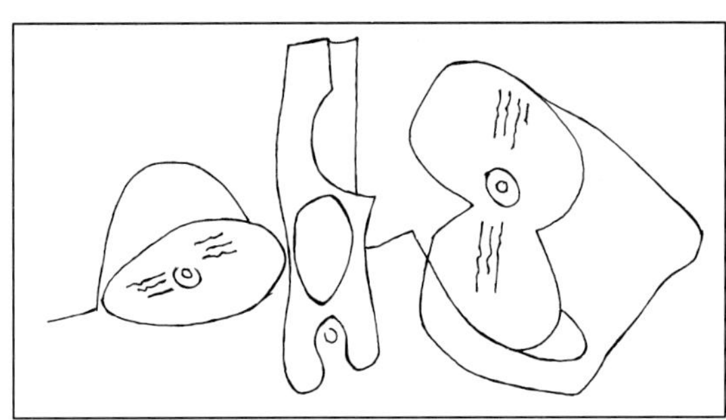

Detail copied from Picasso's *Mandolin and Guitar*, see Illustration II.8.

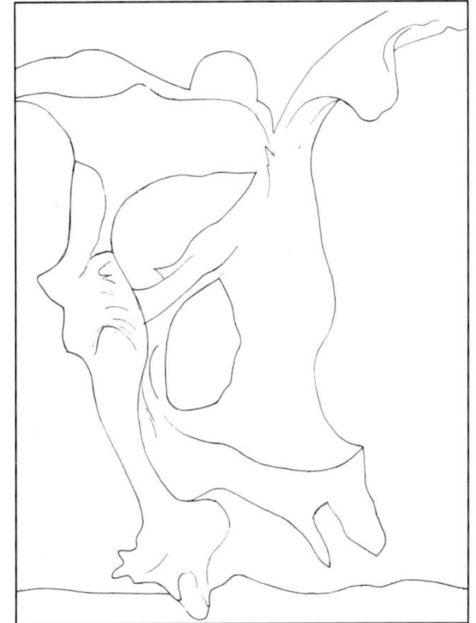

Detail, copied from O'Keeffe's *Pelvis with Moon.*

O'Keeffe magnified the organic qualities in this form. It is precariously balanced and in tension, which enhances its inner life.

In harsh contrast to Matisse, Picasso's aesthetic responses were subjugated to his forceful and intense psychological expression. Picasso was a contradiction to everything in his life and his work. He was intensely interested in world events and their meaning to him, yet, when he painted, he isolated himself from the world. His art was always passionate and never the same. He became a master of using symbols to convey his powerful psychological responses to form. At various times he expressed childlike colors and shapes, classical figures, savage, primitive figures, mythological figures and beasts, and grotesque animals.

All art is a synthesis, a bringing together of creative experience and personal feelings. These feelings should not be tampered with, for they are the sole domain of the artist, but they can and should be understood more clearly to clarify one's direction.

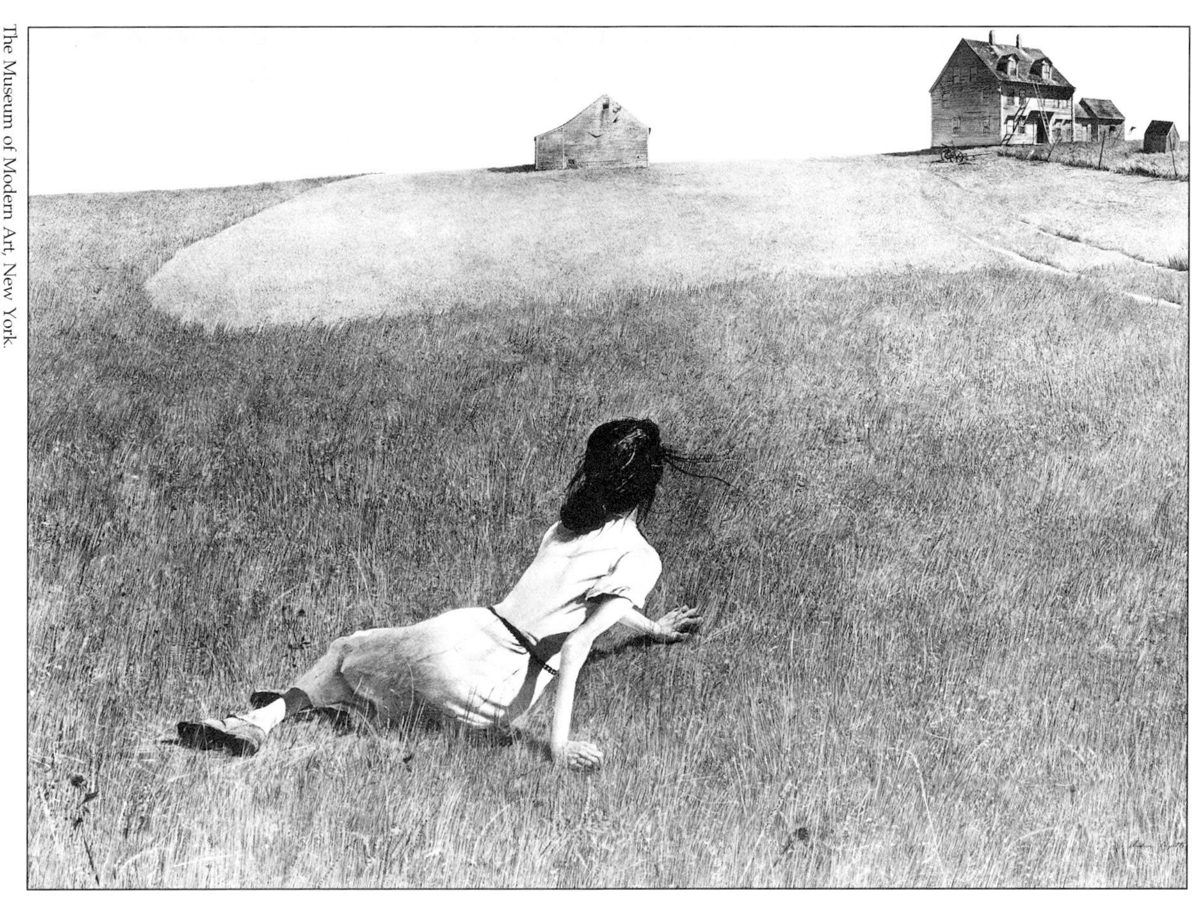

I.40 A Psychological Response to Form.

Andrew Wyeth, *Christina's World*, 1948. Tempora on gessoed panel, 32¼"x 47¾".

The observer responds to the skillful way that the young woman is painted. The beauty of her thin, frail form is made even more precious and solitary in contrast to the immense space of the field. This is an aesthetic response to the traditional use of tonal values and conservative colors. The psychological response is much more powerful. Christina, crippled since childhood, claws her way painfully up the steep hill to the farmhouse where she lives.

The Prisoner and the Irascible Dr. Barnes

A small steam engine belching white smoke pulled the two weathered, wood railway coaches from the hot, slumbering seaport of Bayonne, France, upwards into the Pyrenees Mountains, high above the endless, bleak Atlantic Ocean. It was the summer of 1950. The young artist sipped his Spanish black bean soup and watched chickens squawking in the aisles. He was separated from his homeland by harsh, guttural German spoken by a few tourists, and by the intonations of the soft, native Castillian. The train wound slowly around fog-enshrouded, gray-green mountains, through black, smoke-filled tunnels, over barren, sheep-grazed hills, and descended finally into the burnt orange glare of central Spain's dry dust bowl. In Burgos, he visited the Gaudi-designed, swallow-peaked cathedral, a dark and cool refuge from the shimmering dry heat. Dust clouds billowed from horsedrawn white canvas-topped prairie wagons as they rushed past hostile troops of peasant militia, bayonets fixed, a vignette from America's Wild West.

From Burgos, he travelled to the oasis of Madrid—mechanized, tumultuous, its bullring alive in the white heat of the afternoon sun. There, trumpets blared their high-pitched crescendos and he watched as silver swords plunged into black torsos of death. The impassioned din of the corrida seemed disconnected from the streets suddenly deserted during the noon siesta and the quiet evening music which came later in the parks. He went to the Prado Museum, which stood alone, majestic and imperiously detached with its treasures of El Greco's elongated *Christ* and of Goya's *Majas* and his incomparable etchings of bullfights and the horrors of war. In the main rotunda, the dwarfs of Velásquez still laughed, within their grimaces of pain, at the young American and his ideas of independence.

The young artist was liberated from the regimented traditions of the Academy by these expressive truths. He was faced with new and unknown frailties as he suddenly saw history marching forward, its bold strengths enveloping and stultifying his own ideas of art. He was able to see fierce independence still living within the darkened, aged surfaces of canvas, first at the Prado in Madrid and later in Seville and Toledo, and, finally, in Rome and Florence, where he faced the controlled emotions of the Renaissance. His own feelings were mirrored in the Old Masters' art, but they were imprisoned and inaccessible, for these strengths were beyond his grasp.

Looking back to those days as a student in Europe, I see that the turbulence of new experience was a release from the narrow approach to realism taught in the Academy. Only in retrospect can I appreciate the importance of seeing the Old Masters. The artist is never a student of the history of art in an intellectual sense. He must express his own time, yet he must first intuitively take into account the vivid forms of the past that are important to him, for they are the seeds of future harvests to be reaped. I am amazed by how clearly I remember the inner light and force of Goya's *The Third of May, 1808*, and a small painting by Rembrandt that hangs in a dark corner of the Louvre, of a side of beef.

The full emotional impact, for me, came from the sculpture of Michelangelo and particularly as I contemplated his *Bound Slave* in the Academmia di Belle Arti, in Florence. At that moment, an inspiration came from beyond myself; a shaft of light lifted my senses upward and, within an instant, all my questions and doubts about whether making a life of art would be a purely selfish commitment were answered. I felt a deep sense of enlightenment with the realization that creation can be the highest form of endeavor, beyond any question of self-centered pursuits.

That is how the idea for my painting of *The Prisoner* came into being. In this work there is no similarity to Michelangelo's *Bound Slave*, but the motif, the underlying reason for its inception, was influenced at a subconscious level by the limitations of the Carrara marble and the image of man struggling to be free from the bonds of civilization, to release himself from the stone, and, in my instance, from the confines of paint and canvas.

The strongest influences are never technical, concerned solely with medium, but are related to feelings that cannot be put into words. Very often, the real influences are not recognized until years later. This was true for *The Prisoner*. It was a

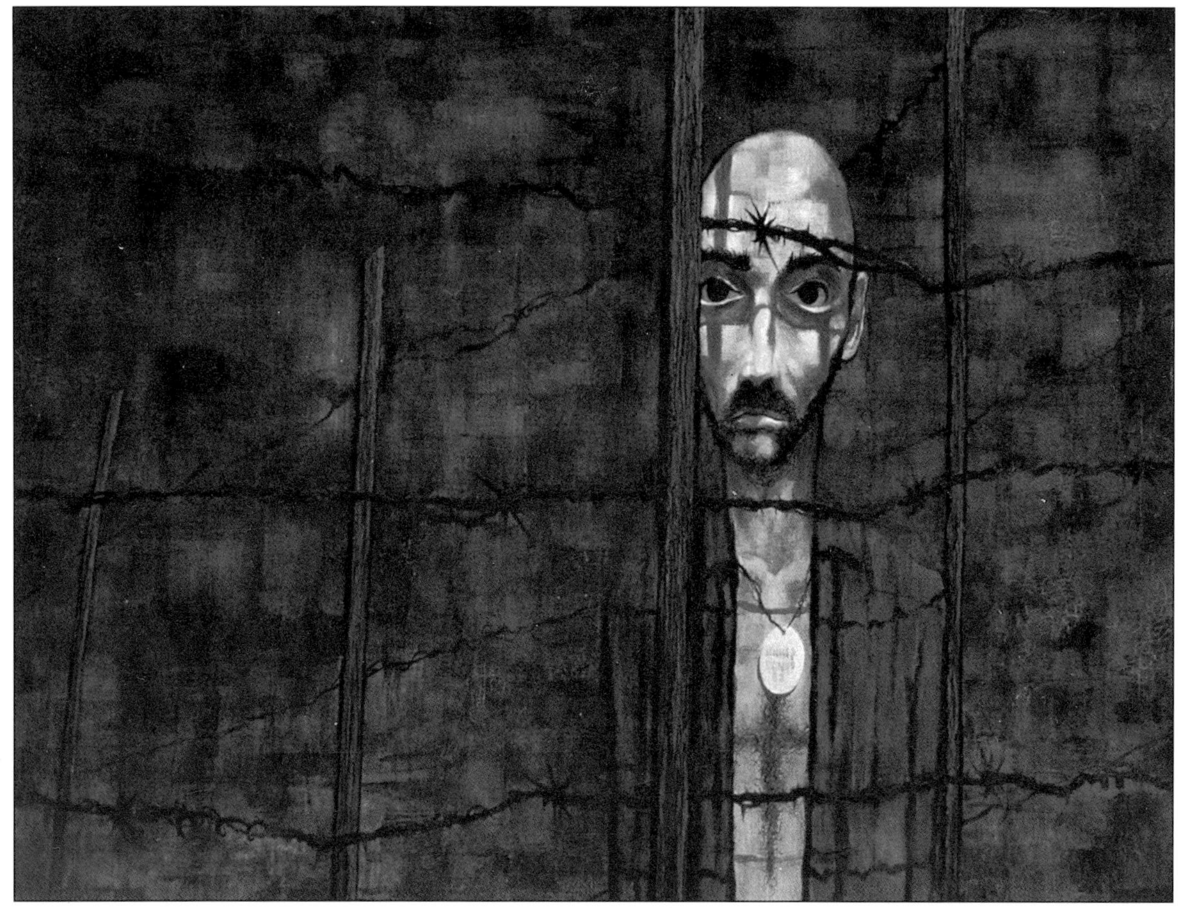

I.41

Henry W. Peacock, *The Prisoner*, 1950.

This painting was both my revolt against the academic dogma that valued the accepted styles and methods of expression, and my response to the horrors of war.

The color green, used in the flesh tones, increases the sense of wasted physical life, contrasting with the harsh red of the pole supports for the barbed wire. The large, deep, purple-blue negative space magnifies the solitary state of the prisoner and helps communicate his suffering. Symbolism is used in the cross of hair on his chest and in the thorns projecting from the barbed wire.

self-portrait of a man confined by his solitary experience. *The Prisoner* was my revolt against academic traditions.

My friend, Ray Twordeska, sold me art supplies from time to time in his little shop in the front room of his house in a small borough on Philadelphia's prestigious Main Line. In retrospect, Ray, myself, and particularly his hardscrabble art shop, were out of character with these surroundings. Ray loved painting. He had been a student at the Academy several years before. He looked like a latter-day Vincent van Gogh, with his red beard and sharp blue eyes. He was married and two little Rays clung around his knees as he tended the sale of his art supplies. Ray Twordeska also worked as a part-time chauffeur for Dr. Albert Barnes from nearby Merion, Pennsylvania.

During my last couple of years at the Academy, there were a good many of us who were veterans of World War II. Roy Lewando especially stands out in my memory, because it was through him that I first heard about the world-renowned Barnes Foundation, which houses possibly the best Courbets, Renoirs, and Cézannes anywhere. Roy was one of the more noticeable vets at the Academy: tall and wiry, with long dark hair, deepset eyes, and a quite prominent pointed beard. He was married to Isabel, whom we called Billie, one of the life models who posed in the painting classes. She was noted for her lanky, tanned figure and blond hair that she had dyed bright green. Roy had applied to the Barnes Foundation to further his study of painting by taking a course taught by Violetta de Mazie, the French-born art director of the Foundation's school. Dr. Barnes personally interviewed each prospective student. He was apparently aghast at Roy's appearance and demeanor, because a short time later, Joseph T. Fraser, director of the Academy, posted a scathing open letter from Dr. Barnes to the Academy on the lobby bulletin board. In his letter, Barnes denounced Roy Lewando as a typical product of the Academy, comparable, he said, to "the man who looked like Jesus Christ, but could not act like Jesus Christ."

Barnes formed his foundation in 1922 as a nonprofit educational institution to teach his theories about painting, which were based on the study of the paintings in his collection and on the ideas of his friend and confidant, the philosopher John Dewey. Barnes had also written a book, *The Art of Painting*, in which he described the process of painting a masterpiece. Interestingly enough, the Lithuanian expressionist painter, Chaim Soutine, whom Barnes took credit for discovering in Paris, stated that his (Barnes's) theories about painting were almost perfect, because he had tested them in a recently finished portrait. Soutine did allow that there was one problem: the painting, although technically perfect, had no feeling.

Albert Barnes was notorious for being the ruthless, ill-tempered multimillionaire who took credit for inventing the silver nitrate antiseptic, Argyrol, as well as for his passion for collecting modern art. In 1912, Dr. Barnes purchased his first Cézannes through his artist friend and advisor, William Glackens, who brought them back from Paris together with paintings by Manet, Gaugin, and Degas. According to the account of a colleague, Barnes could not stomach the Cézannes: "Get them out of here," he said. "Bring me back more Manets and Degas." Glackens told him in reply: "If at the end of one year you still don't like the Cézannes, I will buy them back from you for more money than you paid for them." These new paintings changed Barnes's whole concept of art and he personally went to Paris to purchase all of the Cézannes that were available.

When Barnes first exhibited his collection of European modern art at the galleries of The Pennsylvania Academy of the Fine Arts in 1923, it was ridiculed by the Philadelphia art establishment as outrageous, psychotic, and degenerate. That was the beginning of Albert Barnes's wrath and his vituperative correspondence with critics as well as his notorious feuds with the Academy, The University of Pennsylvania, and the Philadelphia Museum of Art.

Meanwhile, not too long after the Roy Lewando debacle, I showed my painting, *The Prisoner*, at an art gallery where it was seen by Dr. Barnes, who informed me through Ray Twordeska that he intended to purchase it for his Foundation collection. Unfortunately, about a week later, Albert Barnes was killed when he drove his car through a stop sign into the path of an oncoming tractor-trailer.

Sometime later, I had a call from Violetta de Mazie who advised me that the Foundation could not purchase my painting. The Board of Advisors had decided that there would be no further alterations to the collection, but she added that I would be welcome to view the collection without escort throughout my lifetime.

As I reflected on these curious, yet related, events many years later, I suspected that Dr. Barnes was at least partially interested in purchasing *The Prisoner* because he knew I had been a student at the Academy. My painting had obviously defied its conventions, the very same conventions that had infuriated Barnes back in the 1920s.

2.

Color as Vocabulary

Tonal Painting

A tonal painting is one that relies on dark and light tonal values as the principal means to hold the painting together. The Old Masters were tonal painters. Their use of color was restricted, since it was usually applied in thin glazes over a tonal black and white underpainting. As a result, the tonal values of their colors predominated in the structure of their works. Even Rembrandt, possibly the greatest of the Old Masters, cannot be regarded as a colorist by contemporary standards.

Most art schools emphasize tonal structure as the basis for seeing form. This is important. Learning tonal structure the old-fashioned way, with charcoal, chamois, stump, and kneaded eraser, has no equal. But remember, this is only the first step in one's development as a colorist.

Tonal painters, no matter how skilled in handling paint, work with a limited means of expression. Generally, they are both restricted and conservative in their painting because their techniques for making art are limited by their regard for traditional standards. In short, the mind-set of most tonal painters limits their color vocabulary and their understanding of color as a language that can be developed.

In nature, one usually sees the tonal structure of color first and the strength of the color second. Of course grass is green and sky is blue and distant mountains are a pale blue gray, but only the bright colors in flowers can approach the intense range of colors in an artist's palette. This is one of the reasons that most of the world's great photographers choose to work in black and white. With black and white film, they can adjust (mostly in the darkroom) an infinite spectrum of tonal values—maintaining light, losing form in darkness, adjusting focus—to simplify and interrelate tones, to make a stronger image. There is less scope for manipulating colors in photography because the range of colors is limited by the existing hues, values, and intensities, and by the

II.1

Henri Matisse, *L'homme nu*, 1900. Oil on canvas, 39⅛" x 28⅝".

Matisse mastered tonal drawing and painting in his early years, and he relied on this basic knowledge throughout his lifetime. His strong and simplified use of tone was the foundation for the clear and concise color relationships in his later paintings. A black and white photograph of any of his paintings reveals the colors in perfect balance, with a full range of tonal values. One of the main reasons Matisse's paintings are so simple and have such great inner life, is that he restricted his palette to five to seven tones in each painting. His colors varied widely and he used many different combinations, but his tones always showed a range from light to dark.

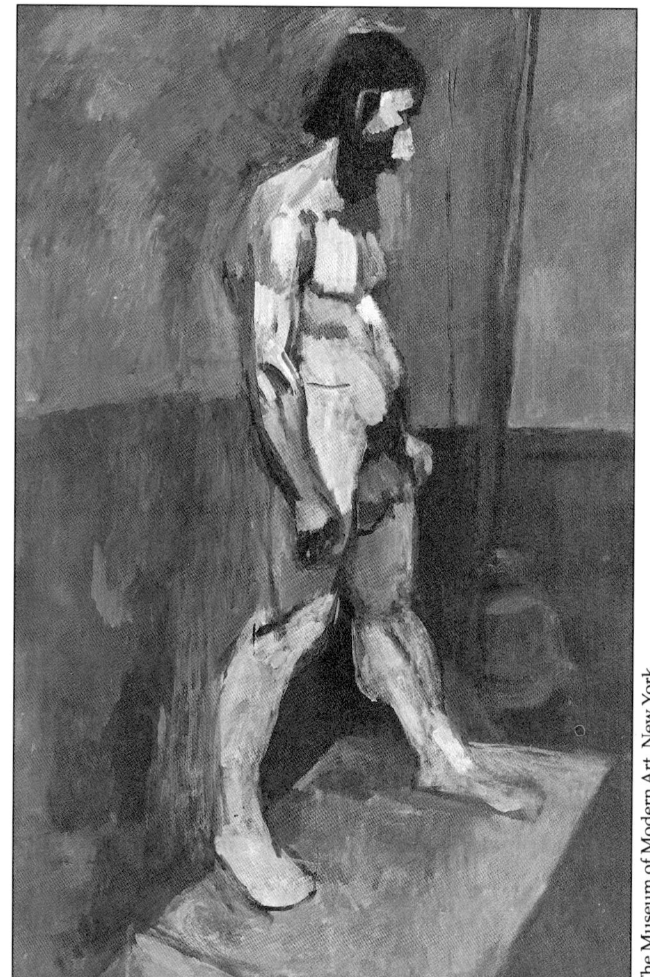

The Museum of Modern Art, New York.

range of colors permissible in the subject itself. Photography should never be confused with painting. Each medium has its own intrinsic value as well as its own limitations.

How We See Color

As light falls on any surface, it is reflected and absorbed. The proportions of the light reflected or absorbed, however, are different at each wavelength of light. As a specific wavelength of light enters the eye, it produces the perception of a specific color. The characteristics of the color, referred to as hue, value, and intensity, will vary according to the wavelength.

Hue is the quality of a color that identifies it as a red, green, or yellow, etc. As the wavelength of light moves along the spectrum, the hue of the color also changes. The spectrum is a series of hues, ranging in order from red through orange, yellow, green and blue, to purple.

The value, or tonal value, of a color refers to its relative brightness compared with other colors. Brightness is determined by the position of the color on a white-to-black scale. White is at the top of the scale and black is at the bottom. Thus a pale yellow is brighter than a darker yellow because it is higher on the scale. A dark red is closer to the bottom of the scale. Most painters and teachers of painting refer to the word "value" as "tonal value" because each color has a specific tone that is synonymous with its brightness.

The intensity of a color is the measure of its hue or lack of grayness. More simply, it is the relative purity of a color. Colors are decreased in intensity by adding various amounts of black, white, or gray to them. Other ways of reducing color intensity include reducing their purity by adding complementary colors or the less intense earth colors such as ochres or browns.

Color Evaluation

Since the eye is able to detect simultaneously the differences between the hue, value, and intensity of colors, and since all the characteristics of a color—including size and shape—affect our perception, a colorist must integrate all of a color's characteristics into a single entity. Color and form in modern painting are inseparable; they have a single, objective physical reality. Hence, I have joined the two separate words, color and form, into a simplified painter's term—"color/form." This basic precept is a departure from the traditional view that color illustrates form or renders form as it is painted. It is a useful concept, however, not only because it reflects more accurately the function of color in a painting, but also because it helps the artist to assess the use of color.

Because the use of color in painting is complex, it is essential to simplify perceptions. First, each color/form, in comparison with others, has a relative weight, according to its intensity and tonal value. Also, by comparison of size, as well as of tone and intensity, it has a relative energy, advancing to or receding from the eye within the picture plane.

Balancing colors in a composition can be simplified by translating them into weight relationships. These weight relationships are at the surface of the picture plane. Obviously, a pale color has a light weight and a dark color a heavy weight. The eye evaluates each color according to its relative tonal value. A cadmium red medium is translated as a middle tone and weight. A pale olive green is darker and heavier than a pale yellow. A large shape of color is heavier than a small shape of the same color. A transparent wash of color appears lighter than an opaque color. A dense black is heavier than a transparent black even if their tonal values are similar.

An evaluation of the weight of any one color is meaningless without a comparison of two or more colors. A color will appear one way on your palette and, because of its relationship to the other colors, completely differently on your canvas. Trust your vision; your eyes and your mind fashion immediate intuitive responses to the comparative weights of colors.

The relative energy of a color/form determines its depth in the picture plane. A color/form of relatively great energy is closer to the eye than one of less energy. The closer colors are termed "positive," while those further away from the eye are relatively "negative." The color closest to the eye can be termed the "primary positive," whereas the color furthest away from the eye can be termed the "primary negative." The relative energy of a color/form is determined by several criteria:

> Warm or hot colors (red and yellow hues) advance to the eye and are positive, provided that they are the same size as cool and cold colors (blues and greens), which recede from the eye and are negative.

> Bright, pure colors advance to the eye and dull colors recede from the eye.
>
> A large color/form has greater energy than a small color/form of the same color.
>
> A color painted as an intricate shape has greater energy and is seen as positive when compared with the same color in a more passive shape.
>
> A color in focus (i.e., with hard edges) advances to the eye; a color out of focus (i.e., with soft edges) recedes from the eye.

Any color's temperature is relative to those of the other colors. Thus a warm blue tends toward red, a cool blue tends toward green, hot red tends toward orange, and a cool red tends toward blue. Green, which is a mixture of blue and yellow, can tend toward blue (cool) or toward yellow (warm) or be midway between them. When warm or cool colors are mixed with the neutral colors—white, black, or gray—and with any mixtures of these or other colors, the interpretation of temperatures becomes more difficult.

Reading the relationships of colors is much like reading words in a sentence: the eye instantly accommodates all the letters in a word, then the words in a sentence, and the brain interprets their meaning. The eye seeks coherence and sees color and its inherent form always in context of the other colors and of the whole.

Spatial Intervals In Nature

The colors of the countless forms in nature all vary in hue, tonal value, and intensity. There is no way to describe adequately their subtle harmonies or their startling contrasts. Nature's colors never appear flat or manmade. The golden yellow of a New England autumnal oak leaf may have a delicate spatter of yellow-green, a tinge of burnt sienna, and a blush of deeper red at its edges. This leaf con-

II.2 Spatial Intervals.

Our ability to evaluate the relative depth of colors in a painting is similar to our ability to evaluate the distance between a near form and a distant form. For our purposes, I call the depth between two colors a spatial interval.

The depth of the spatial interval between a hot color and a cold color of the same size is an extreme.

Colors that have extreme temperatures clash.

As the spatial interval between two colors of the same size is decreased, they become more harmonious.

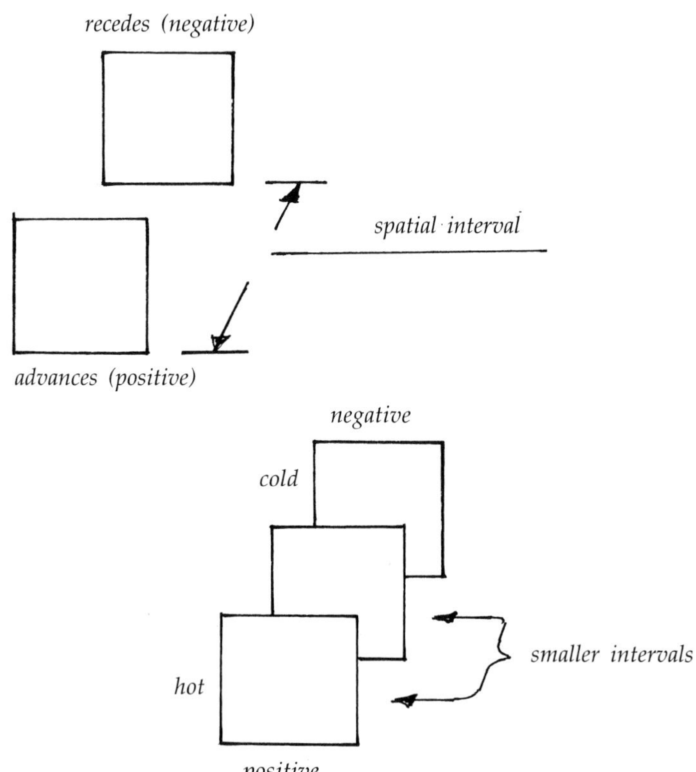

trasts with other deeper toned olive green, burnt red, and deep crimson leaves. All these colors are in the same warm "family" of color. Their spatial intervals are close together and, regardless of how they are arranged, they are in perfect harmony. As the season changes from fall to winter, the colors in the leaves also change, and their harmony is maintained until the trees are bare.

The same harmony exists among the colors of a tropical rain forest, desert, plain, savannah, steppe, tundra, beach, or morning-misted mountain. Each particular environment in nature has a range of colors that is in concord with its own range of temperatures. The baked Indian red in the southwest United States would be entirely out of place in the color environment of Scandinavia. A jungle orchid would not relate to the colors in an Arctic environment.

Nature is an extraordinary teacher for the colorist.

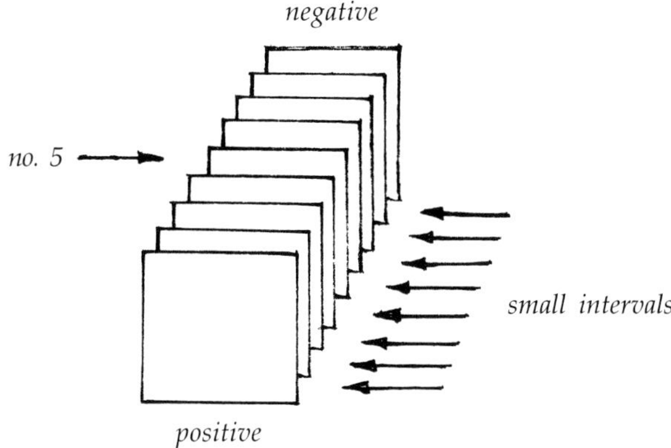

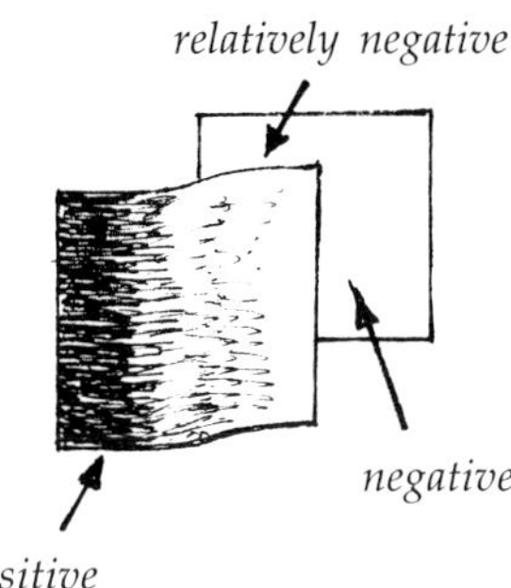

II.2 *continued.*

Modulated colors have minute spatial intervals and are in harmony.

A color that exists halfway between the positive and negative color (no. 5 in example) appears relatively neutral.

A true neutral color is neither warm nor cool. It can be black or white or any mixture of the two.

A plane composed of gradations of color is activated, or curves, advancing to or receding from the eye. This alters the spatial interval between the gradated color and a second color.

We can learn and be inspired by the natural laws that govern its harmony, but we must also learn that nature's laws cannot be equated to the creative problems inherent in the interaction of colors on a canvas. Painted colors don't look back at you in the same way as do the colors seen in nature. They must be seen as part of pictorial structure with their own objective reality.

Color Interaction

There are three fundamental ways that colors interact and influence each other in painting.

Integration: As each color/form is integrated with an adjoining color/form, it becomes a part of an integrated whole. There can be variations among the parts, but none are discordant or separated visually from the others. Forms that are well integrated have a sense of belonging to each other. Changes are subtle rather than dramatic. Colors are in accord. They are neither brash nor compelling because of forceful insistence, but rather are quietly modulated so that the eye can move smoothly from one passage to the next. Tones and temperatures of colors are in harmony with subtle variations from light to dark and warm to cool.

Opposition: Conversely, color/forms can oppose each other with startling contrasts, and by lesser contrasts as shapes and colors are modified. A brilliant red dramatically opposes a pure black and an off-white, or a brilliant cobalt blue contradistinguishes a pale lemon yellow. Bold shapes and colors interact and confront the eye and each color/form is seen with its own degree of insistent energy.

Saturation: Minute points of color are scattered in and about a field of contrasting color, producing a quality in the combined scheme that words cannot describe. As the tiny particles of color are further sprinkled and finally merged into the underlying color, they make a fully harmonious transition from one color to the other. In certain respects, the way that the Old Masters gradated tonal values from light to dark is similar to the idea of saturating one color into another. Because of the extremely subtle way that they gradated tones, light had the effect of glowing out of the dark. Saturated colors can also produce the effect of glowing, but it is the color that glows and not the illusion of light such as that depicted by the Old Masters.

All three color interactions can occur in a single painting. Color/forms can be softly integrated as well as oppose each other and edges of forms can be diffused with the saturation of color. The appearance of colors can be deceiving because all colors influence each other to a greater or to a lesser extent. Here are some considerations:

Colors appear lighter on a dark background and darker on a light background. A cadmium red medium appears light when painted next to a dark green and much darker against white.

The size of a color/form affects its energy as well as its relation to other shapes. For example, make a small circle of yellow and surround it with a large area of black. Rather than the yellow losing energy as one might suspect, it becomes a strong focal point because of the contrast. The same yellow surrounded by a very pale gray would hardly be seen. Thus as a shape becomes larger, it does not necessarily become stronger. The same small circle enlarged to a six-foot diameter, surrounded by white, would tend to float.

The background of a color changes the appearance of its tone and temperature. A brilliant yellow can make a rich medium green look dark and cool, whereas the same green appears lighter and warmer next to a dark blue.

A color will appear brighter and more energetic by painting it next to a neutral white, gray, or black. Bright contrasting colors are also pleasing in this scheme because the spatial intervals between them are decreased by their juxtaposition to the neutral color. The neutral color serves as a buffer. Its temperature is intermediate, or in between the temperatures of the brilliant warm and cool, or hot and cold, colors.

Pale colors painted on a neutral background appear more intense than when surrounded by bright colors. A pale, cool green, for example, looks more colorful against white than it does when surrounded by a bright blue.

Two different colors painted side by side that have similar tonal values appear to blend together because they are seen—regardless of their different hues—as similar weights. As the tonal value in one of the colors is increased, it separates from the second color.

When two colors painted side by side have equal intensities (equal energy), the eye is attracted to both simultaneously since it does not know which color to see first. This is a static relationship that can be changed by either increasing or decreasing the intensity in one of the colors. A bright red and a bright green, painted side by side, can create a pleasing relationship because they are complementary colors. At fullest intensity each has a similar tonal value, so that both colors are seen with equal amounts of energy. The two colors appear to quiver at their adjoining edge. This phenomenon is termed simultaneous contrast, which in effect is a negative after-image of each color acting equally on the retina.

It is easy to remember distinct colors if they have been used successfully in paintings, bearing in mind that the colors are remembered in association with other colors and an image of the whole painting. Specific color retention is difficult, if not impossible, if one tries to remember colors independently as in samples or color chips. Using colored paper to explore the various problems inherent in color interaction should not be confused with the process of painting.

Mixing paint is a time-consuming, disciplined process that relates directly to intentions. One must visualize a color before mixing it. The choice of color is an emotional response, generated by relationships of painted colors combined with all the characteristics of brushwork, such as texture, surface qualities, and movement. Thus, the appearance of a color cannot be separated from how it is painted. Colors appear differently at different times and in different lights.

I found that the best way to critique color relationships in students' paintings was by comparison, placing their works on the floor next to each other. In this way one can see each work objectively in the context of all the other paintings. Are the colors too dark or too light? Is the painting too weak? Are the colors wishy-washy, without feeling? Is the painting too strong? Are the colors overly stated?

Are the colors harmonic, resonant? Are the colors dissonant? If so, do they express a whole, valid feeling? Are the colors balanced? Are they plastic? I walk around the paintings, looking at them sidewise, upside down. I might separate one from the others to see it independently. A good way for any painter to evaluate a single painting is to see it on the floor in contrast to his other paintings.

A systematic exploration of color interaction, using different combinations of color in different paintings, can lead to an entirely new appreciation of color as an unlimited language.

The Discoverers

Here we will consider the work of Cézanne, Picasso, and Matisse, not for the purpose of teaching art history or art appreciation, but to tear apart and diagram their painting to enhance visual awareness and demonstrate color interaction.

PAUL CÉZANNE

The oil painting, *La Montagne Sainte-Victoire* (1903–04) by Paul Cézanne, influenced Georges Braque and Pablo Picasso, the two artists who founded cubism. An overview of the composition shows three distinct horizontal areas of color: a narrow, reddish tan and beige foreground, deceivingly simple; a wide, more complex middleground composed of deep greens, some of the reddish beige from the foreground, some very pale blue-violets, and a few accentuating planes of orange-red; and the medium-wide area at the top of the painting, generally composed of a soft blue-violet and other echoes of colors from the middleground.

Cézanne was obviously aware that any view of nature, at least as far as the eye could see from a single vantage point, has structural integration. All the parts belong to the whole and no changes in the shape of form or in color are abrupt. His concept of composition was an integrated design on a flat surface. Consequently, there is a soft transition from foreground to middleground to background. Each area belongs to the next area, yet each can be seen independently.

Cézanne used space to hold the painting together. The entire surface of the painting is an orchestration of form correlated to space—more like music than any paintings done up to that time. The individual brush strokes that make up the integrated structure were each spatially oriented; that is, interrelated by means of color advancing to or receding from the eye. Cézanne used dark lines to define form in space.

The large middleground of this painting is almost identical to the broken up, fragmented forms used by both Picasso and Braque in their early cubist paintings. The noteworthy difference was in Cézanne's overall image of *La Montagne Sainte-Victoire*. It had more color, was softer, more out-of-focus than either Braque's or Picasso's works.

Turn Cézanne's painting of *La Montagne Sainte-Victoire* on its side and compare its large, middle section of color to Picasso's *The Mandolin Player*, painted in 1911 (see

II.3

A pencil sketch by the author of a photograph of Cézanne when he was about thirty-six or thirty-seven years old. He is dressed in his ordinary rough painting clothes and carries heavy painting equipment on his back. He frequently hiked many miles to his various outdoor painting locations and worked incessantly, weather permitting. On rainy days, he painted in his studio.

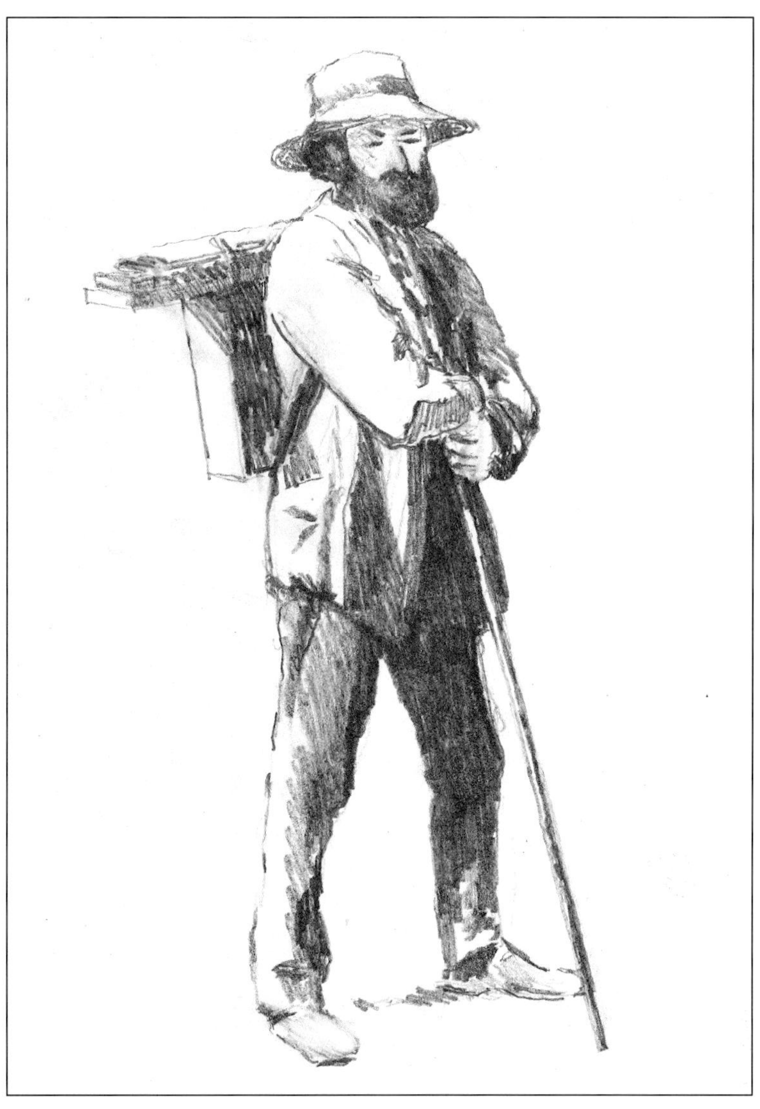

Illustration II.7). Picasso could not have painted *The Mandolin Player* without studying the way Cézanne developed space.

Picasso intensified depth relationships by shading overlapping planes with blurred, extremely dark shadows, mixing his colors with additions of grays and black, pulling the observer's eye in and out of the picture plane. In addition, he further emphasized the angular, geometric shapes that Cézanne suggested in his painting and, to make it more exciting, he used variegated brush strokes as an integrated textural counterpoint.

Regardless of their subject matter, Braque's and Picasso's cubist paintings looked much alike. Both artists used somber earth tones, touches of ochre and sienna, browns, slate grays, and blacks. In the spring of 1910, Picasso's dealer, Daniel-Henri Kahnweiler, said that Picasso had repeatedly tried to give color to structured forms, but each time he was forced to paint out the color he had used. Whereas Cézanne's work had evolved slowly but surely to a synthesis of color more pure than that used by any of his contemporaries, Picasso, despite his enormous talent and aggressive nature at this stage of development, remained a tonal painter. Cézanne was able to use pure color as dark and light tones because of his ability to translate the light in nature into harmonic color relationships. He was inventive. A pale orange-red rooftop sings and comes forward in the picture plane as a focal point. A soft olive green was used to add depth in the sky juxtaposed with an advancing pale, warm violet. Cézanne's color advances to or recedes from the eye, creating a sensation of volume in space, breathing and pulsating within the confines of the picture plane.

Cézanne and his colleague, the French painter Emile Bernard, carried on a more or less regular correspondence. On April 15, 1904, Cézanne wrote:

> Let me repeat what I told you here: you must see in nature the cylinder, the sphere, the cone, all put into perspective, so that every side of an object, of a plane, recedes to a central point. The parallel lines at the horizon give the extension, that is a section of nature, or, if you prefer, of the spectacle which the "pateromnipotens aeterne Deus" spreads before our eyes. The perpendicular lines at that horizon give the depth. Now to us nature appears more in depth than in surface, hence the necessity for the introduction into our vibrations of light, represented by reds and yellows, of enough blue tones to make the atmosphere perceptible.[16]

II.4

Sketch of Paul Cézanne's *La Montagne Sainte-Victoire*, 1903–04.

Cézanne's composition is divided into three major areas: sky and distant mountain, dominant middleground, and a small foreground.

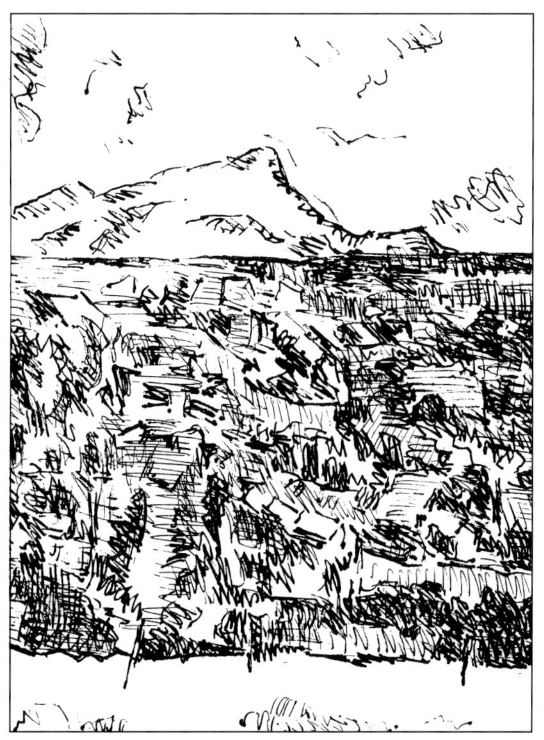

La Montagne Sainte-Victoire cropped at the top and viewed sideways, illustrating spatial characteristics similar to those in Picasso's *The Mandolin Player*.

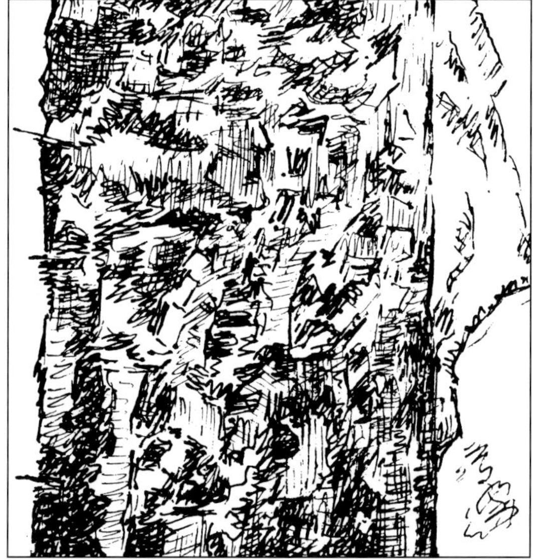

Again on July 25, 1904, Cézanne wrote Bernard:

> For progress towards realization there is nothing but nature, and the eye becomes educated through contact with her. It becomes concentric through observation and work: I mean that in an orange, an apple, a sphere, a head, there is a focal point, and this point is always nearest to our eye, no matter how it is affected by light, shade, sensation of color.[17]

In one of his last letters to Bernard, Cézanne wrote this advice, which even today is good guidance for a representational painter:

> One cannot be too scrupulous, too sincere, or too humble before nature; but one is more or less master of one's model, and above all of one's means of expression. One must penetrate what is in front of one and persevere in expressing oneself as logically as possible.[18]

PABLO PICASSO

Picasso's genius rested in his ability to synthesize visual experience—not just from his own creative painting, but from innumerable sources. From Cézanne he was able to understand a whole new concept of form and space made up of structural planes rather than being shaded conventionally and seen as rounded volume in deep space. But more importantly, Picasso deliberately rejected the laws of true perspective in his attempts to unify the picture plane. It was almost as if his vision came from inside Cézanne's mind, for this was the direction in which the master of Aix-en-Provence was headed in his last paintings.

In 1921, Picasso stated emphatically, "Cubism is dead!" He was telling the art world with great pride that he had finished painting cubist pictures. Picasso knew that he, more than Georges Braque, Juan Gris, or any of the other cubist painters, had finally taken cubism to its inevitable conclusion. Suddenly and dramatically, he combined his creative experiences of the past twenty years of painting into simple, powerful masterpieces such as *Mandolin and Guitar* (Illustration II.8), done in 1924.

GEORGES BRAQUE

The simplest kind of color combination contains several different values and intensities of a single hue. This is commonly referred to as a limited palette. Most of Picasso's and Braque's cubist painting was limited to simple earth colors and black and white. Because they chose not to work with bolder, contrasting colors, their paintings not only looked similar, but also held together with a consistent harmony. Apparently Picasso and Braque both recognized that the creative problems in their newly invented style of cubism would have been almost untenable with the additional problems of bold, contrasting color combinations.

After he stopped painting cubist pictures, Braque used variations of his limited palette during most of his career. He became a master of painting strong depth relationships in an inventive way, varying his subdued colors with a subtle interchange of tone and intensity. His magnificent painting, *Kitchen Table With Roast* (see author's sketch, Illustration III.14), is a typical Braque, with all the colors based on a subdued red-orange. The derivative colors include a pale salmon pink, a pale reddish brown, a rich chocolate brown, and a pale ochre, with all of these colors offset by an off-white and tones of gray from light to dark. The richness of this simple color orchestration is strengthened because each color is illuminated by its contrast to the next color and the temperatures of all of the colors are adjusted accordingly. Because the temperature variations of his colors are not extreme, Braque learned to vary his brush strokes from soft and dragged to hard edged, suggesting diverse textures and surface qualities, further enriching visual interest in his orchestration of a unified whole.

In his early cubist period, Braque used black as shadow to create an illusion of depth. In his later, more mature work, he used black and all other colors as planes in space.

Georges Braque limited his colors by using a restricted palette. Most of his color schemes in his later work were developed from the knowledge of tone that he gained as a cubist. Although he developed into a superb colorist, his use of color was discerning and reserved. He rarely used bright colors. The inner life in his painting was largely achieved by subtle temperature variations (small spatial intervals) used in contrasting mass relationships of color. He became a master of using varying tones of line to create focal points as well as to articulate the edges of forms.

HENRI MATISSE

Henri Matisse painted a small still life in 1899 that he called *Le compotier et la cruche de verre*, which depicted nine oranges, six of which were in a white compote, the other three on a tabletop with a tall glass pitcher and a teacup and saucer. By today's standards, this painting would not appear radical. The arrangement of the forms was conventional, yet this painting was a marked departure for Matisse, and challenged the whole idea that color must be attached to form. He no longer was concerned with traditional side lighting that illustrated form as volume with distinct tonal values. All the forms were painted as simply as possible. Four of the oranges were painted as flat shapes, not as fruit to eat, but as the color orange. The other five oranges were painted with a paler, more yellow orange and a deeper red. The tabletop was gradated from light rose in its lower corner to a deep, purplish blue. The pitcher was yellow-green, the cup and compote white. These were counterbalanced by a flat orange in the lower right side; a pale yellow and deep rose were painted in the upper left corner. The foreground was extremely simple—an off-white interrupted with a few splashes of color.

Matisse's choice and use of color was no longer directed toward a reproduction of observed fact, but instead was determined by an innovative, developing interrelationship of colors, brush stroke by brush stroke, balanced and counterbalanced to achieve a cohesive unity. This straightforward and refreshing still life can be seen as a turning point in the journey that Matisse was to take through the twentieth century. It was a departure from tradition and a highly original beginning for the development of his art.

II.5

Pen and ink sketch of Henri Matisse's *Le compotier et la cruche de verre*, 1899.

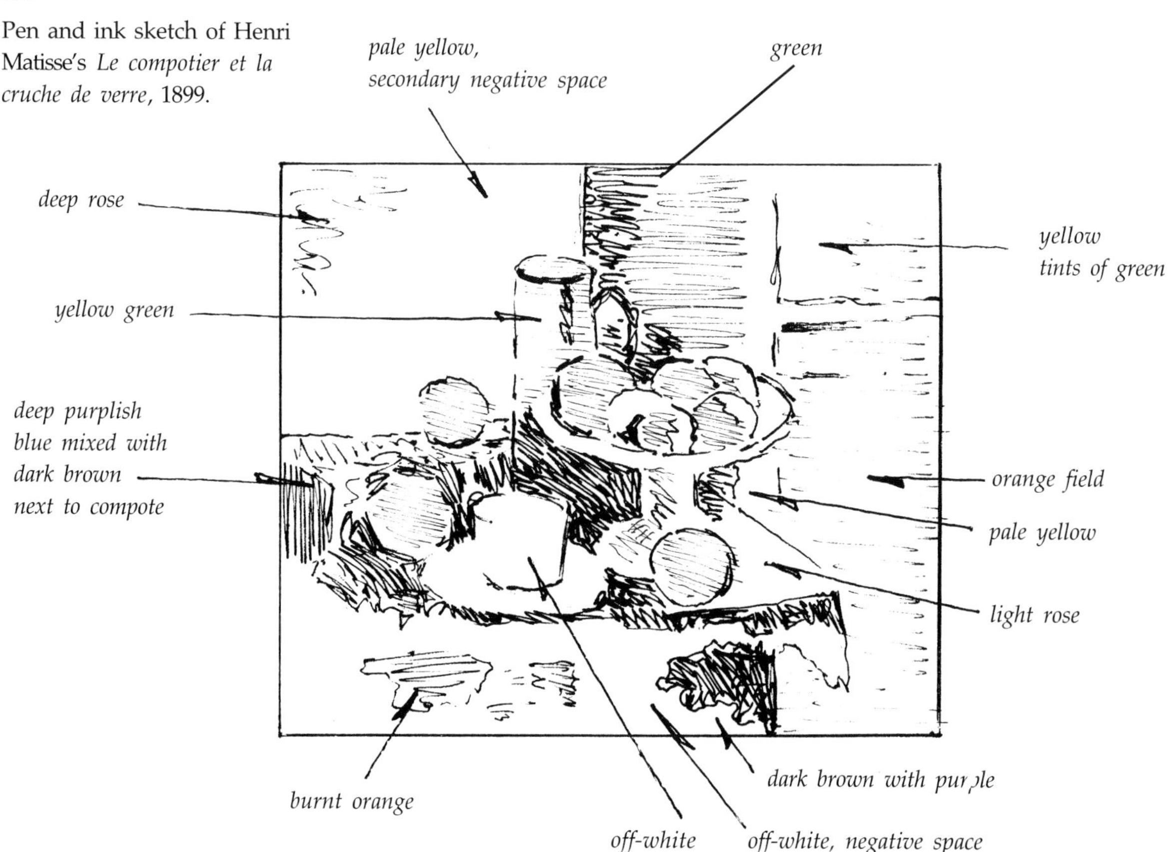

From that point in his life, the use of pure color became an all-consuming passion. An exhibition of Islamic art in Munich, which featured Persian miniatures, further influenced Matisse's concept of painting. His concept of space was dramatically changed as the entire surface of his painting became more important. The idea of a harmonious and unified pictorial pattern became synonymous with composition. As he developed his work, his search for more distinctive ways to use color led him to a childlike simplicity in composition. Matisse then said: "This all or nothing is very exhausting."[19] He also said: "Painting is always hard for me . . . always this struggle . . . is it natural? Yes, but why so much of it? It is so sweet when it comes naturally."[20]

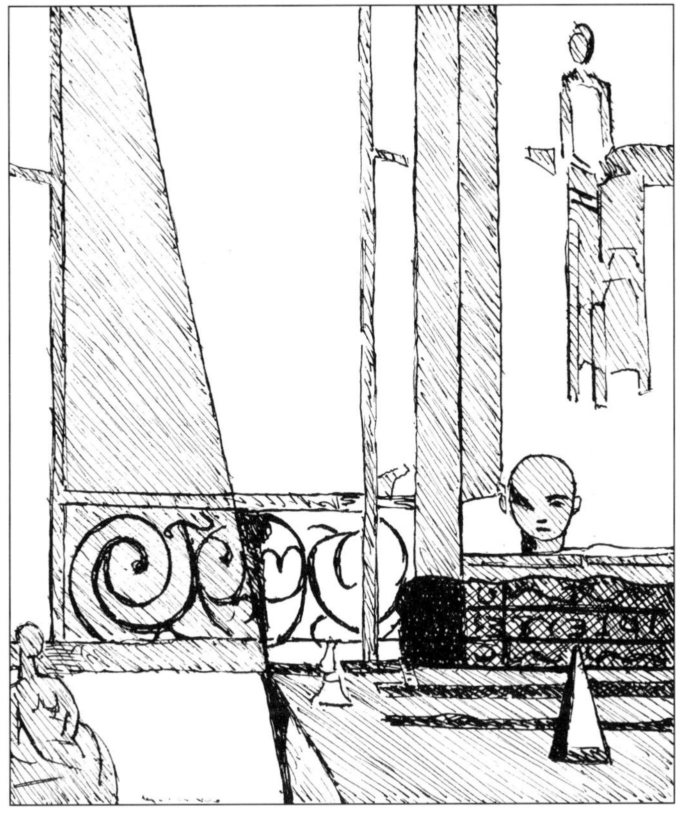

II.6

Sketch of Henri Matisse's *La leçon de piano*, 1916.

The shaded areas are composed of green, pale blue, orange, rose, off-white, and a small amount of black. The remaining white area shows the large (up to eight-feet-high) dominant color of pale gray. The large, dull color of the gray effectively counterbalances the smaller areas of brighter colors. The sculptural figure in the lower left corner occupies the area that Matisse apparently had difficulty with when completing this painting.

Why did Matisse find his painting such a struggle? The interaction of colors in composition is not determined entirely by known factors, and any formula is the antithesis of innovation. What was so unusual was his ability to see each painting as a whole new problem of color and form. Therein lay both his mastery and the difficulties he created for himself.

There is a corner in one of Matisse's paintings with which he had difficulty. This is located in the lower left section of his large oil painting called *The Piano Lesson* (see above). A reddish nude figure is sketched into the corner as a counterbalance for the white figure that is isolated by the gray background in the upper right area of the painting. The remainder of the painting is fluid and totally intuitive in its execution, but this corner is unresolved. Despite this weakness, it is a magnificent painting.

These anecdotes, the little things like that corner, help us understand painting. If you have the will to be a creative painter, you have allies. Both Cézanne and Matisse struggled. You can sense their humanity. Although I did not know it at that time, it was for this same reason that I bought a biography of Cézanne back in 1950 at a bookstall on the west bank of the Seine in Paris. I had to know about this business of painting, what it was all about, from a master. I needed Paul Cézanne as my ally, to reinforce my own ideas about form. As we paint, the Old Masters look over our shoulders.

> The apparently effortless lightness of touch, which, as Matisse said, in fact cost him a lifetime of labor from morning to dusk, was the sign of confidence and contentment with an actual situation.[21]

During the same period that Picasso and Braque were painting with restricted color schemes, Matisse was forging ahead into a whole new world of color problems and creative solutions. In 1906, Matisse painted a remarkable self-portrait that demonstrates the use of neutral colors between hot and cold colors (Illustration II.11). The passage of colors from the shirt to the background on the right side shows a streak of brilliant red (hot) next to an off-white (neutral), next to a black (neutral), next to a gray-blue (cooler), next to the black in the background (neutral), next to the deep green (cool), next to a blue (cool), next to a pale blue (cool, echoes in shirt), next to the pale pink-orange (warm). Matisse painted pale red as flesh tones next to very warm greens in the lighter shadows and cooler, darker greens in the deep shadows. The reds appear brighter by placing them next to the deeper shades of complementary greens. All the colors are seen in perfect harmony simply because Matisse instinctively limited the spatial intervals between all these colors.

Matisse continued to use neutral colors in much of his painting throughout his career, always intuitively, for greater harmony. His "papiers decoupes" (paper cutouts), done in the 1950s, which in many ways were the fulfillment of his desire for pure color in his painting, often employed neutral white as the buffer zone between bold, flat and brilliant warm and cool colors. Both *L'escargot* (Illustration II.17) and *Souvenir d'océanie* (Illustration II.12) show turquoise (cold), brilliant magenta (warm), orange (hot), deep orange-yellow (hot), and ultramarine blue (relatively cool), all used as pure hues, seen against large areas of white, negative space.

The knowledge a painter absorbs by working with the creative problems of color and form in each painting, little by little, adds to and expands his visual vocabulary, which in turn increases his expressive potential. This kind of knowledge is not gained through theory or from what I am writing here; it is gained only through painting itself, or from finding out yourself how these ideas relate to your personal expression. Otherwise, they are only meaningless ideas. Matisse went far beyond Braque and Picasso as a colorist because he regarded color/form as the most essential ingredient in modern art. The critics can decide who was the greatest painter in the long run, but our purpose is to understand how the interaction of color has developed, and what can be gained from this understanding.

Single Color Dominance

Matisse's red period culminated in *Le studio rouge* (Illustration II.13). The entire foreground and background in this huge canvas were painted a brilliant, flat, medium-toned red that boldly contrasted with the various forms that identified it as a studio: a stack of canvases, a chair and a table, paintings on the wall, all seen as minor notes that complemented the immense amount of red. In this work, Matisse was in search of simplistic definition. He needed not a family of colors derived from a single color as observed in nature, but a single dominant color, painted as a continuous environment that enveloped everything. Matisse had discovered that a single pure color conveyed its own deep meaning and controlled all of the other colors in the painting. For the first time in the history of painting, the energy of a color, magnified because of both its brilliance and relative size, fairly leaped out of the picture plane into physical space. *Le studio rouge* paved the way for his climactic series of flat, brilliant-colored paper cutouts that he created forty-odd years later.

There was a monumental quality in this painting that Matisse had never achieved before, and its impact provided him with an insight into the process of color simplification for new canvases. His painting of *The Piano Lesson* (Illustration II.6) is an excellent example of how a huge field of color, in this instance a warm light gray, can influence the entire range of remaining colors that comprise the whole, and balance the smaller yet more intense hues, producing a perfect, harmonious interrelationship. The neutral gray advances in the picture plane, and, because of its relatively large size, has an insistent energy, despite its lack of intensity.

The idea of a single color dominating a canvas is not new. Monet, as early as 1874, had learned from closely observing nature that an effective color mood could be both simplified and intensified by using one color as the basis for his composition as well as for the source of all his other colors. The seascapes that he painted during that period created an effect of infinite atmospheric space made even more perceptible by the presence of water. He used orange, for example, as the dominant color in a Le Havre harbor sunset, and a blue-green as the controlling color in a channel beach view. These paintings, typical of Monet's early color explorations, provided the basis for his future painting that ultimately ended with his unparalleled union with nature at Giverny. His last canvases of his beloved ponds and water lilies revealed an incredible insight into the transitory yet exquisite color states of nature, each dependent on a singular color mood.

As I was writing this explanation of how color dominance works, my wife called me excitedly to see, through our front picture window, the vast panorama of sky and water just after the mid-December sun had disappeared in the west. The sky and water were combined as a huge field of deep blue-gray, and the horizon that remained was revealed by a broad, jagged path of intense Chinese red-orange—a spectacular and uncommon view. I immediately asked her which color dominated, the blue-gray or the red, and she replied without hesitation that it was the red. It fairly screamed at us,

II.7

Pablo Picasso, *The Mandolin Player*, 1911. Oil on canvas, 162cm. x 71cm.

Cézanne's concept of planes of color advancing to and receding from the eye provided Picasso with the insight to develop a more formal, geometric concept of space.

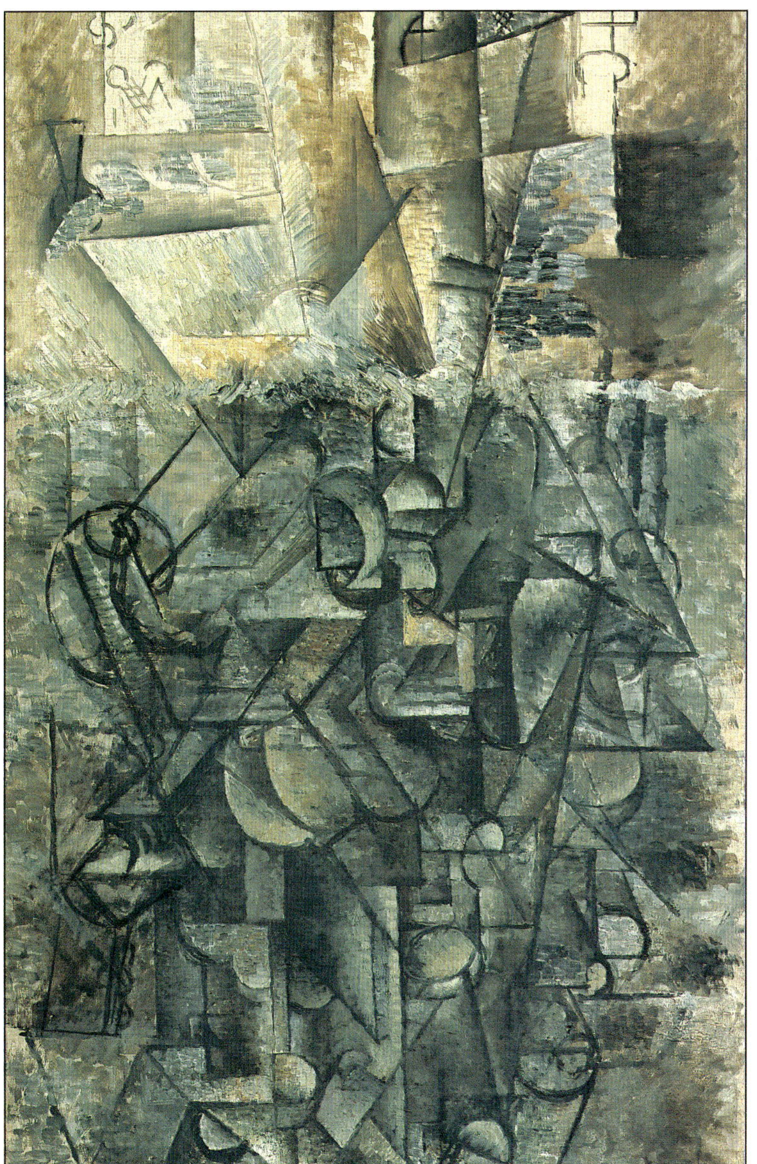

II.8

Pablo Picasso, *Mandolin and Guitar*, 1924. Oil with sand on canvas, 55⅜" x 78⅞".

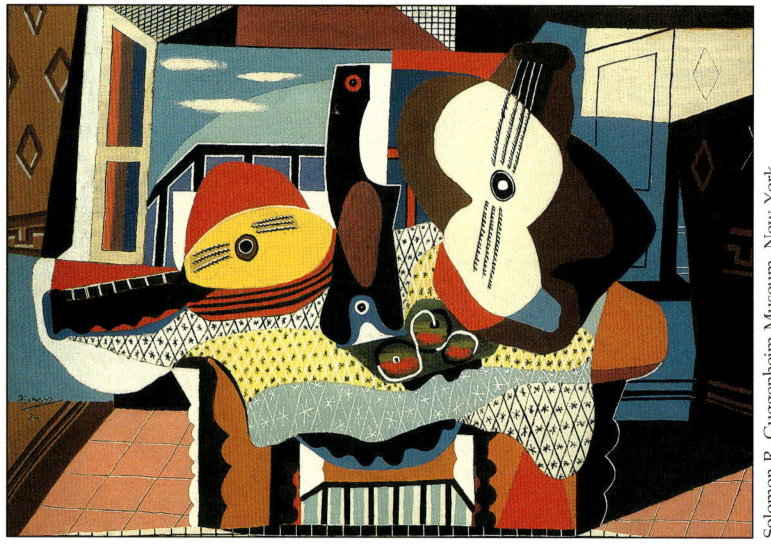

Solomon R. Guggenheim Museum, New York.

BALANCE
Mandolin and Guitar
Squint at the whole. The entire painting pushes and pulls the eye; all the forms are balanced effectively in terms of surface, weight relationships, and corresponding spatial intervals with varying depths and degrees of energy. Tonal range and distribution from light to dark produce strong contrasts and accompanying strength. The predominantly light tones, coupled with the prevailing warm colors, generate an extraordinary light radiating from within the painting. The cool tones of blue further magnify brightness and warmth. Patterns are counterbalanced as they are repeated in the floor tiles, balcony railing, diamond shapes, and assorted textures—all generate visual interest as well as pull one's eye from various depths to the painted surface. Colors are counterbalanced as they are repeated in various places in the picture plane—a means of distributing colors to create harmony.

II.9

Detail of *Mandolin and Guitar*.

Picasso's genius for creative synthesis of prior experience, combined with an ever-increasing need to use pure color, overcame his dependency on the more easily used dark and light tonal gradations of his cubist period. He composed *Mandolin and Guitar* with flat, bright, contrasting colors, each seen with their own indigenous energy. They do not illustrate the forms; the only gradated colors are in the three apples that act as a focal point, counterbalanced by four other focal points seen in the remaining circles.

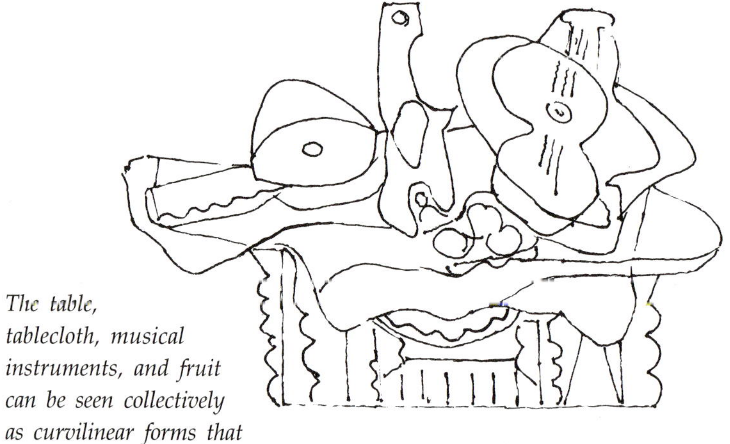

The table, tablecloth, musical instruments, and fruit can be seen collectively as curvilinear forms that dominate the composition—these are counterbalanced by the purely geometric patterns of light and shadow within the room and the distant sky and clouds.

II.10 More Detail.

Whites

Primary Positives

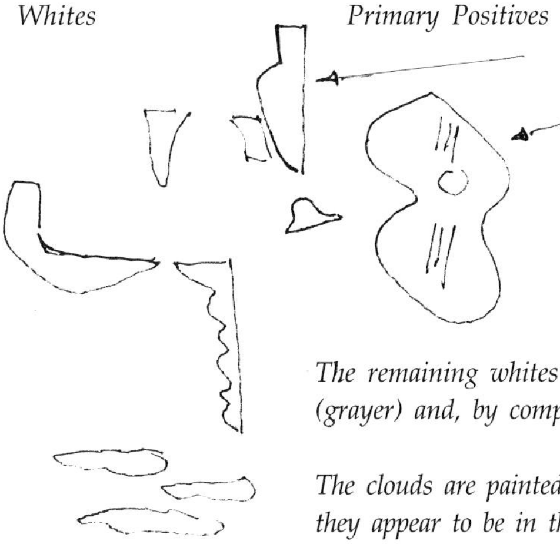

Brightness is increased in guitar and shape to its left (whitest whites) because of contrast to the dark, adjoining shapes. Curvilinear qualities attract the eye.

The remaining whites are slightly desaturated (grayer) and, by comparison, recede.

The clouds are painted with soft edges so that they appear to be in the distance (out of focus). The large warm shape of white in the upper right recedes when compared with the guitar.

COLOR SEEN AS FORM

An analysis of *Mandolin and Guitar* in terms of its depth relationships.

Yellows, oranges, reds, Secondary positives All advance in the picture plane. The large expanse of warm rose at the bottom firmly anchors the composition. Reds, oranges, and yellow effectively counterbalance the strong blacks, whites, and cooler colors.

Browns Recede in contrast to the lighter, brighter, warm colors, and are cooler and relatively negative. Note how much red is mixed into the deep brown next to the white guitar, uniting this color to the surface plane of the canvas while it is simultaneously seen as an intermediate dark negative. A cooler brown, mixed without red, would appear comparatively dull and recessed in the picture plane.

Blues, Secondary negatives Of all the blues, the deep blue adjoining the guitar is the most negative. Note that the white to its left advances sharply to the eye and the red-brown, adjoining it on the right side, tends to merge with it because of the similarity of tonal value. A closer look reveals the red-brown well in front of the blue. The two blues in the upper left window are paler and grayer and recede from the eye when compared with the distinctly brighter blues used in the shadows of the interior.

Blacks, Primary negative Although the blacks are seen as the primary negative in the picture plane because of their extreme contrast to adjoining colors, it is possible to perceive them, with a conscious effort, as advancing to the eye as primary positives. At first glance, the extremely dark brown, painted adjacent to the black on the right side, is seen as a continuation of the black, but it can be further perceived as Picasso's means to adjust the balance of the overall composition. If the entire shape of dark had been painted black, the right side of the painting would appear too heavy. Both black and white in this painting, because of their neutral temperatures, decrease the intervals between the warm and cool colors, producing a harmonic interchange between them.

II.11

Henri Matisse, *Self-Portrait*, 1906. Oil, 21⅝" x 18⅛".

Both the light and dark, relatively neutral colors, enhance the harmonic interchange of the reds and greens.

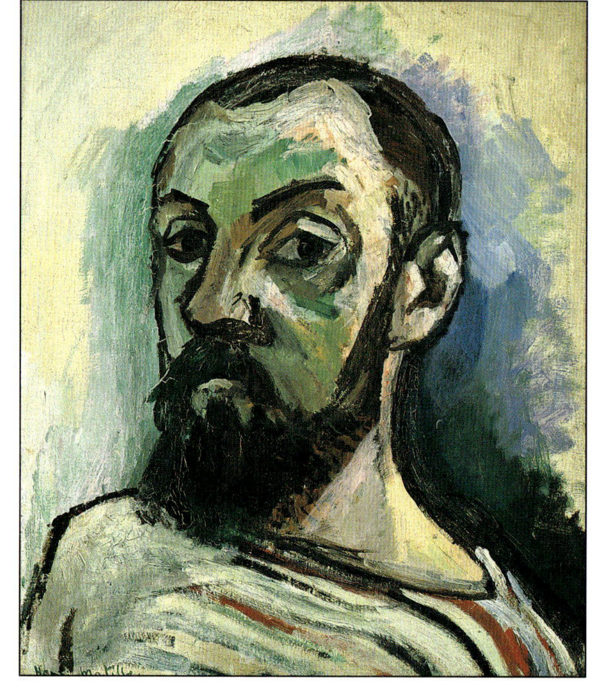

Statens Museum for Kunst, Copenhagen, Denmark; photo, © Hans Petersen.

II.12

Henri Matisse, *Souvenir d'océanie*, 1952–53. Gouache and crayon on cut-and-pasted paper, 9′4" x 9′4⅞".

Nonobjective imagery by Matisse. A balance between the positive physical presence of form and space. The oppositions of color are bold and flat, resulting in simplicity and expressive power.

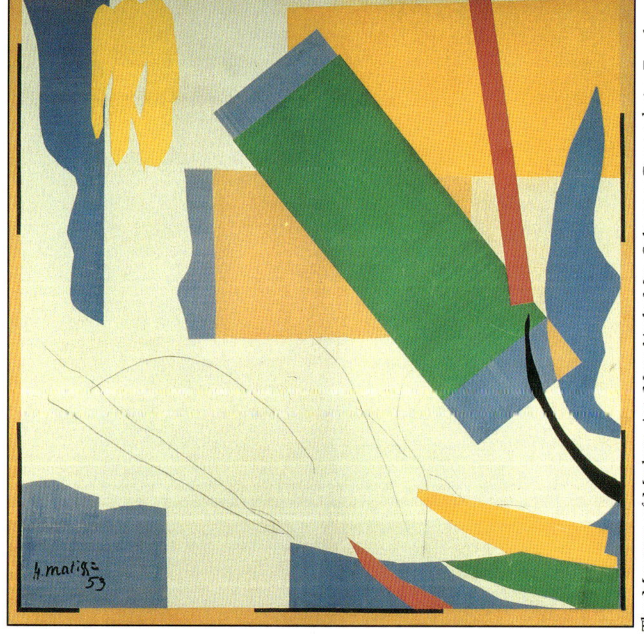

The Museum of Modern Art, New York; Mrs. Solomon Guggenheim Fund.

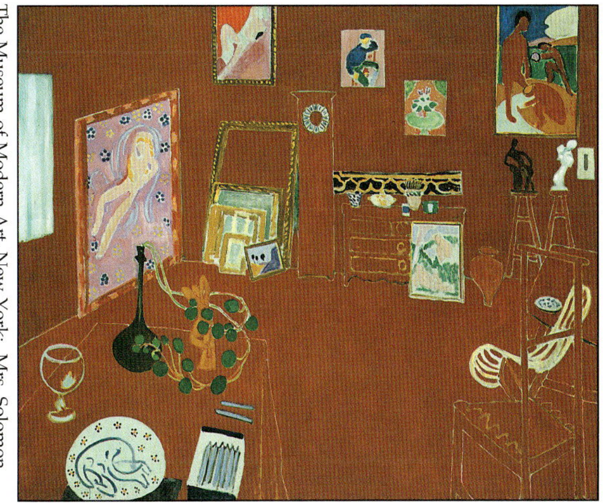

The Museum of Modern Art, New York; Mrs. Solomon Guggenheim Fund.

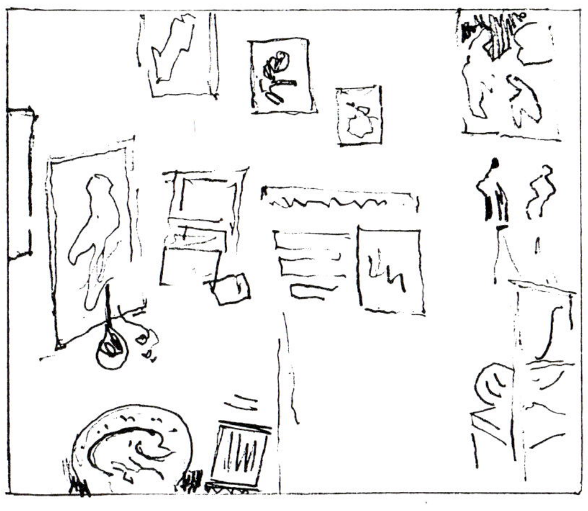

II.13

Henri Matisse, *Le studio rouge*, 1911. Oil on canvas, 71¼" x 72¼".

Because of its size and intensity, the red is seen as positive, but with a closer look, one can perceive the smaller forms, because of contrast, advancing to the eye, and the red seen as negative.

II.14

Pablo Picasso, *Still Life*, 1919. Oil on canvas, 31⅞" x 39⅜".

Any strong color has its own individual character. In this instance, the eye responds to the bright red as a dominant form that leaps forward in the picture plane, separating it from the strong tonal characteristics in the rest of the painting.

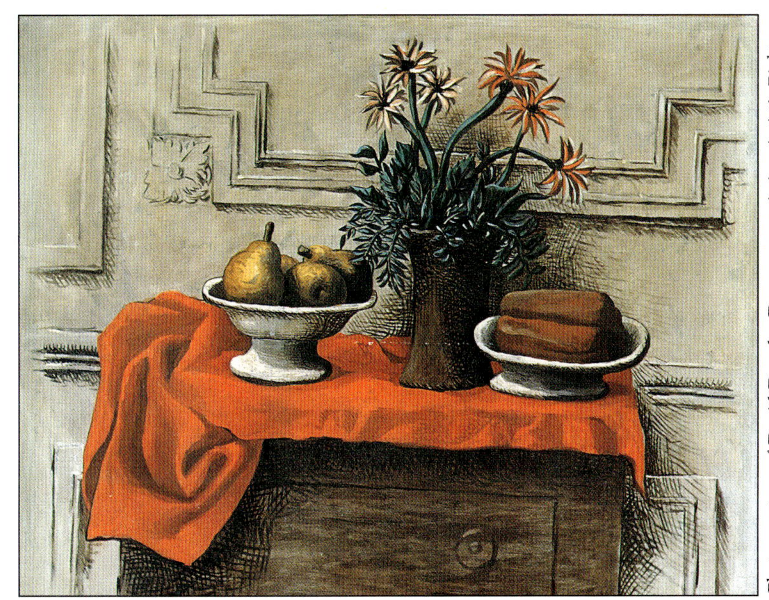

Photo courtesy of David Douglas Duncan; permission Artist's Rights Society, New York/SPADEM, Paris.

II.15

Henri Matisse, *Studio, Quai St. Michel*, 1916. Oil on canvas, 58 1/4" x 46".

BALANCING COLORS
A comparison of two paintings by Matisse.

Two totally different kinds of pictorial structure with coinciding perplexities of color balance are demonstrated in Matisse's semirepresentational painting of his studio model, pictured here, and his nonobjective painting, *L'escargot*, pictured in Illustration II.17.

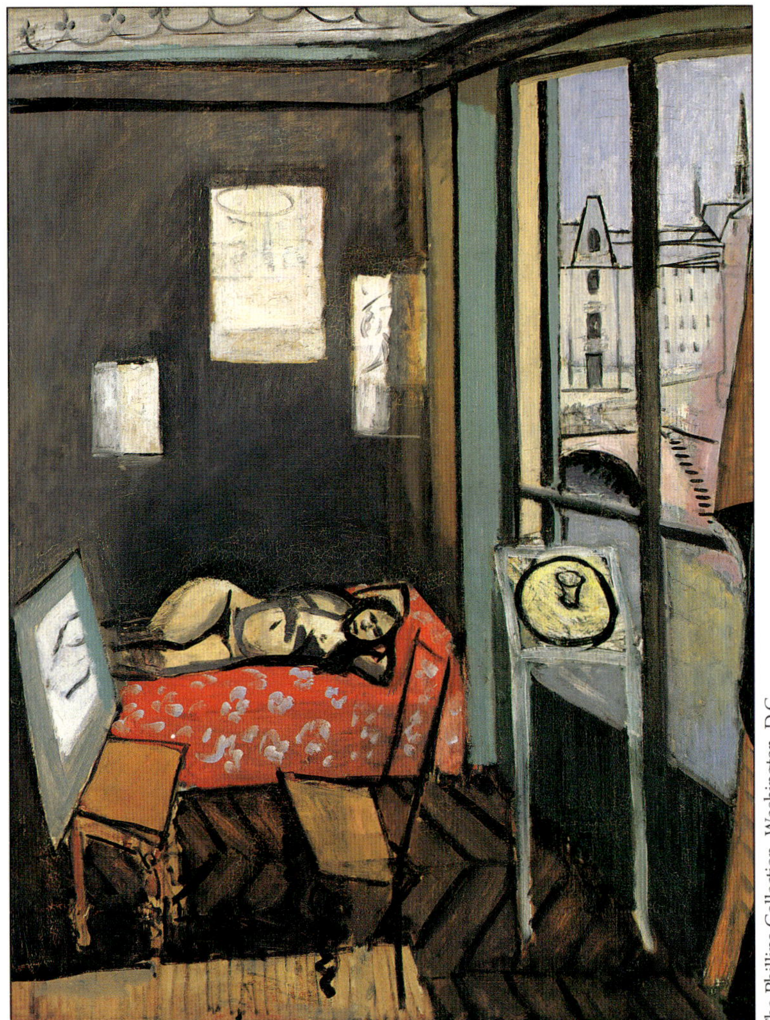

A COMPOSITE PICTORIAL STRUCTURE
Matisse counterbalances hollowed-out deep space composed with tonal gradations by flat planes of more intense colors in the bedspread, the chairs, throw rug, and tray. Lines are used to reinforce planes and accentuate focal points. The spatial intervals between the colors are modest. The pale yellow, burnt oranges, warm red, and varying gradations of cooler browns are in the same family of colors and are harmonious.

II.16

Diagram of *Studio, Quai St. Michel.*

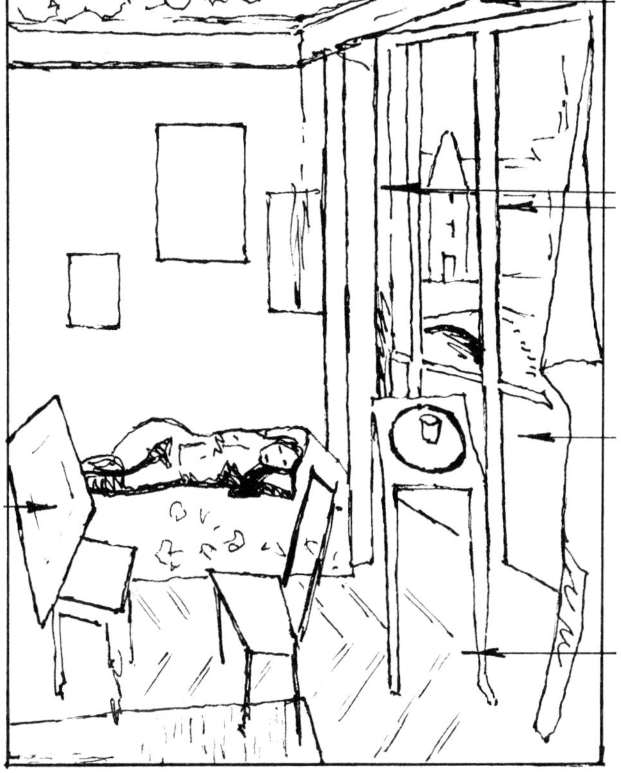

OPPOSITIONS OF TONE AND COLOR

The eye enters the painting at the lower left, attracted to the strong gravitational base. The throw rug takes the eye movement upwards, via the distorted true perspective in the two chairs, to the figure that is seen as the primary focal point. The eye then moves to the right, attracted by the round yellow tray, then upward via the strong verticality in the window and back to the left via the perspective of the cornices at the ceiling, and finally back down to the figure via the pictures on the wall.

The counterclockwise eye movement is in contrast to the clockwise movement usually seen in traditional Western painting.

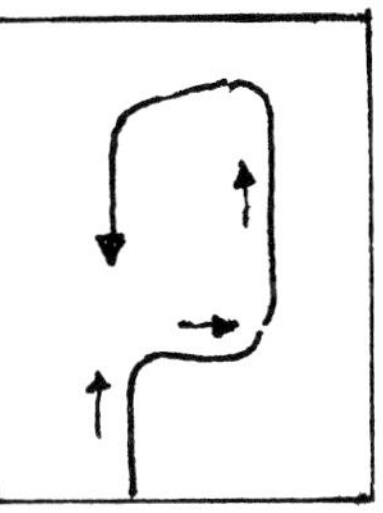

Place your finger over any one element in the composition, and note how the painting becomes out of balance.

II.17

Henri Matisse, *L'escargot*, 1953. Gouache on cut and pasted paper, 112¾" x 113".

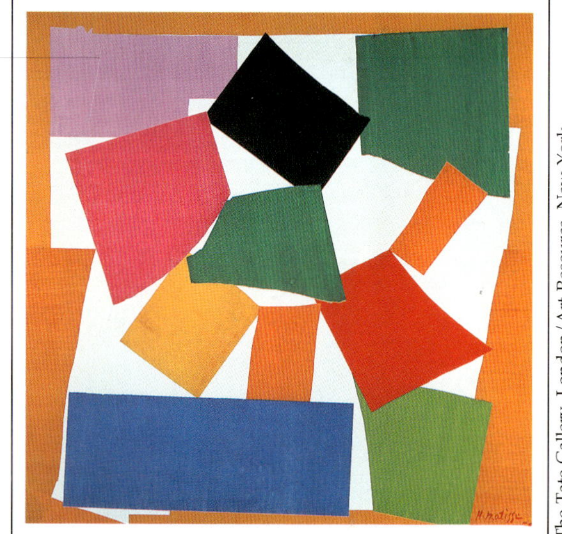

The Tate Gallery, London/Art Resource, New York.

BALANCE OPPOSITIONS OF PURE COLOR

The small arrows show how the eye is directed into the painting. Because the corners are securely anchored by the geometric repetition to the corners of the picture plane, the composition has strength and stability. There is a positive pull from the strong lower-left corner to the strong upper-right corner. The tonal values of the other two corners are weaker, approximating that of the orange.

II.18

Diagram of *L'escargot*.

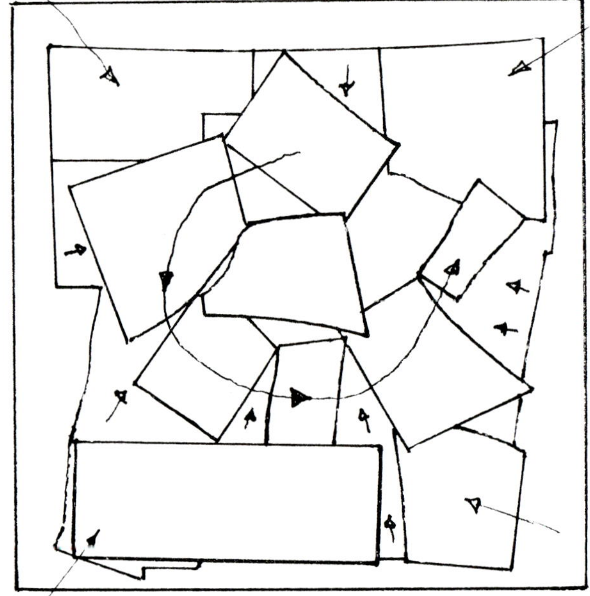

The warm blue, because of its intensity, size, and weight, is the dominant form in the painting (primary positive), establishing a heavy gravitational base. The smaller shapes of black (secondary positive), green, two reds, yellow-orange, and orange oppose and counterbalance the blue. The orange at the perimeter of the painting, the largest area of color, effectively frames all the other colors. Note how the smaller shapes of color, starting with the black at the top, are arranged counterclockwise, each with a sense of motion when compared to the larger, more stable, shapes of orange and blue. The white field (primary negative) is opposed by the weights of all the remaining colors. The white is seen as neutral, its relationship to the other colors in perfect harmony regardless of their different energies.

SPATIAL INTERVALS

Matisse increased and decreased spatial intervals to move the eye in and out of the picture plane. The deep rose in the upper left is seen as negative next to the slightly darker, warmer orange, and positive next to the cooler white. The red (relatively cool compared with the brighter red on the right side) in turn comes forward; the yellow-orange recedes almost to the same plane as the white because of its light tone; the orange comes forward and the bright red moves even further forward. The two cold greens are essential to the balance of the overall composition. Place a finger over both greens and note how the color mode of the entire painting changes from warm (pleasing) to hot (oppressive).

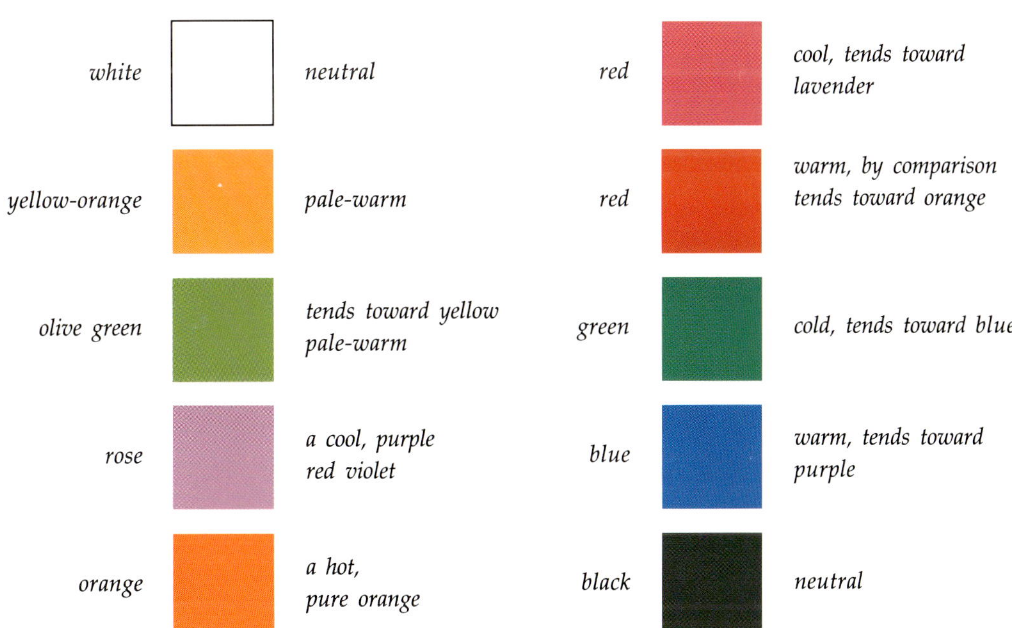

II.19

Diagram of tonal value range of *L'escargot.*

II.20

John Marin, *Movement: Sky and Grey Sea*, 1941. Watercolor, pencil, and charcoal on paper, 15⅛" x 20⅞".

Wet into wet, dry, dragged—Marin's brush, water, and color were the malleable means for spontaneous discovery, pushing and pulling the eye in and out of the picture plane.

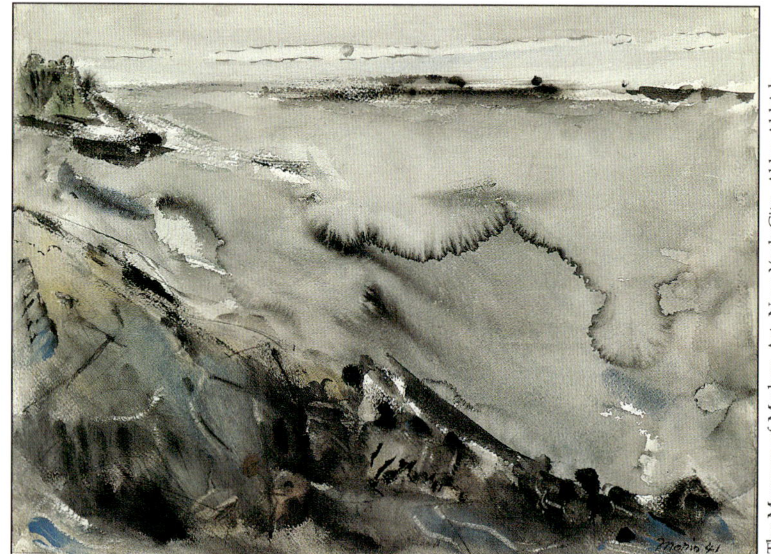

The Museum of Modern Art, New York City. Abby Aldrich Rockefeller Fund.

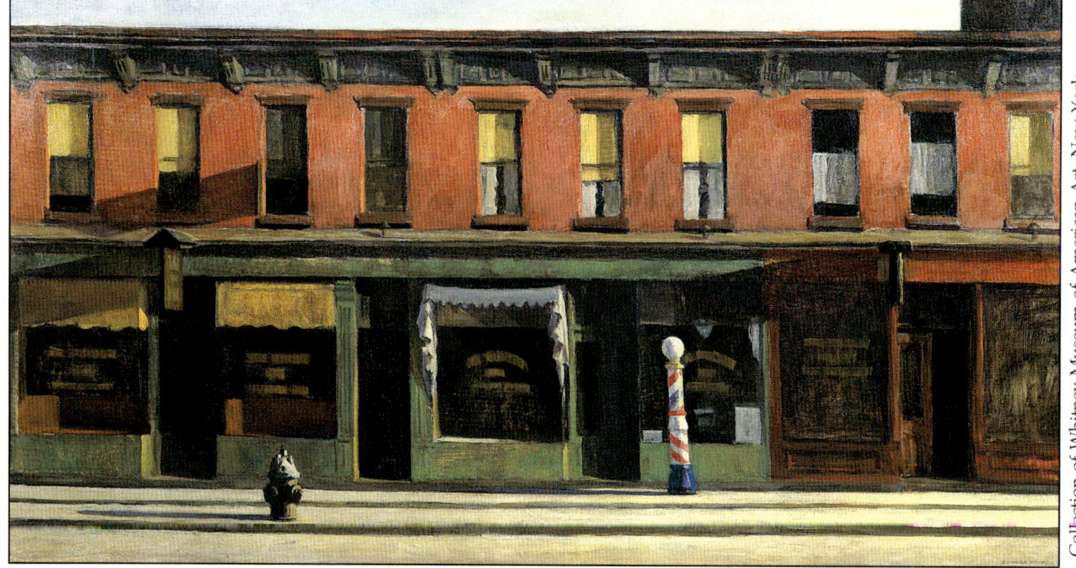

Collection of Whitney Museum of American Art, New York.

II.21

Edward Hopper, *Early Sunday Morning*, 1930. Oil, on canvas, 35" x 60".

Colors and forms are interdependent and are seen as solid masses that produce both a sense of interior light coming from within the painting and an illusion of early morning sunlight. Hopper worked with the principle that light is warm and shadow is cool. Each nuance of color is essential to the whole.

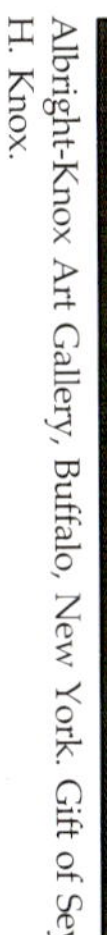

Albright-Knox Art Gallery, Buffalo, New York. Gift of Seymour H. Knox.

II.22

Clyfford Still, *1954*, 1954. Oil on canvas, 113½" x 156".

The black comprises more than two-thirds of the area of the entire canvas. This is obviously the dominant color and is the primary positive. The off-white, raw cotton canvas is the primary negative. The bright orange-reds on the left and right sides effectively counterbalance the massive dark positive. Because of its power, the black advances from the picture plane into physical space, but if one's focus is then directed toward the two orange-reds, they become positive and the black becomes negative by contrast. This kind of interaction between positive and negative color fields is one of the components in dynamic, contemporary color orchestration.

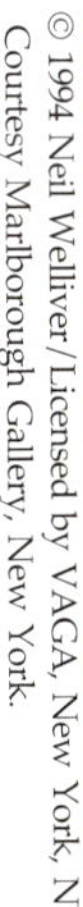

© 1994 Neil Welliver/Licensed by VAGA, New York, NY. Courtesy Marlborough Gallery, New York.

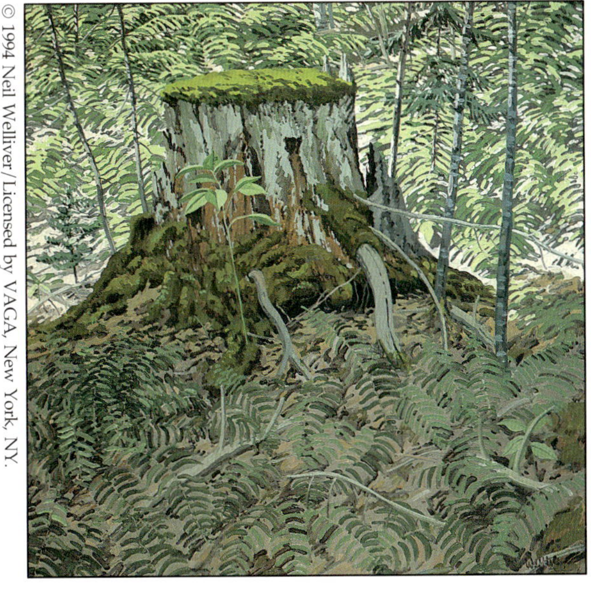

II.23

Neil Welliver, *Stump and Ferns*, 1974. Oil on canvas, 60" x 60".

The eye penetrates the painting from the surface, by seeing color/forms in front of and behind each other.

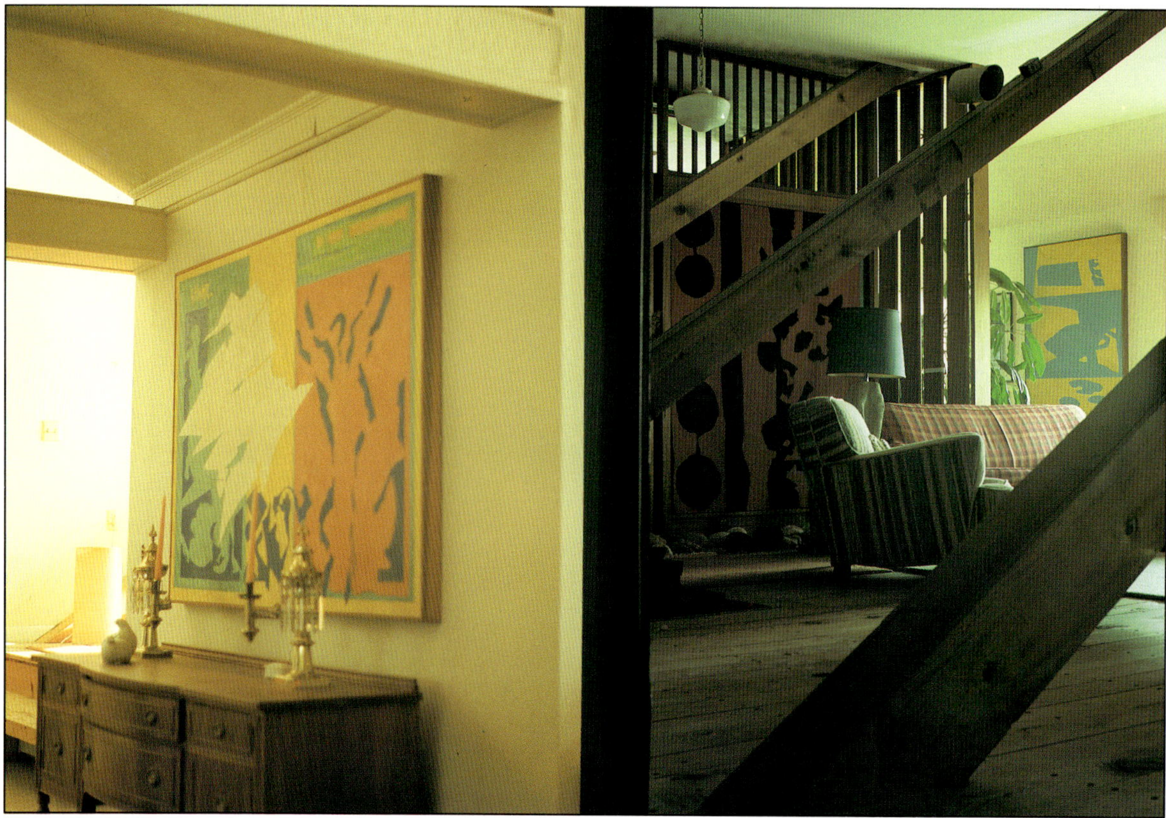

II.24

Strawberry Factory interior, showing the east living room (left-hand photo) adjoining, with a step up, the west living room (right-hand photo) that overlooks the Chesapeake Bay.

particularly because it was further intensified by the surrounding field of the deep blue-gray. The eye was drawn as if by a magnet to this vibrant source of energy.

The artist, however, must learn to perceive color and its relative size, shape, and intensity in terms of relationships. Depending on how one looked at it, the brilliant red could be seen as a small area of intense energy opposed by a much heavier and larger field of energy. The relative weight of the blue-gray was in direct proportion to its tonal value and size. The artist responds to nature's wonders, but also sees things differently from others. He has learned to see in terms of "visual equations." In a painting of this dramatic sunset, the brilliant red could be perfectly counterbalanced by an immense area of the deep blue-gray.

There is no pigment, however, that can equal the dazzling brilliance of the red-orange. A thin wash of this color painted over a pure white ground would appear the brightest, particularly if it were contrasted by a heavier, slightly opaque consistency of pigment mixed for the blue-gray. It is the appearance of these colors on the canvas that is the important consideration.

A substantial characteristic of Matisse's painting rested in his ability to make his colors "speak" to each of the others with luminous authority. Very often he painted thin washes of color or he left hints of the white ground shining through—or, as in *The Piano Lesson*, he painted a brilliant medium-cool shade of green, modulated by a paler yellow-green to give it a sense of inner life. He often articulated the edges of color masses with suggestions of a lighter color, and, at times, strengthened edges with wisps of a dark line.

If the red-orange that we observed at sunset were painted brilliantly, but were deliberately softened at its edges, taking it out of focus, it would move back slightly in the picture plane. But if its perimeter were pronounced, with either hard or jagged edges, it would jump right out of the painting.

The concept of a single color dominating all of the other colors in a canvas can lend strength and harmony to a composition. The remaining colors, then, are subordinated and controlled by the dominant color. The effect suggests a singular color mood. At times a single color can be seen as a dominant color in a landscape, hence the expressions, "a gray day," or "a blue day." All colors seen within one's view are strongly influenced by a particular color.

Early morning summer light can often be tinged with rose, so that in a subtle way the entire landscape is influenced by the sense of rose light. On the same day, during a clear sunset, the colors are hotter, permeated by the brilliant orange setting sun into shades of orange and red. Again, the landscape is transformed by the change in the dominant color with a subtle saturation of orange or red.

As the sun sinks below the horizon's rim, one can look into the depths of a dominant color such as the dark green in summer fields and trees, and perceive that the greens are tinged with lavender. As the sun sinks further below the horizon, the greens become imperceptibly darker and cooler and the sensation of lavender is replaced by a suggestion of purple, and then, finally, as the light disappears, the greens turn to black.

During the summer months in the country, greens can permeate one's view of nature—brownish greens, olive greens, strident yellow-greens, cool blue-greens and dark black-greens. Vast acres of brilliant green winter wheat, or the intense green seen in a large field of sod, rise up and can overcome the senses, fairly shouting, "I am green and beautiful!"

As the field of a single color is enlarged and dominates a composition, its energy is magnified. An enlarged color can stimulate certain responses in us. We are affected both psychologically and aesthetically. A large field of pale yellow bathes receptive feelings with a warm, bright light, or a field of red pulls and hammers at the senses; a field of blue, although more serene than the red, can envelop and permeate the mind. Each dominant color can stimulate a certain mood.

Painting with a single dominant color for a long period of time can expand one's understanding of a much greater range of color. This, for example, can be done by working in a blue period first (because it can be seen as the most traditional of the primary colors), and a year or so later, working in a red period, perhaps followed by a yellow period.

In essence, as the artist explores his expressive potential by working within the limitations of a single color dominating the whole, he discovers hitherto unknown qualities in the range of the particular color that he is using. He learns how it interacts with other colors that are subordinated to it. His color vocabulary is expanded by means of these explorations. Thus, the artist comes to know a whole range of blues, for instance. This knowledge, because it has been gained expressively by means of painting, is understood in terms of both its aesthetic and its psychological implications.

By working within the limitations of individual dominant color periods, the artist can develop a more comprehensive understanding of how all colors interact with each other. Painting with two predominant colors, for example, is a natural extension of painting with single color dominance. A combination of red and green, or of blue and yellow, might dominate. Variations are endless.

By limiting the colors in a painting, the colorist gains expressive power because:

- As the use of color is restricted, there is an inherent simplicity in the work. A painting can be seen as more open and frank.
- There is an obvious consistency in the particular language of color used from one painting to the next, regardless of the various color combinations.
- The repeated use of simple color relationships fosters a more intimate knowledge of how to solve the creative problems in painting.

Of course, a teacher can only suggest ways to expand a student's individual color experience, for what will work must be derived from the student's own creative experience. The student must be eager to grasp this new kind of experience. It is not an intellectual exercise.

Seeing Color/Form as Structure

One does not become a colorist simply by "socking" a few bright colors into an otherwise drab painting. Tonal painters who want to give more life to their work often do this, but usually without realizing that at the same time they are also destroying pictorial structure. Picasso's *Still Life* (Illustration II.14), painted in 1919, is an excellent example. He obviously tried to balance the bright orange-red tablecloth with the dark brown table and vase, but the orange-red leaps out of the picture. This is essentially a tonal painting with a single brilliant color.

One of my landscape painting students, working outdoors on location, was carried away by a bright, deep blue sky. It appeared in harsh contrast to an old, weathered, silver-gray barn with fieldstone walls. She painted the barn with great expertise with almost neutral colors. Why not paint the sky a vivid blue? Like Picasso in 1919, her idea of color was limited to illustrating form. When I critiqued her painting in an attempt to help her solve the structural problems, she was defensive about her use of the blue. She could not understand how the single strong color could be seen as dissonant, interrupting the entire continuity of her painting.

In both instances above, the intense psychological responses to the subject (giving it meaning and greater feeling by adding a strong color) dominated the artist's visual idea of the paintings. In fact, each artist (forget that one is Picasso), because of his or her limited creative experience with color at that time, and perhaps even more importantly in Picasso's case, because of his superb confidence and undeniable skill as a tonal painter, was unable to see the painting objectively in terms of color structure.

A bright orange-red is a trumpet blast. It is powerful. It advances, leaps into space. If this vigorous note is not answered by other kinds of color, composed to counterbalance its strength, then the color structure of the painting falls apart. In a similar way, the intense blue in the landscape painting dominated the composition because of its strength.

Suppose I paint three brush strokes of blue on a small white canvas. If these marks are similar in size, my eye is confused; I do not know which one to look at first. But if I enlarge one brush stroke, I have created a simple opposition of one versus two. Each brush stroke is seen as a positive form in the negative field of the picture plane. The large form comes forward to the eye and is seen as positive, while the other two brush strokes are seen as further away from the eye and are relatively negative. The plane of the white canvas is now seen as a deeper space. The three brush strokes of blue can be readily balanced by seeing them as weight relationships as they are painted. A surface relationship is thus established as the heavy blue is counterbalanced by the two lighter blues; the blues can also be balanced as depth relationships in space by adjusting their brightness or focus (hard- or soft-edged.)

Now, if I add a red that is brighter than any of the blues, the red immediately comes forward and all of the blues recede. Each addition of color makes the composition more complex. The rule that must be understood and observed is that every particle, every nuance, every shape of color in a painting, is part of its visual structure. A brush stroke of color should never be taken for granted, nor should brushwork be done so quickly that its relationship to the whole is lost.

Above all, color is a vehicle of expression. The choice of a color or a group of colors and the way you push them around is a highly personal matter. I paint a pale yellow a certain tone and hue because at that instant I have responded to a feeling for a particular color and shape. This has meaning to me only because it is a product of my own experience as a colorist, yet it is also a response to other colors held in my mind's eye, or to colors that have already been objectified on the canvas.

The sensations of color created by light, as they are seen in nature, are transposed into expressive variations on the canvas. Color in contemporary painting *is* light. Each color/form has a relevant light quotient, or a degree of dullness or brightness, or a change in hue and tonal value that is consistent with a particular concept of light.

Painting with pure color is like playing a game of chess; the visual mind responds not only to each move, but also looks ahead to see how the next move will be affected by the immediate play. Any move, then, is related to anticipating as much as possible, the developing whole field of play. As I sock the pale yellow into my painting, I respond to it emotionally first. The yellow produces a simple psychological effect of light, of brightness and warmth. I also see it structurally as an advancing form. Other colors interact. My control of the painting requires balancing all of the relationships as they are developed. Yet my control of color is also related to my visual idea of an inner light in the painting. So much has to do with keeping one's vision intact. The painting is a product both of the idea that inspired it and of the creative development of that idea.

Of course, control in painting is based on intuitive response. There has to be an easygoing reciprocal give-and-take between all the elements in a painting as it is developed. For each force there is a reciprocal force. Warmth demands coolness, dark demands light, dullness demands brightness. Each element has its own intrinsic qualities, its own energy. Drawing can be related to color, as the work is developed, by retaining the pictorial balance of its qualities, the weight of the line, its movement, and its interrelated role to the masses of color.

A painting can be composed of flat planes of color (both positive form and negative space are flattened). There is a simple continuity in this kind of structure and if the colors and forms are painted with consistency, the painting should hold together.

A flat painting is the simplest kind of visual approach, but what happens if this kind of structure is inadvertently changed during the process of painting? A student might treat color passages in other ways that interrupt the consistency of the composition. Colors, for instance, may be gradated in some areas of the painting, creating a sense of volume that conflicts with the flat planes of color. At this point the painting gets out of balance and begins to fall apart. Any further work on the painting tends to compound the problem. Control of the painting can be regained only through a recognition that the structure is muddled. This kind of problem is common in student work.

Basically, this is a spatial problem. A flat plane of color that is seen as a positive, in turn, demands flatness in the corresponding negative space. By contrast, any modulated form (a form in a painting that conveys a sense of depth by means of color gradation) demands a corresponding depth in the negative space.

The question immediately arises: Is it possible to paint flat colors and colors that are variegated and modulated all in the same picture? Of course it's possible, but the key for unification is to retain continuity in the development of the painting. If the idea of the painting is to fashion contrasts of flatness and volume, the work will hold together as long as each element in the painting is balanced in relation to the whole as it is developed.

As you expand your color vocabulary, you must be willing to explore new relationships, which, to a large extent, are based on a visual knowledge gained through experience with color interaction. This development happens best through painting. There are no theories or formulae that can teach how much cadmium yellow light is needed to intensify a yellow-green, or how much pale yellow is needed at the edge of the green to further illuminate it next to a deep crimson.

My general advice is to weigh carefully what I say here—toss it around in your grist mill—and then use what is appropriate for your needs. When you paint, forget completely what you have read and, instead, rely solely on your instinctive response to the developing color interrelationships. No one should ever tell you how to put down a brush stroke of any color. The width of the stroke, its direction, the amount of paint on the brush, the brush dry or wet, and particularly the color itself are all part of the substance of painting, and are personal considerations.

Balancing Color

The distribution of color reveals how a painting is balanced between the extremes of (or at the extreme of) bright or dull, strong or weak, light or heavy, hot or cold. All color properties—hue, value, and intensity—must be considered as factors in the basic organization of color relations and their balance.

Tonal value differences are possibly the most effective component in balancing colors. A range of tones from light to dark can establish a basic balance in color relations: tending toward light, perfectly balanced, or tending toward dark. The color mode of the painting is correlated to this relationship, as well as correlated to choices of hues and related intensities. There are no rules. The intent here is to make one aware of balance as a means to control expression.

Varying kinds of oppositions can be used to attract the eye and balance and counterbalance color/forms. For example, a large, dull color can be counterbalanced by a smaller, bright color; a large color can be effectively counterbalanced by smaller shapes of the same color lending harmony to an arrangement of colors.

Temperature variations in colors affect interval relations and cause them to reveal the finest differentiations.

II.25 Fundamental Factors.

Size and Temperature
The weight and relative energy of a color is increased as it is enlarged, bringing it forward in the picture plane.

Two colors with unequal energies can be balanced by enlarging the size of the weaker color.

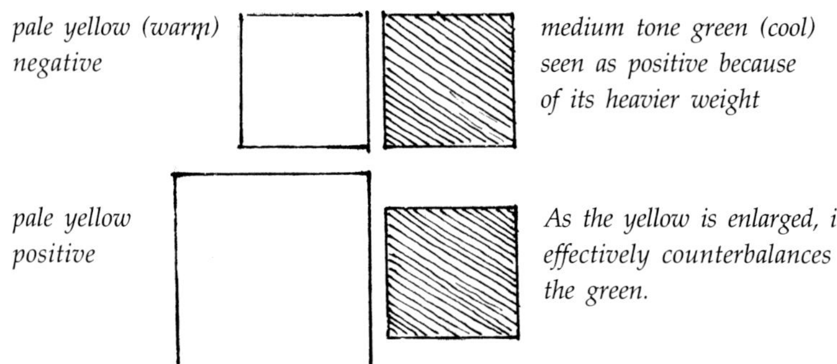

Colors can be balanced spatially by making them warmer or cooler. When two colors of the same size are placed next to each other—a warm green, for example, tending toward yellow, is placed next to a cool green, tending toward blue—the warm color is dominant, or positive. Any adjustment in the temperature of either color affects both their harmony and spatial relationship.

Pictorial space is increased as temperature variation is increased, affecting push-pull and relationships to all the other colors in the painting.

This effect is diminished as the tonal structure becomes more important than the color structure. As colors are desaturated, tending toward neutral, temperature variation is also increased.

Control of color temperature in relation to overall balance is essential. A painting can be too hot (oppressive) or too cold (unfriendly and bleak).

Color Effects

A layer of color on a high-gloss surface will appear more brilliant and luminous than the same color painted on a matte surface. In watercolor painting, for instance, colors appear more alive and fresher on smooth paper than they do on rough paper.

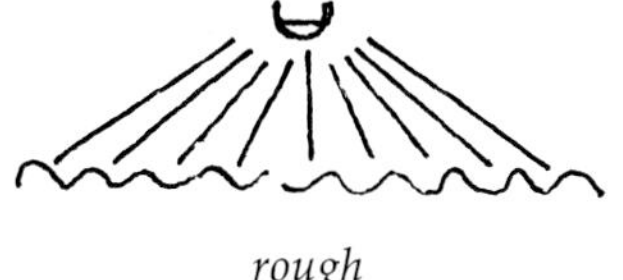

rough
x percent of color is seen

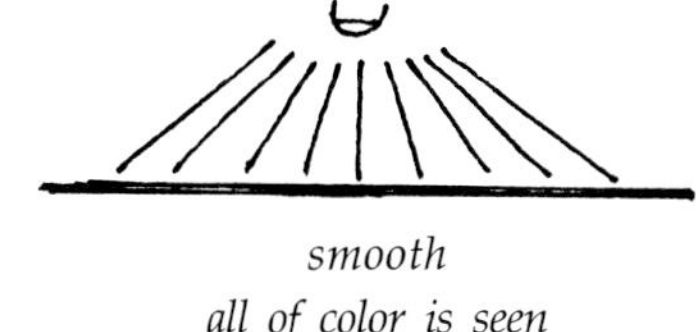

smooth
all of color is seen

II.26
Color on rough and smooth surfaces.

Light is either absorbed or reflected from the support surface. The greatest amount of absorption of light accompanied by the least reflection happens when light falls on a rough-textured black surface. A brilliant white, smooth surface will reflect the most light. As the white surface of the ground is tinted to a deeper tonal value, the amount of reflection will decrease according to the relative darkness of the ground. Furthermore, a matte surface absorbs light more than a high-gloss surface, because its surface is porous or broken up into minute particles.

A single layer of color painted on a brilliant white ground is more transparent than multiple layers of color painted over the same ground.

A color painted over a black ground absorbs the light and appears duller and darker than the same color painted over a light ground.

Mixtures of opaque colors are duller than transparent washes of colors. As any two pigments are mixed together, the minute particles of each are intermingled and reflect a certain amount of white light, which decreases the intensity of the mixed color. The addition of more colors further dulls the mixture.

As pigment is thinned with medium, its brilliance and luminosity is increased as it is painted over a white ground; conversely, as a pigment is thickened by the addition of an opaque white, it appears less brilliant when painted over the same ground.

When a thin, transparent color is mixed with a dense, opaque color, the reflection of light comes mostly from the opaque color (the opaque color is dominant and controls the mixture). For example, alizarin crimson, which is a thin color, when mixed with an opaque titanium white, is absorbed by the strength of the white and its tinting power is practically negated.

Because of these considerations, some colorists have learned through experience to limit their use of white. Consequently, their work appears fresher and more alive. In watercolor painting it is advisable to limit your number of overlaying washes to two, or at most three. Similarly, in oil painting it is good practice to limit paint layers on the canvas and work as directly as possible.

The relative degree of transparency or opacity in colors is best learned by using them; see how they thin with the addition of medium and how they flow on the canvas or paper.

The cover of this book shows a color chart I made for my own use as well as to show my students an example of a tone, hue, and intensity range using an extended, virtually unlimited palette. I used a full range of cadmiums—light, middle, and deep—and all of the blues, violets, and magentas. All of the colors are well integrated in groups from cool at the bottom to warm at the top. The bright warm colors communicate energy and light. The relatively neutral colors in the middle group are neither warm nor cool. Each color was mixed in comparison with its adjacent colors as well as worked out with an eye for the whole. Dark and light colors and bright and dull colors were deliberately separated to gain strength by contrast in a checkerboard effect, providing visual interest and a means of organization.[22]

The Americans

JOHN MARIN

John Marin has long been viewed as the greatest American watercolorist since Winslow Homer. He was one of the first painters in the United States to forge an original style, derived from post-impressionism, fauvism, and cubism. John Marin, a self-effacing, rather conservative printmaker who made representational etchings of landscape motifs, was inspired when he traveled to Europe in the early 1900s and saw the paintings of Cézanne. After he returned to the United States, his own expressiveness, hitherto locked within, came to life, literally exploding on paper and canvas, showing his deep feeling for nature and, particularly, for the Maine seacoast.

Marin attacked his painting like a fencer, jabbing and parrying with his brush, dancing back and forth in front of his easel, which he wedged into the rocks and weighed down with automobile chains so it would not blow away in the sea breeze. He painted four, five, six small watercolors in a day and saved only his best ones. These were usually fleeting glimpses of the fast-changing moods of nature.

When I owned an island in Maine, I came to understand and deeply appreciate John Marin and his work. For many years I painted alone and with my students near Newagen on the southern tip of Southport Island, down east of Small Point where Marin painted. When you live and paint by the sea, you quickly learn that the tides, the breaking waves and rocks awash, and all the colors are seen only briefly—momentary glimpses of nature's evanescent conditions. John Marin had an uncanny ability to capture shadows moving quickly on the ocean, or light breaking through the clouds, or fog rolling in over off-shore islands, all in a free, shorthand way. A few deft lines defined the intrinsic character of a Gloucester fishing schooner seen in the distance, or blurred wet into wet washes, accented with dry brush lines, revealed an island fringed with blue spruce—not just any island, but a pristine Maine island. With all the abstract qualities seen in his paintings, his colors were always remarkably convincing; as he painted they were inseparable from his deep feeling about form. The reddish rust of wet granite and salmon pinks and cooler grays or a hot orange sun are each seen as clear harmonic tones in the white space of his paper.

John Marin's expressiveness evolved through spatial movement—space expanding and contracting with perfect cohesion to positive form. In his words, "Taut, taut, loose and taut . . . electric . . . staccato."[23] There was a pulse in his work, a rhythmic beat. He used negative space to define strong forms and weaker distant forms, always suggesting the innate quality, the intrinsic life in each form in his own simplified way. His expressiveness grew from his early cubist-patterned imagery into highly inventive and free statements in his later years.

GEORGIA O'KEEFFE

Along with John Marin, Georgia O'Keeffe was one of the few figures in American art during the 1920s and 1930s who painted in her own way, unlike anything painted in Europe. O'Keeffe's paintings, distinguished by their flowing, rhythmical shapes and a certain femininity in their cleancut tidiness and subtle finish, ranged from varying forms of semi-abstraction to an absolute nonobjectivity.

Although O'Keeffe's idea of enlarging form in her work was inspired, at least in part, by the photography of her famous husband, Alfred Stieglitz, over a period of time she developed her own unique style of painting that was deceptively simple and unpretentious. Her series of six *Jack in the Pulpit* paintings done in 1930, from the first realistic version to the last that showed only the "Jack" from the flower, reflected her objective to enlarge and further simplify the form. As each painting in the series becomes stronger, it becomes less factual and more abstract. All of these paintings make the statement, "Let there be no doubt about it, I am Jack-in-the-Pulpit!"

O'Keeffe learned to use the concept of single-color dominance in a variety of subjects throughout her lifetime. In her tiny oil painting on canvas of the *Red Poppy*, the brilliant red dominates the composition and the poppy is seen as a monumental form, squeezed into the picture plane. This painting reflects the strength of O'Keeffe's resolve to express only what was essential to her. As O'Keeffe blocked in the brilliant red in her painting of the poppy, her "idea" of the painting was objectified. The shape of the red and her emotional response to it became a distinct reality.

> It is surprising to me to see how many people separate the objective from the abstract. Objective painting is

> not good painting unless it is good in the abstract sense. A hill or a tree cannot make a good painting just because it is a hill or a tree. It is lines and colors put together so that they say something. For me that is the very basis of painting. The abstraction is often the most definite form for the intangible thing in myself that I can only clarify in paint.[24]
>
> —Georgia O'Keeffe

Many of Georgia O'Keeffe's paintings depended on strong tonal relationships with varying gradations (see *Black Rock with Blue III*, and *Black Cross, New Mexico*, Illustrations III.6, 7). On occasion, as in her painting, *Red Poppy*, she worked with pure color with a limited number of gradations. The visual structure in each of these modes of expression changed according to her feelings about her subject matter. Each style was expressed with clarity and a simple purposefulness.[25] O'Keeffe fully understood that there were limitations in each kind of structure.

EDWARD HOPPER, THE CONSUMMATE REALIST

Over the years I have repeatedly used the paintings of Edward Hopper to show my students how a painter portrays the natural light in landscape as color, transposed into simple, powerful weight relationships.

Hopper had a natural gift for composing solid forms. They were massive and severely simplified. Each element in his design was essential to the whole. There were no unnecessary details. Hopper painted colors as varied, flat planes that opposed subtly variegated color planes. A sky, for instance, was seen as pale and flat against deep, changing bands of color in the water. Each plane represented a specific kind of light, or shadows out of the light. He composed with "weights of color."

Hopper's authority lay in his ability to transform a landscape into a powerful composition, built on straight lines and severe angles. He most often utilized a strong horizontal base, in contrast to less regular, more complex forms in the middleground or beyond.

Hopper's work merits intensive study. Place your hand over any element in any one of his paintings—a telephone pole or a tree—and see how the structure of the painting is weakened without this essential form. His paintings were never static. He never painted windows in the same way; for example, in his painting *Early Sunday Morning* (Illustration II.21), a shade is painted up or down, or a window open, or he painted a different play of light on each window. His paintings lead the eye into the picture plane. His vision was always first in the abstract.

There is a beat here, a visual rhythm—a three in the middle, a two at the left, a one at the right, a two and one and a one, and a half. These are focal points, the brightest colors seen in full light, of window shade and awnings and a fire hydrant and a barber pole. Picasso once said that the Americans did not have the intellectual capacity to paint cubistically. Bah! Hopper's realism has all the depth of cubism and a primary focal point, counterbalanced by lesser focal points. He has full control over the observer's eye. Remove any one detail, any nuance of color, any focus, hardness or softness at the edges of the forms, and the painting is lessened.

Most of his mature oil paintings were planned in a series of preliminaries. He deliberately interpreted his subject loosely and freely in these sketches so that he would not have the tendency to copy them and spoil the concept in his mind's eye. They were also sketched in black and white so that he could see a deliberate, powerful tonal structure. This method in turn permitted him to interpret these tones as fresh color and with greater spontaneity as he worked.

Hopper said about Cape Cod, where he and his wife lived in a starkly simple, shingled house overlooking Massachusetts Bay, "There's a beautiful light here . . . very luminous . . . perhaps because it is so far out to sea; an island almost."[26]

CLYFFORD STILL

There is nothing to show that Clyfford Still was directly influenced by Matisse's ideas of color dominance, other than a brief statement acknowledging and then dismissing the European modernists. Nevertheless, by the 1950s, Still's painting was distinguished by his ability to counterbalance immense areas of color with much smaller shapes of boldly contrasting colors. Single color dominance increased the power and simplicity of Still's large paintings. When his canvases are seen collectively, each painting, because of its combination of size and sheer audacity, is astonishing. But when they are seen in the context of each other, there is an interrelated color interaction producing contrasting energies in physical space. The effect is one of a monumental symphony.

During 1931 and 1932, Henri Matisse completed two versions of a gigantic mural for the Barnes Foundation in Merion, Pennsylvania. (When the first version was completed, a mistake in measurements required him to paint it over again.) The subject of *La danse* revolved around figure and field, painted as a dynamic interaction between positive and negative color fields in blue, black, and pink. For the first time in painting, there was a balance between the

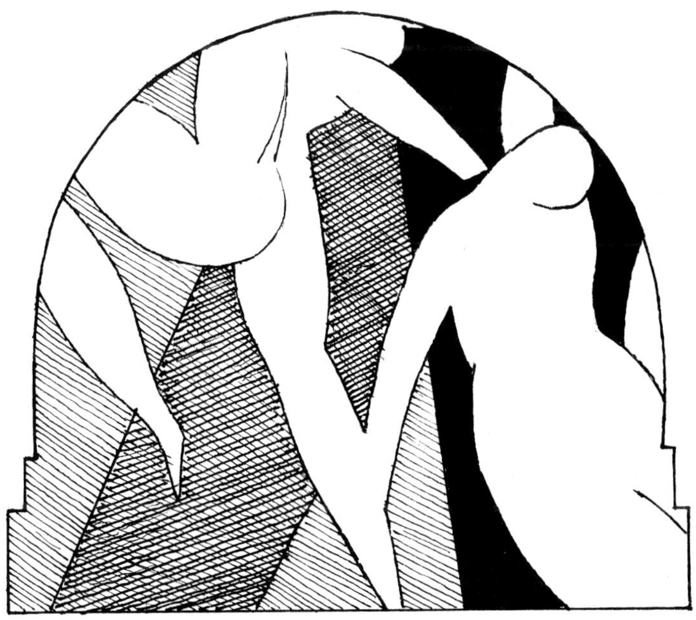

II.27

Author's sketch of section of Henri Matisse's *La danse.*

The mural Matisse was commissioned to paint by Dr. Albert Barnes for his foundation in Merion, Pennsylvania. The reciprocal interrelationship between the positive and negative elements of the composition is interchangeable. The figures come forward as positive because of psychological responses to them as form, and then if one concentrates on the powerful shapes in the background, they in turn become positive and the figures are seen as negative counterparts.

positive physical presence of the figures and the negative areas between them.

In the act of painting, there can be a duality between positive and negative. The artist must be keenly aware as he paints of how his vision encompasses the whole as directed by a balanced coordination of both positive and negative. Each shapes the other. The eye must account for interrelated color hues, intensities, tonal values, and shapes. The balance of figure and field remained a recurrent theme in much of Matisse's work that followed.

Although Clyfford Still never painted figure and field—he was a completely nonobjective painter—he balanced and counterbalanced positives and negatives according to the same principles used by Matisse in his Barnes Foundation mural. Each artist had learned from his own explorative work how to see color as a form of relative energy.

What distinguished Still's painting from all the others was his unparalleled use of color as the source of energy through extreme variations in the size of the relative color fields. The immensity of the black in *1954* creates a dynamic and dominant field of energy; this simple, monumental shape is counterbalanced by the pure orange-red. At first glance, this balance appears disproportionate, yet the colors, each nuance, each detail, belong to each other. A thin contrasting line or a flick of pale yellow further articulates the major mass relationships.

Still limited the number of colors he used. This is typical of all of his work. He was highly selective in his choice of colors. He was also keenly aware that a harmonious interchange between colors was an essential ingredient in his painting. The spatial intervals between his chosen colors in any one painting are fairly close together.

A Still painting does not evoke a strong sense of drawing, at least not in the conventional way of a Matisse painting, and yet there is a mastery in the way that Clyfford Still shaped his masses of color—much like a sculptor hewing out a positive form that in turn locks it to the adjoining negative space. Not only were his color/shapes balanced proportionally to fashion a whole, but each individual shape also retained its own balance that was based on its own innate verticality. At times, his painted forms hover in space and other kinds of forms are solid and imposing. His compositions, invariably based on verticality, are the simplest kinds of visual structure, as if in each there is an underlying common geometry that increases its physical presence.

> Everywhere in his work there are underlying rhythms surging back and forth like ocean tides or cadenced rivers. At times, internal activity intensifies and one thinks of molten lava, but the paintings are never specific representations. Having nothing to do with landscape or any recognizable subject, they frankly exploit all possible means to make the painting itself the entire experience. The painting is the sum total and to search beyond that is to invalidate the meaning of the work.[27]

NEIL WELLIVER

Neil Welliver's painting, *Stump and Ferns* (Illustration II.23), has all of the inner and outer penetration of space seen in the finest cubist paintings, but he has achieved his pictorial order in modernist terms, without the cubist mannerism of gradating tonal values to create an illusion of depth.

Welliver moves the eye in and out of the picture plane by painting forms in front of and behind each other as well as by varying the spatial intervals between the colors that can be seen as planes with relative amounts of energy. Thus the forms can be seen in two ways: realistically, with the ferns in front of the underlying dark brown soil and the stump in front of the distant trees, and abstractly, as shapes and colors that have indigenous hues, tones, and temperatures. Cool patches of pale blue-gray lichen, in strong contrast to the adjoining deep, brownish green in the stump and the lightest tones in the distant trees, dance forward and are seen as focal points.

There is a lot of drawing in the painting of the stump, but with all the seemingly profuse detail, Welliver directs the eye throughout the painting to establish a composition that is cohesive and well-balanced. Welliver's underlying drawing was used as a guide for the brush and paint and nothing more than that. He does not render the paint between the lines but rather paints directly, with incredible patience and discipline, each detail, each branch, each flicker of light as solid forms, which vary in tone and temperature, to create his own visual world. Each nuance of color has an indigenous weight that is correlated to the tonal scheme of the whole.

Welliver paints with a limited palette that consists of eight colors: white, black, cadmium red scarlet, manganese blue, ultramarine blue, lemon yellow, cadmium yellow, and talens green light. It is important to understand that Welliver was able to select these colors from the wide range of available colors only because of his prior experience with color experimentation in his abstract painting. There is nothing arbitrary about the way Welliver uses color in his paintings. Each painting has a specific range of colors derived from this limited palette, and a distinctive color mood that is in accord with a particular time of day and light condition. He generally favors a middle light condition that reduces harsh tonal contrasts and intense colors because this increases his sensitivity to subtleties in tones and temperatures. Thus, grays can become more blue, or more brown, or more pink, as their tonal values change; or greens can change from deep olive to pale yellow, or to cooler and bluer, or to grayer and more neutral. He mixes his earth colors from the cadmiums because he is after a luminosity that hc cannot duplicate with earth colors.

> I never, never try to copy the colors out there. If I mix a color and put some of it on the object I am painting, on leaves, for example . . . it looks bizarre. I am not interested in "painting from nature." I am not interested at all in that.[28]

The Painter's Light

A painter's light, a term that refers to a particular artist's use of light in his paintings, is the unique result of all his personal experience, influences, environment, and creativity. The colors in Matisse's paintings, for example, celebrate the vivid, warm light of the Mediterranean, whereas Picasso, because he usually painted at night, often used cold colors to offset the warm effects of incandescent bulbs.

The best light for a pure colorist is a north light flooding through large, vertical windows or a steeply sloped skylight. There cannot be enough of it. North light, theoretically, is a neutral light, devoid of the warmth of the sun.

A sunny studio produces dissonant color relationships because of the constantly changing light conditions such as cooler light in the morning and warmer light during the afternoon. Temperatures in color mixing are subconsciously adjusted by the artist to suit each light condition. Most often, without any realization of it as he paints, he loses control of color harmony. As the day wears on and the light continues to change, the color relationships appear false. Later, after dark, when the painting is seen under incandescent lighting, it still does not hold together. This can be a frustrating experience.

Because of the slight temperature variations in the colors, tonal painting is not as severely affected by changing light conditions; in fact, many tonal painters work with incandescent light as a principal light source, day or night.

For a final evaluation, a painting should be viewed under different light conditions, including north light, outdoor light (in shadow), warm south light, and incandescent light. If the colors interact properly, the painting will "work" under each kind of light condition.

For these reasons, some painters prefer to work on cloudy days. They know that at the end of the day their color choices will appear consistent and correct. When working outdoors on a cloudy day, or, even better, a "gray" day, I have found that colors in nature have more depth because as you look into mass relationships it is possible to see subtle variations of both tones and temperatures that would be impossible to see on a sunny, bright day. In effect, the light is filtered by the neutral quality of the atmosphere.

Invariably, over a period of time, the true artist learns to control his working environment. He instinctively gravitates toward his own set of rules, regardless of what kind of artist he is, or which medium he works in. Thoreau's cabin at Walden Pond, for example, was a by-product of his strong philosophical beliefs—a simple, working cabin that fit his frugal needs as well as a mansion for his expression. The cabin was not a result of his circumstances, any more than Picasso stumbled by accident upon his great chateaux. Picasso's Villa La Californie in Cannes not only was a castle to showcase the results of his prodigious creative energy, but the great rooms with their high, arched doorways also served as an incomparable working environment that offered an infinite variety of inspiring subject matter.

Generally, painters are classified as studio painters if they work within a controlled light environment, or as outdoor landscape painters if they work as directly as possible from nature. Monet painted light as color by breaking up his tangible, concrete views of nature into a multiple scheme of colors—yellows, violets, oranges, greens, and blues—to create an illusion of light and shadow in space. Toward the end of his life and at the height of his expression, he came to understand the water and reflected sky in his Oriental lily ponds as a spatial environment, nourished by a mystic quality of color—tinged with pale violet or permeated with rose and lavender. He was deeply involved in a close fusion with nature. His paintings were drenched with the warm, bright, outdoor light of Giverny in southern France.

The Purkinjee Effect

By mid-June, the late afternoon sun has swung an arm's length to the north on the western rim of the Chesapeake Bay. This is the most intense light of the year and it fairly floods through the large windows on the west side of our Strawberry Factory into the great, high-ceilinged living room. The space comes alive. The vibrant colors in my large paintings hanging on the walls are pierced with brilliant shafts of light—with shimmering, moving patterns. The colors bounce around in space—a huge field of pale, cool yellow opposed by a brilliant magenta, wine red, and black reverberate in opposition to the deepest blue and sienna-stained colors in my mural, *Dance of Life*. On the opposite side, a brilliant Chinese red is opposed by a dark purple-blue fabric in a decorative screen that I fashioned as a counterpoint to our Maine rock garden.

We have many visitors. Most are perplexed by my oversize colorful abstractions (the few who like them love them), but all are impressed by the space and our view of the Bay. Many openly talk about the qualities of a "great" space. Of course, the colors affect them psychologically in a warm, positive way, but most of our visitors are unaware of this.

As the sun sinks toward the horizon in the west, the interior light gradually changes into cool, dim tones, and as the light further changes, the colors in the paintings seem to vibrate and quiver. Tonal values are reversed. Bright oranges and reds turn very dark and the cooler blues and greens appear light and iridescent.

This puzzled me until I read that Matisse witnessed this same phenomenon in his paintings at twilight. He called in his friend, Edward Steichen, the photographer, for an opinion and Steichen referred to it as the Purkinjee effect, a rarity that could take place only during that particular change of light with oppositions of pure warm and cool colors. Steichen confirmed what Matisse had seen and explained that as the light faded and at the same time grew warmer the colors reached a balance point at which a complementary reflex within the eye made them jump and vibrate. Once he understood this, Matisse was no longer disturbed.[29]

3.
Composition

The Conceptual Image of Form

> That glimpse or vision is what makes art a matter of inner experience . . . therefore sacred, and no less but rather more individual in this age I assure you than ever before.[30]
>
> —Frank Lloyd Wright

Ideas occupy the creative mind and are as difficult to subdue as a restless wind churning the ocean. As they are channeled, they chime through interaction. A conceptual image is the seed of a new work of art, born from an inner need for expression. It is a vision computed by the mind of a fleeting, nevertheless concrete, image of the work to be done.

An artist who wants to make an original drawing or painting and who does not know where to start may doodle with a pencil without any kind of preconceived idea. The doodle is not drawn consciously but draws itself, and becomes an intuitive search for a whole image. The "Eureka!" comes when possibilities and their interaction fuse into a whole in a process that is beyond any kind of conscious effort. The conceptual image comes from an exploration that requires the peeling away of inhibitions and constraints, permitting the inner nature to express itself. It is an inspiration.

Most importantly, a conceptual image can be a result of exploring questions about the meaning of form. Albert Einstein said simply, yet with significant implications: "The formulation of a problem is often more essential than its solution, which may be merely a matter of mathematical or experimental skill. To raise new questions, new possibilities, to regard old questions from a new angle, requires creative imagination and marks real advances in science."[31]

An inspired vision is often the result of a spontaneous response to a new, objectified image (the actual form the eye assimilates and registers as a specific reality), or to a synthesis of several objectified images. Or, possibly, it comes when one part of a sketch triggers an idea for the whole that the pencil quickly completes. An image may be seen during waking hours in the early morning, or perhaps during the day while the mind is engaged in a more routine mode of thinking. The image seen by a student in a life drawing class may be a simple line drawing, while a more experienced artist may visualize the same scene as a completed painting.

It is essential in creative art to probe, search, and discover. All are necessary for visual expansion. Ideally, the image encompasses the fundamental relationships of volume, space, color, and light. Some artists, inspired by the image in their mind's eye, start the painting directly to work with maximum freshness and spontaneity; others make preliminary studies to determine more accurately the size and proportions of the finished work, its support surface, and specific technique.

In preparation for major oil paintings, Georges Braque made extensive pencil preliminaries in a small sketchbook that was divided into squared grids by his printer for the purpose of expanding accurately the proportions of the sketch to the large painting. These drawings were straightforward arrangements of all the major shapes and their interrelated movements and of their definition as positive and negative within the specific shape of the picture plane.

The Maine realist, Neil Welliver, has developed a somewhat unique method for composing his paintings. He treks deep into the Maine woods to find his inspiration and explores the possibilities for painting a particular scene, often returning over a period of months until he has finally absorbed it. Only then does he begin to paint in oil a preliminary picture, usually about forty-by-forty inches, which may take three days or so to complete. The preliminary, which in itself is a well-composed, complete painting, is then used back in his studio for expanding his concept to a double size, often ninety inches square, oil on canvas. Welliver then spends a lot of time drawing in line and great detail on a full-sized sheet of paper (commensurate to the canvas proportions). He transfers this expanded image to his canvas by a process of perforating and pouncing.[32]

In his own unique way, he begins to paint from the top of the canvas to the bottom. He paints wet into wet, finishing

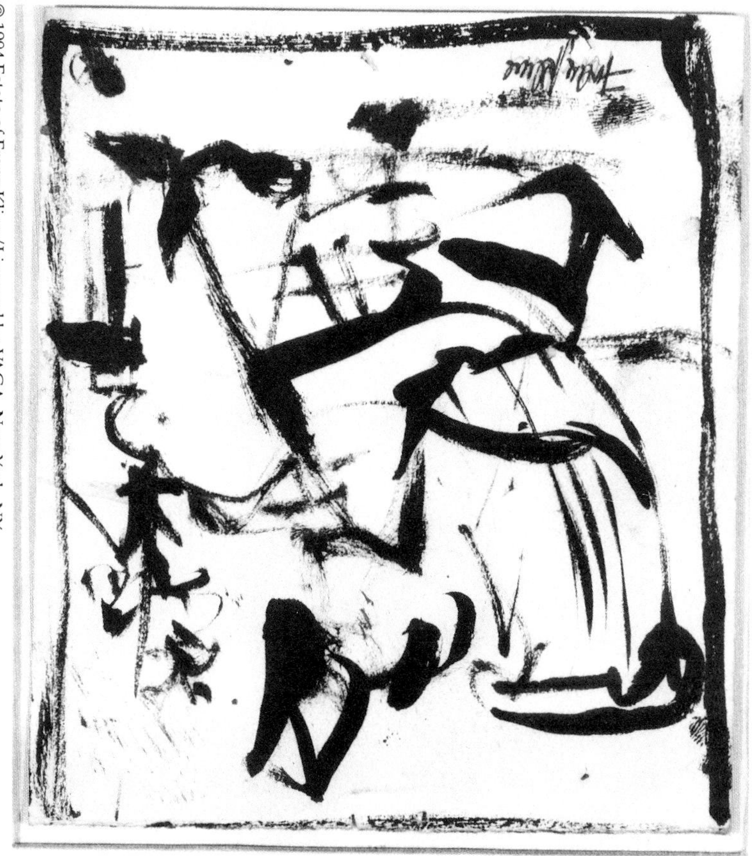

III.1

Franz Kline, *Elizabeth in Rocking Chair*, ca. 1948. Ink on paper, 5" x 4".

Shown below as original and above as seen enlarged when projected inverted on a wall from a Bell-Opticon projector.

Franz Kline's most famous drawing was of a rocking chair, a fluid, quick sketch done in brush and ink. As the story has been told, one evening after a few drinks with a friend, this sketch was placed in his friend's slide projector and its image expanded upside down on the wall. Kline became excited by the abstract qualities he saw in the enlarged, powerful shapes. That was the beginning of his famous abstract expressionistic style of painting. Kline had a clear-cut conceptual image of his painting, enlarged in his mind both expressively and in actual scale, from the tiny sketch.

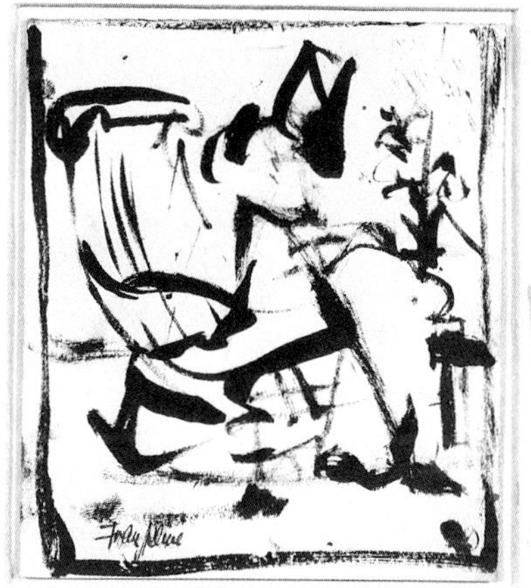

III.2

Two Neil Welliver preliminaries:

Study for *Base of Falls*, 1989. Oil on canvas, 24" x 24".

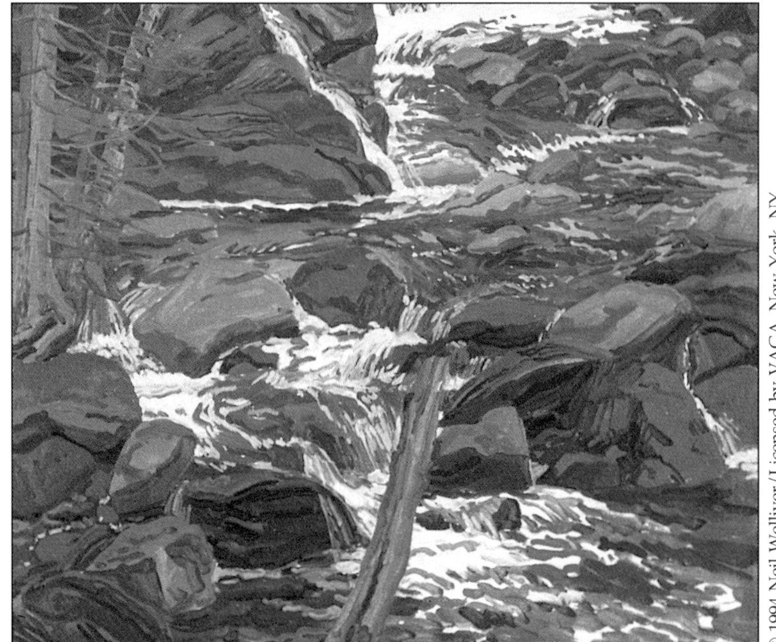

Study for *To Clair Island*, 1990. Oil on canvas, 24" x 24".

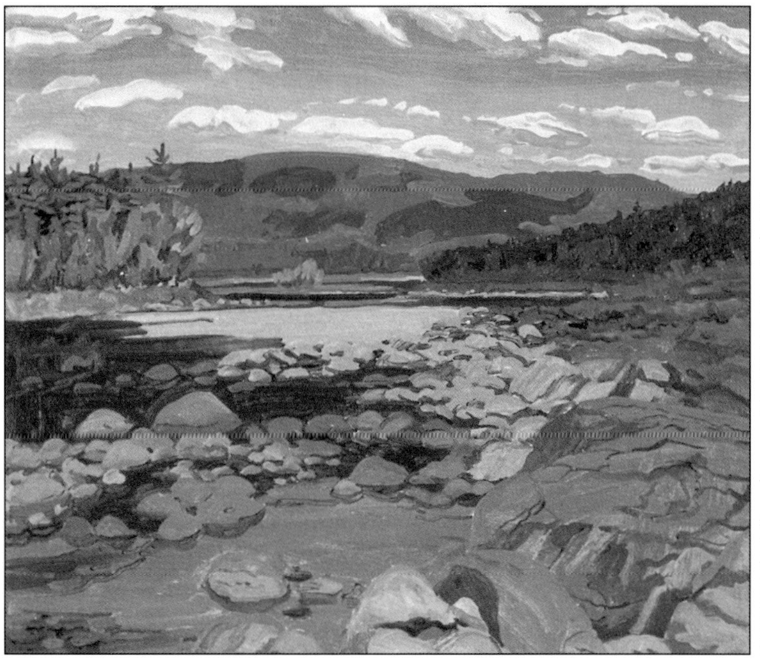

each area as he proceeds and does not make any corrections or alterations. When he gets to the bottom, he is finished.

The Value of Preliminary Sketches

> The idea in a painting is like a launching cradle for a ship . . . After the ship is built, it floats; it has left the cradle useless and forgotten. The idea for a painting is similar. You use the idea to build, to guide, and when your painting is strong enough, it goes off. It floats, it no longer needs the idea to uphold it. It goes off to lead its own life, as the ship does.[33]
>
> —GEORGES BRAQUE

Preliminary sketches measuring from two to five inches wide at their outside dimensions, often referred to as thumbnail sketches, are an effective way to explore possibilities for composition. The tiny size makes the whole field of play easily discernible. Because of the size, the arrangement and choice of forms are limited; the movements are basic and the shapes are large since there is little room left for detail. The whole idea is to shape the primary aspects of the subject matter in a simplified way in accordance with the limitations of the picture plane. The process is flexible. The picture plane can be adjusted to the expressive meaning of the form and vice versa. It can be made higher, wider, or square, in keeping with an imaginative concept of the subject. Form can be juggled about, drawn from different angles and viewpoints, readily changed from a low, worm's-eye view to an overhead view, made larger or smaller, or simplified by deleting or moving some forms. Composing and drawing become synonymous. The pencil explores as the eye envisions. The purpose of the tiny preliminary is to clarify intentions.

There are no rules. Some artists develop more accurate, larger preliminary drawings after exploring the basic structure from small-scale sketches. Preliminary drawings can be composed from many sketches of landscape done on location, or from figures in separate studies.

The choice of a medium to be used in the prelimi-

III.3

Two preliminary studies by the author.

The author often makes preliminary studies in black and white tonal values. Imagination is not restricted by the factual representation of color, and there is greater freedom to explore the possibilities of color interaction in the painting. Each tonal value in the preliminary sketch has a specific weight, which, when compared with the other tones, can be interpreted as a color.

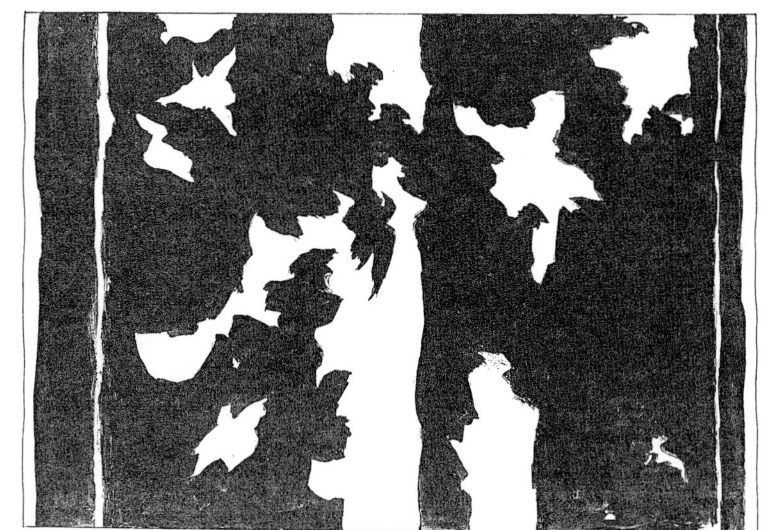

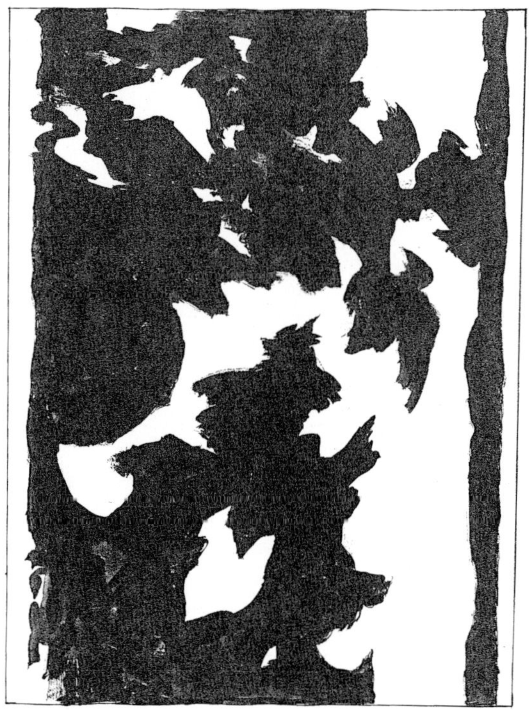

nary sketch is often dictated by an image of the finished painting held in the mind's eye. A wet into wet watercolor technique envisioned in the painting, for example, may demand exploring the subject matter in the preliminary with a similar spontaneous technique. Some painters who picture the use of pure color in their finished work might do their exploratory work in oil or acrylic, not only to correspond to the appearance of the finished painting, but also to explore color combinations more accurately. It is often an advantage to fashion preliminaries that are structurally in accord with the idea of the painting. The image of a final work envisioned as pure mass relationships, for example, can be confused by shaping the preliminary with lines. A vision of line and tone should not be explored in terms of mass relationships. The key is to work as consistently as possible from the small scale to the larger painting.

Many admirers thought Edward Hopper was a "realist" who portrayed literal interpretations of form. His methods for composing paintings, however, were far removed from copying subject matter. Many of his preliminary sketches were fresh and vigorously drawn with black or red conte crayon, emphasizing the structural simplicity of his subject. His oil paintings were often composed as a composite of many impressions from nature. Complex paintings were, on occasion, composed from thirty or forty preliminary studies.

Picasso drew over forty-five studies for *Guernica*, most of which were summed-up insights from his many earlier styles of drawing and painting. A disemboweled horse, sketched in 1917, was the basis for the screaming horse that he painted in *Guernica* twenty years later.

Basic Composition: Eastern vs. Western Ideology

There are three fundamental ways to envision form in a composition, and each pertains to the abstract order of form and space. The relative sizes of positive form and negative space determine the overall impression of a composition:

- Space dominates the composition and the importance of material structure is diminished; subject matter is seen in the distance.
- Form dominates the composition and the negative space is a minor supporting dimension; subject matter is enlarged and generally seen up close.
- Form is placed somewhere between a near view and a faraway view; this is the most common method for composing subject matter.

These three choices of composition are influenced by the traditional roles of form and space in Western and Eastern cultures and it is important to understand how these traditions affect your work.

In the Eastern tradition, truth cannot be fully understood; it must be felt. The view of space in art is related to Lao-tse's early Eastern philosophy, Taoism, which extols the subjugation of the material in favor of the aesthetic, the temporal in favor of the eternal. Tao is perceived through nature. To practice Taoism, the oriental artist prefers landscape as his subject matter. He lives in harmony with nature and never seeks to dominate it, for it is the predominant power in his universe. The seemingly realistic painting of the Eastern tradition is an abstraction in which positive form is subjugated to the larger reality of negative space.

The Western tradition has emphasized the progression of scientific knowledge to improve human life. Spatial concepts in art have been related to the importance of material reality. In traditional Western art, form was regarded as the principal dimension in composition, and space was a minor supporting dimension. In Renaissance sculpture, painting, and architecture, space was simply a by-product of the form. In painting, the importance of material reality was heightened by the illusion of a strong foreground, a middleground, seen further away by the eye, a background in the distance, and, finally, a deep space. This type of image was conveyed through the use of aerial perspective. It was magnified by the use of true perspective after being discovered and used by Raphael.

The French Impressionists ultimately rejected this tradition. They were struggling to find a new, less restricted art form in the late 1800s when they first saw Japanese art at the Paris World's Fair in 1867. This fresh, exciting view of art had a lasting effect on their creative vision. Ultimately, it changed not only their ideas about nature, but also, through the evolution of their work, the course of Western art in the twentieth century.

Both the Eastern and Western views of composition have advantages and limitations. It is particularly important in one's early stages of development to look beyond the surface characteristics of painting to see the underlying framework of a motif. Your particular view of subject matter is all-important.

When Space Dominates the Composition

When space in a composition completely dominates form, the space takes on a role of objective reality. Space flows, embraces, and envelops form; it makes the objective form more diminutive, and thus produces a more sensitive reciprocal relationship between form and space.

Since most people are conditioned to seeing visual reality by the identification of objects, the idea of space used as a predominant form is often perplexing. In the least, any vision of space is regarded as subjective. Which is more important: a bird seen in flight or the space in which the bird flies? When space is viewed as important, its relative proportions, its weight, and its innate energy are perceived more clearly and one can see an image of composition in reverse. As it dominates the composition, space can be viewed as positive and, in turn, the coexisting form can be regarded as negative.

Much of the work of the Impressionists was composed with space as the dominant element. This view was in keeping with their concepts of light being broken up into color components. As subject matter is painted from a distance, the importance of space usually increases.

Cézanne painted *La Montagne Sainte-Victoire* from a vantage point on a high ridge overlooking the distant valley and mountain. Since the fabric of his compositions was made up of brush strokes in spatially oriented structures, he saw space as the most important part of nature; and, in the Eastern tradition, he accepted nature as an all-pervading force. "Nature for us is revealed more in depth than in surface," he said.[34]

Matisse painted various distant landscapes during the early 1900s in his fauvist period. Many of his landscapes were inspired by Cézanne's concepts of space, but, unlike Cézanne, he invented form with color and line to suit his composition. As he became more aware of how space interrelated with positive form, Matisse flattened space into larger planes of color. As he simplified space, it became structurally more important.

A generally valid criticism of painting that views subject matter from a distance is that the composition is weak because the painting relies on details or complex brushwork to give it vitality. Consequently, the composition lacks simplicity and corresponding structural strength.

John Marin painted islands and ocean waves, most often from a distance, and also painted cityscapes of Manhattan from a distant vantage point. He did a few paintings of the Hudson River with the New York City skyline in the distance as seen from his house, high up on the Palisades on the New Jersey side of the river. The fundamental difference between Marin's painting and that of a primitive painter was that Marin directed every brush stroke according to the spatial demands of the composition. He never painted detail to tell a story or for its own end.

Most painters who are worth their salt learn to simplify their work to strengthen it compositionally and increase its expressive power. For example, some years after she had painted her somewhat detailed cityscapes, Georgia O'Keeffe painted the skull of a steer with its large horns curving upward in an immense spatial background in New Mexico. There are distant mountains at the bottom of the painting and just above them a few streaks of horizontal blue sky. The space is greatly simplified, painted almost flat, producing a corresponding structural strength that imparts a surrealistic quality.

In 1963, O'Keeffe painted a picture she called *The Winter Road*, which shows a beautiful, slender, dark reddish brown form curving simply through an enormous, pale gray space, almost disappearing into a thin line at the top of the painting with a zig to the left and a zag to the right. The space is almost flat and is very simple. It has a luminous quality. Although it was inspired by her view of the sweeping, curving road as seen from her house in Abiquiu, New Mexico, this painting is essentially nonobjective. O'Keeffe reduced form and space to their essences. This painting feels subjective and imparts a mystical aura. There is a perfect balance between the dynamic, curving, diminutive form and its coexisting immense space. As space is enlarged, the psychological effect of the form on the viewer is magnified.

When Form Dominates the Composition

As form is enlarged, the negative space becomes a minor supporting dimension; this is in keeping with the Western tradition because material objects gain optical strength as they are enlarged. This is a more "objective" approach to painting compared with the "subjective" view of space controlling the form. In representational painting, expressive power is increased because the form is invariably simplified as it is enlarged. The supporting role of space is increased as it is made smaller and compressed by larger forms. As the space is squeezed, its energy quotient is increased.

As form is made bolder and the painting is simplified, the concept of the image of the painting and its entire structure can also be simplified in the mind's eye of the artist. Expressiveness and empathy with the subject matter then can be enhanced because one's psychological response to the very size of the form is magnified. Contemporary paintings composed with immense forms and correspondingly

III.4

Georgia O'Keeffe, *Summer Days*, 1936. Oil on canvas, 36" x 30".

Space and form are portrayed as realistic entities, each in terms of illusionistic volume so that there is a total visual continuity in the way they are painted. O'Keeffe was obviously moved by the huge vistas of space in New Mexico. *Summer Days* shows an influence from surrealism, which depicted illusionistic and diminutive positive form floating in deep space, hence the quality of "time" in its imagery.

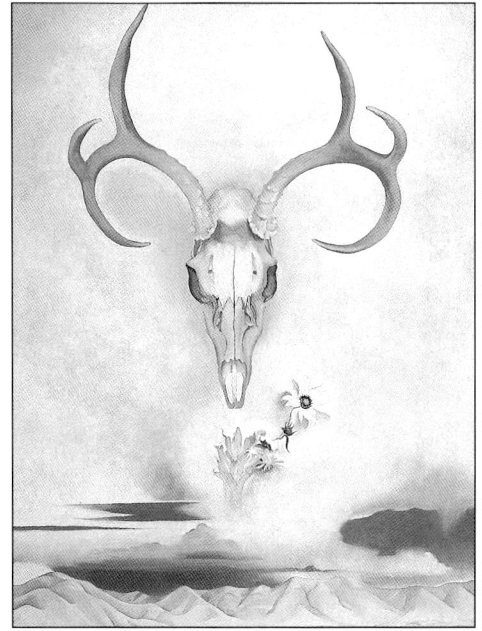

SPACE DOMINATING THE COMPOSITION

III.5

Georgia O'Keeffe, *The Winter Road*, 1963. Oil on canvas, 22" x 18".

Space and form are projected as flat, pattern imagery. In contrast to her earlier painting, *Summer Days*, O'Keeffe's conceptualization in this painting was based on a nonobjective (to the viewer) portrayal of the winding road and endless space near her New Mexico home. This is a purely aesthetic response to form (positive vs. negative) as it is shaped. The primary reality to O'Keeffe was the "objectivity" of the line and its coexisting large area of space.

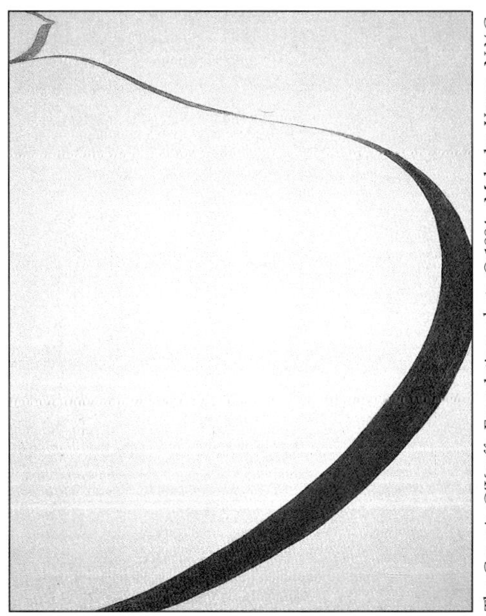

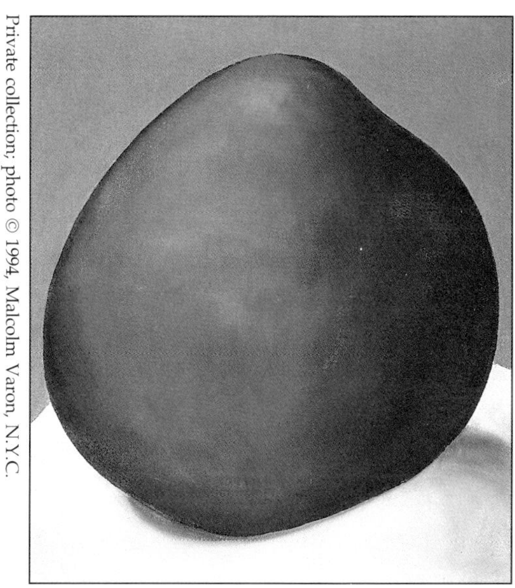

FORM DOMINATING THE COMPOSITION

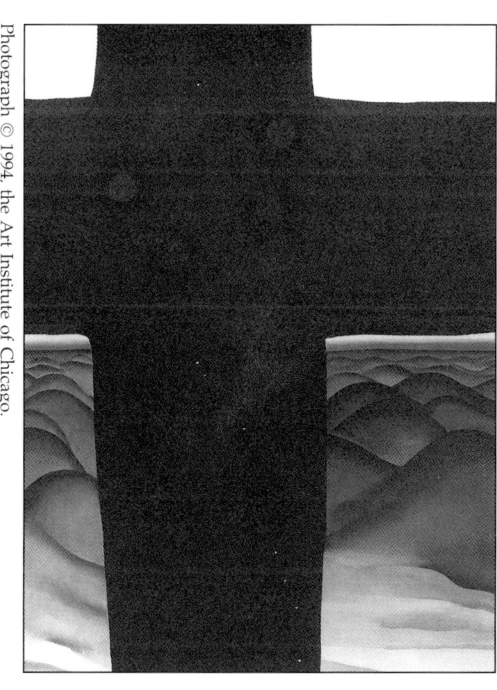

III.6

Georgia O'Keeffe, *Black Rock with Blue III*, 1970. Oil on canvas, 20" x 17".

Although there was a forty-one-year span between the times that O'Keeffe painted these pictures, her simple love for her subject matter determined her concept of form as the dominant element in each composition.

"The black rocks from the road to the Glen Canyon dam seem to have become a symbol to me—of the wideness and wonder of the sky and the world. They have lain there for a long time with the sun and wind and the blowing sand making them into something that is precious to the eye and hand—to find with excitement, to treasure and love."[35]

III.7

Georgia O'Keeffe, *Black Cross, New Mexico*, 1929. Oil on canvas, 99cm. x 77.2cm.

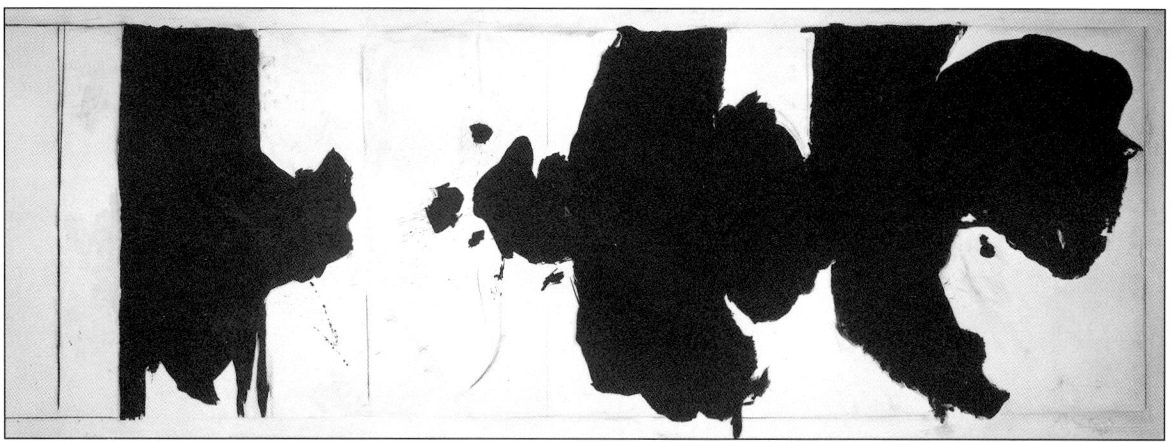

III.8
Robert Motherwell, *Reconciliation Elegy*, 1978. Acrylic on canvas, 120" x 364".

The belligerent vitality of the immense black shapes that Robert Motherwell painted in his canvas, *Reconciliation Elegy*, fairly leaps across the huge interior space. The pure energy of these massive organic forms is magnified by the large size of the painting. Motherwell painted over one hundred variations of his "Elegy" theme, each distinctly expressive of variations in his feelings about this monumental subject. In each instance the black positive and the white negative are fashioned as reciprocal forces, each shaping the other.

diminutive space dominate the viewer with the innate power in the painted form and energize the accompanying space. Forms can be painted flat, or almost flat, in both positive and negative color fields to increase their simplicity. In nonrepresentational painting, gravity plays a lesser role in composition. Positive form can be painted as free-standing or floating within the confines of the picture plane. As it is enlarged, the form takes on its own material reality or "objectness." Negative space is not perceived as an illusionary deep space, but as a reciprocal force.

A Mid-view of Composition

The most commonly accepted way to compose form is from a mid-distance. Neither the large extremes of space nor form dominate the composition. It is a more normal point of view. The eye generally encompasses a greater amount of form than that seen from the extreme viewpoints; therefore, composition is more flexible because there are a greater number of choices and more options in their interpretation within the limitations of the picture plane. Moreover, there is invariably more visual interest in this viewpoint than in others. For these reasons, a mid-view of subject matter is used for most representational painting.

To demonstrate different ways to explore composition, make a simple viewfinder by cutting out a small rectangular shape, about $1\frac{1}{4}$"-by-2", from a piece of mat board. First, view your subject matter up close, deliberately squeezing the accompanying negative space. Then take a view from several intermediate distances, and, finally, from far away. By making thumbnail sketches of each view you will quickly find what is important in the basic imagery. In each instance it is your fundamental idea of a composition, as it is seen broadly, in relation to spatial conceptions, that permits a clearer understanding of inner feelings for order.

Reading Paintings

Any painting can be read from a glance at its basic imagery, and the distinguishing qualities of a first-rate painting can be recognized instantly. This immediate perception should not be confused with a full appreciation of a painting and all its complexities. The way a painting reads varies from picture to picture because the artist is able to control the observer's eye by the basic imagery and the related sequence of movements in the composition. Music and literature differ from painting in this respect because they both require a certain length of time to absorb their content.

In traditional Western painting, the eye is usually led into the painting at the bottom because it is attracted by a substantial, gravity-oriented base. It then swings clockwise, up to the left and then to the right. Both gravity and the conditioned method of reading literature, from left to right, appear to influence Western representational composition. Traditional oriental painting, in contrast, reads from the top to the bottom, apparently as a result of reading literature vertically. Gravity is not a factor in composition because material content is subdued.

As Eastern and Western cultures have interacted, there have been more crossovers in the arts, resulting in a greater blend. In nonrepresentational painting, the traditional extremes of both sides have been more or less rejected. Gravity either plays a lesser role or is ignored. Nonrepresenta-

III.9 The Picture Plane.

Kandinsky's Theory (about 1914)

Left: According to Wassily Kandinsky, an empty picture plane has two positive poles of energy, one in the upper-left corner and one in the lower-right corner. The eye is attracted to each, which produces a slight field of energy between them.

Right: Traditional Western composition has a clockwise movement starting at the bottom of the composition as a counterbalance to the energy field between these two poles.

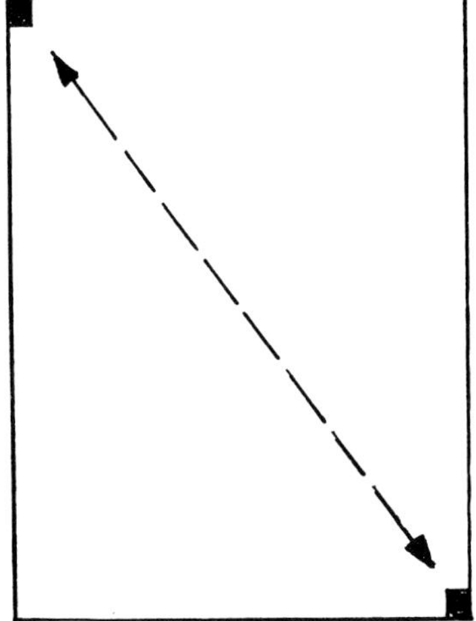

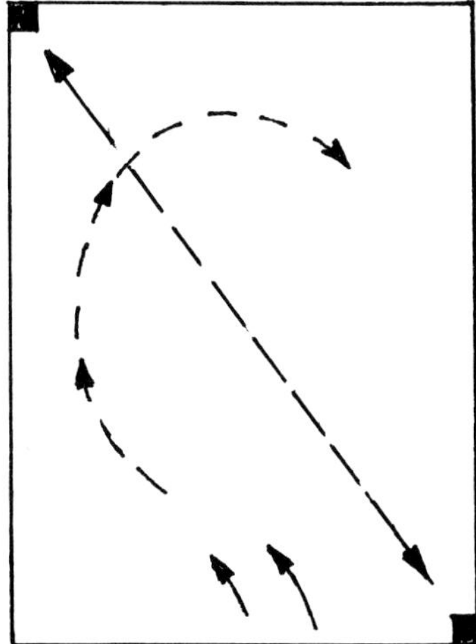

tional paintings can be read in various ways. As modern artists have become more receptive to alternatives, they have found greater freedom.

The Distance Factor

Generally, easel paintings, regardless of their size, should read well from various distances; their imagery should communicate directly to observers regardless of their viewpoint. The exceptions to this adage are extra-large paintings composed with large forms that must be seen at a distance to communicate their imagery or loosely handled, deliberately out-of-focus paintings from a near point of view. "Closet painting" is a term used to describe paintings that can only be read at close range and fall apart at a distance. This effect is usually a result of painting either within a confined space, or of painting too close to the easel for prolonged periods of time.

A rule of thumb is to evaluate constantly the basic imagery and movement sequences in your work from both a near view and a far view as you paint. This criterion is particularly important for developing large paintings. All

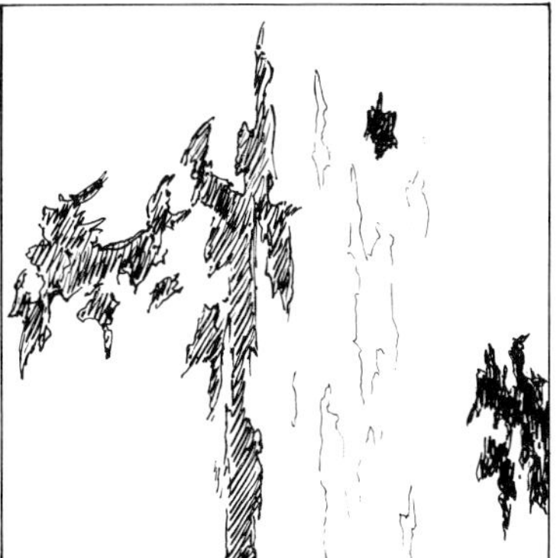

III.10
Sketch of Clyfford Still's
PH-580, 1965.

Sketch of a Still painting that reads from left to right. The negative space is the controlling dimension. The positive forms float in space.

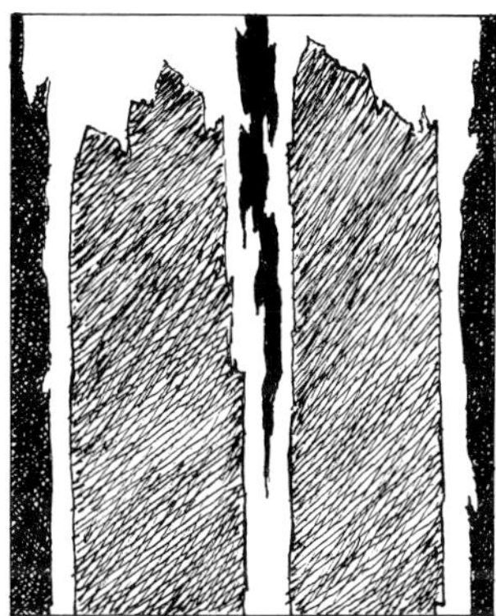

III.11
Sketch of Clyfford Still's
PH-827, 1971.

Still varied the way he composed his paintings. This one "reads" from the gravitational, heavy base at the bottom to the top. Here, positive form is the controlling dimension. The much smaller amount of negative space actively supports the heavy positives.

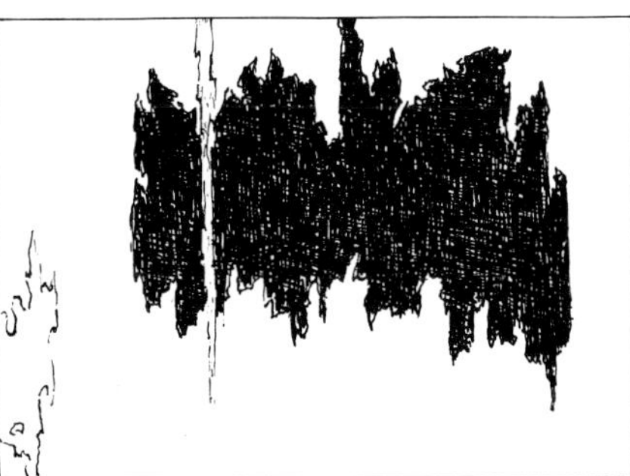

III.12
Sketch of Clyfford Still's
PH-1081, 1960.

Sketch of a Still painting that reads from the upper right to the bottom left. The negative space is the controlling dimension. The positive forms float in space.

major decisions for composing a painting are best made from a distance. That is why some painters deliberately place their palettes away from their easels.

The Picture Plane: Size, Shape, and Subdivision

The choices of the size and the shape of a painting should be regarded as fundamental to the creative process of picture making. During the early stages of their development, most artists are content to work with conventional sizes and shapes of canvas or paper, usually rectangular shapes in small or moderate sizes. These choices are usually determined by conservative, traditional concepts of composition. The choice of smaller sizes is logical, because smaller works are easier to control.

As artists gain experience, they will find that the image held in the mind's eye of the finished painting, regardless of whether or not it is distinct, most often determines its size and shape. Dimensions are seen either in their entirety as an image, or as an idea that has been clarified by preliminary sketches.

Attraction to a subject and how one sees it often trigger an emotional response to the question, "How can this motif be projected?" A tall shape might demand a narrow, tall, vertical canvas, while a broad, panoramic view of landscape might demand a large, wide canvas. In each instance, choosing a specific size and shape is one of the first steps in creative picture making. Certain paintings that I can visualize as compositions have to be large oils. Others may be small watercolors; still others as full sheet, twenty-two by thirty-inch watercolors. Inner feelings control these visual decisions. A few inches added onto one end of a conventional rectangular canvas may be essential for composing a particular subject, whereas another subject may demand a more conventional rectangular shape.

Certain artists prefer particular shapes and sizes. Welliver almost always paints immense eight-to-nine-foot square canvases. His principal idea is to envelop the viewer in a realistic image of his beloved Maine scenery. Cézanne invariably worked with rectangular shapes of conventional proportions. These canvas shapes were usually predetermined by a numbered code that was standard in all French art supply shops. Not until his late years did Cézanne vary his format by working with less conventional, larger canvases. Many of Matisse's early fauvist paintings were small, almost all conventional rectangles. During his mid-years he painted hundreds of conventionally shaped larger horizontal and vertical canvases, but it wasn't until his last truly heroic period that he varied both the size and shape of his pictures to amplify his mastery of painting.

Generally, large paintings impart more energy than smaller ones, but there is no rule of thumb. A small drawing, print, or painting can generate an amount of energy disproportionate to its size. A tiny Goya etching, *The Prisoner*, comes to mind, which, from a distance of fifteen feet, projects its incredible strength across the interior space.

> To paint a small picture is to place yourself outside your experience, to look upon an experience as a stereopticon view or with a reducing glass. However, when you paint the larger picture, you are in it. It isn't something you command.[36]

Properties of Basic Shapes

- A square canvas projects an image of matter, solidity, and strength. The square is the foundation for the rectangle, which is either horizontal or vertical. It may be a conventional shape or an extreme shape with lengthened proportions. Rectangular pictures are generally popular, not only because of their traditional imagery, but also because they fit conventionally shaped walls.
- A square placed on its corner is a diamond shape. As such, it loses its solid gravity-oriented base and tends

III.13 Subdivision of the Picture Plane.

<u>Basic Principle</u>—Static shapes tend to cancel each other out, so for legibility compose with shapes that contrast in size.

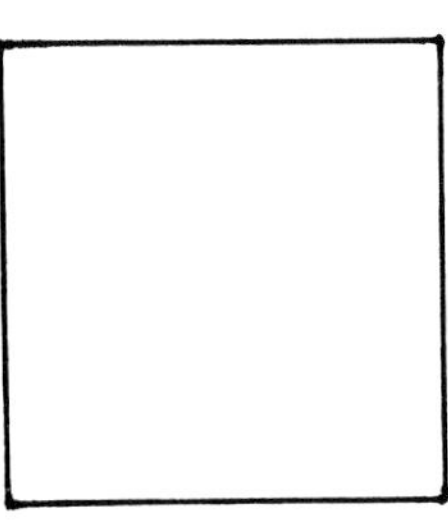

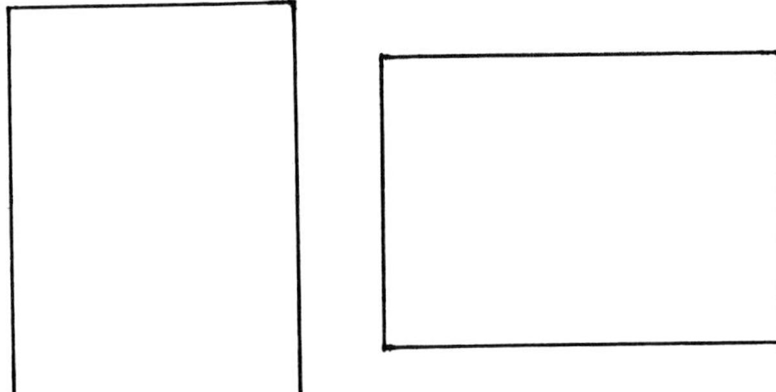

A square picture is a more stable shape than a rectangular picture · plane because all four sides are the same length.

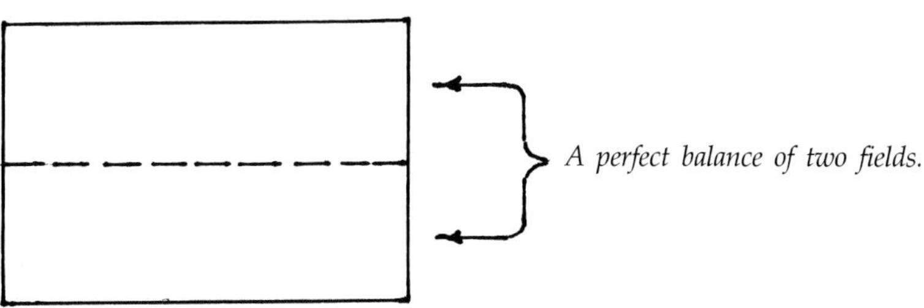

The picture plane should never be divided equally when composing, because this creates two static shapes. In representational painting, this means you should not start your composition by placing a horizon or line of trees or buildings, etc., at the centerline of the picture plane.

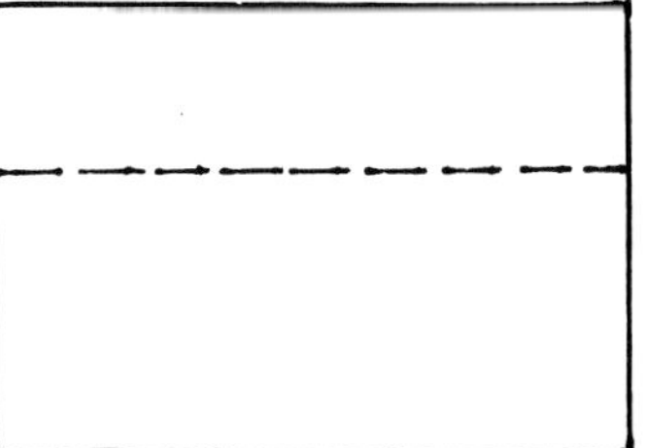

A horizon line is often placed about two-thirds of the way up in traditional representational painting. This establishes a very broad gravitational base.

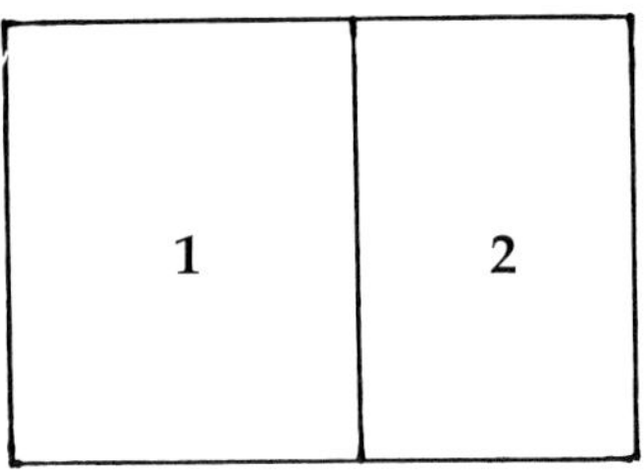

III.13 *continued.*

This basic composition "reads" from left to right because the area of field #1 dominates that of #2 and attracts the eye first.
Lines or shapes within the picture plane that parallel the sides or top are stable and are seen as perfectly vertical or horizontal.
Consequently, they do not convey lateral movement and relative energy.

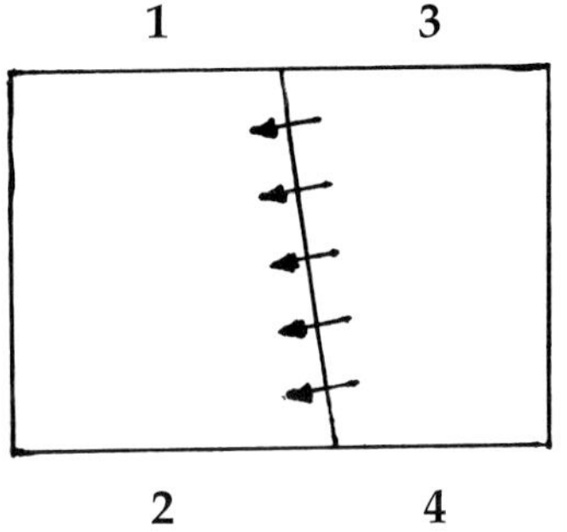

This composition is less static than the one illustrated above because the sides of the two shapes numbered 1 through 4 are all different lengths. The small arrows show the flow of energy produced by the diagonal line.

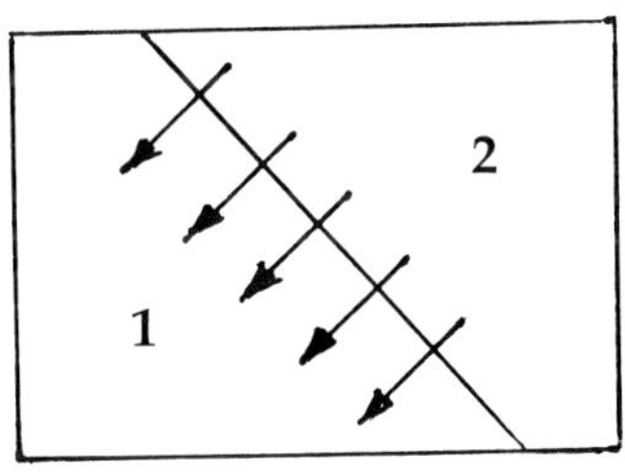

These shapes convey more lateral energy than those illustrated above because the diagonal line that separates the two fields is less stable. As the speed of the diagonal is increased, spatial pressure is increased in fields #1 and #2 and there is a stronger opposition between them.

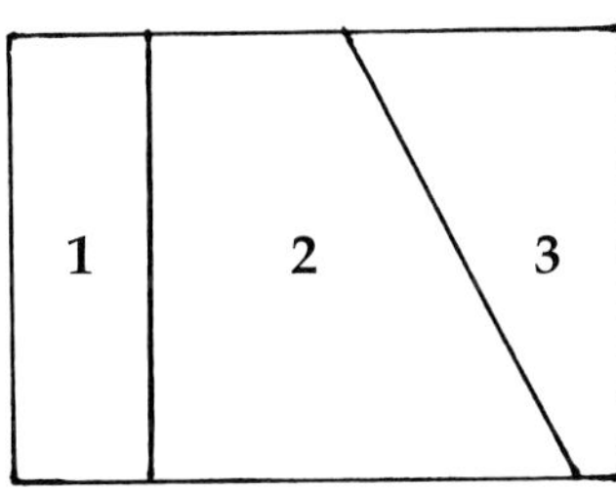

Field #1 is perceived as a stable shape. Stable lines or shapes can be used in composition to "anchor" other lines or shapes that have greater energy. Field #2 is more stable than Field #3 because it is larger and has a broad gravity-oriented base.

to float in space. This shape is best suited to nonrepresentational composition.

- Triangular canvases symbolize thought and momentum as well as direction. A triangular painting also connotes geometrical precision.
- A circular canvas symbolizes closure, representing the effect of movement undivided within. The circle is the foundation for the oval or for an elliptical form.

Canvases can be shaped to create geometrical combinations such as three canvases shaped as a square, triangle, and circle hanging side by side. Canvases can also be other kinds of geometrical shapes. Support surfaces for painting need not be limited to traditional geometric shapes; with the use of new materials they can be shaped as free-form images.

The Three Basic Types of Composition

A composition of *horizontal and vertical forms* is the easiest to compose and the most commonly used. The forms can be created as line, mass, or combinations of both. Diagonal and/or curvilinear shapes are often used to impart inner life to these otherwise relatively stable forms.

Composition based on *diagonal forms* usually appears energetic and alive because these forms convey energy and speed. A triangle, for example, can be used effectively as a foundation for a composition. As a general principle, any one diagonal demands counterbalancing by a reciprocal diagonal. Horizontal and/or vertical forms can be used in combination with diagonal forms to increase interest and anchor or provide stability to the composition; curvilinear forms can be added to provide excitement and rhythmical interchange.

Composition created with *curvilinear forms* is the most difficult to compose as well as the least common type. Curved forms are generally associated with flowing rhythms, which give an inner vitality to a composition. Obviously, horizontal, vertical, and/or diagonal forms can be interspersed with curvilinear forms to produce visual interest and strength.

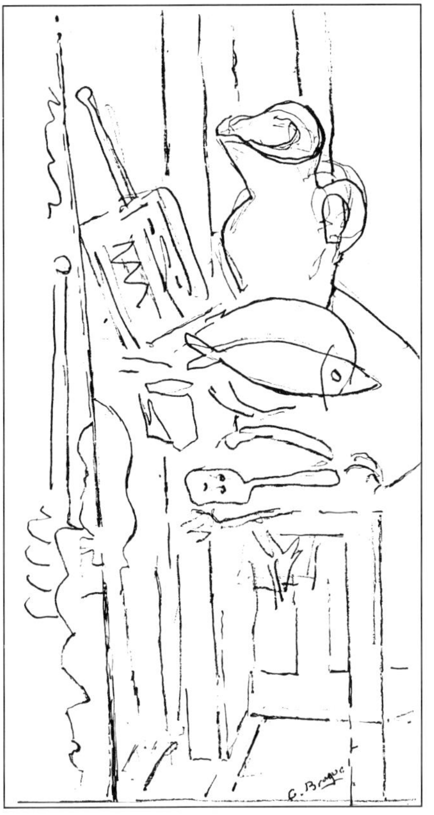

III.14 Sketch of Georges Braque's *Kitchen Table with Roast.*

The slightly angled line subdivides the picture plane and increases the sense of inner life. The broom handle works as a counterbalance against the angled line.

This sketch of Braque's oil painting, *Kitchen Table with Roast*, shows how the artist used the vertical shapes to stabilize his composition. Notice how he used both angled and curvilinear shapes to increase visual interest toward the tabletop, fish plate, and cooking implements. These are the focal points in the painting. The composition is obviously vertical, combined with the lesser elements of diagonals and curves. Braque's signature in the lower right is used as a final balancing note in the composition. The broad masses of color were blocked in first and details were added and pronounced as the painting neared completion, articulating the major forms.

One of the essential characteristics of Picasso's, Braque's, and Matisse's painting is their handling of geometric shapes, often suggested or reinforced with line and painted freely without mechanical aid. Their edges are always changing, kept visually alive because of their subtle variations.

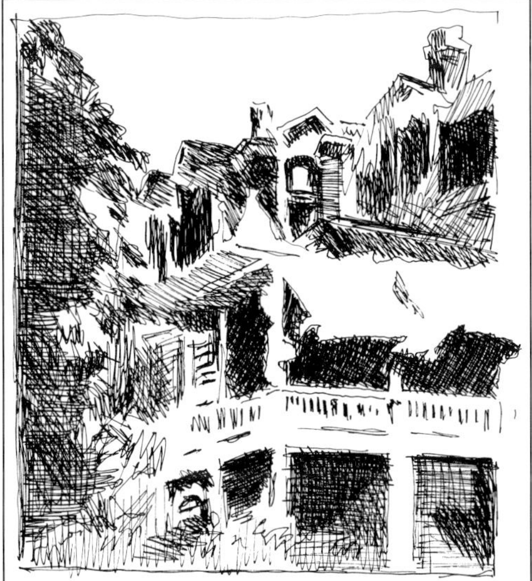

III.15 Detail from Edward Hopper's *The Mansard Roof.*

This detail, copied from Edward Hopper's *The Mansard Roof*, 1923 (watercolor, 14" x 23", Brooklyn Museum, New York), shows simplification of masses. Blacks become negative, pulling lights out to the observer's eye. There is a beautiful flow in these abstract forms; all is interrelated. This is a horizontal and vertical composition interrupted by the few diagonals that produce movement and life. Note how much life there is in the negative space of the sky.

III.16

Edward Hopper, *Early Sunday Morning*, 1930. Oil on canvas, 35" x 60".

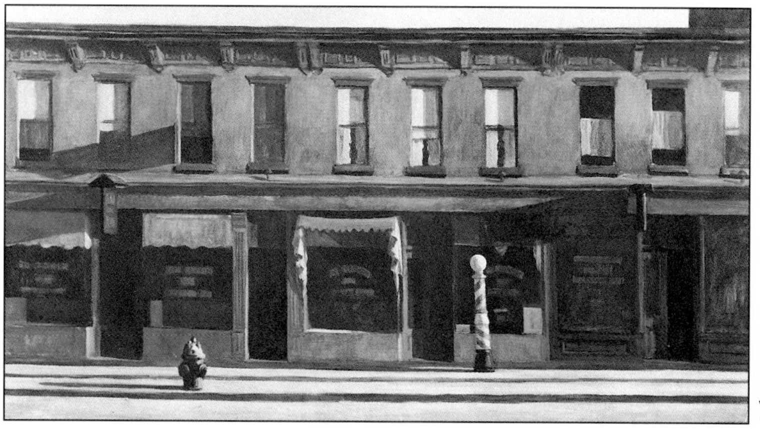

Whitney Museum of American Art, New York.

The composition is based on the strong horizontal mass of the building, composed of storefronts, roof, and cornice, which are interrupted by the vertical windows, barber pole, and fire hydrant. Hopper used similar compositions in several paintings, which he wrote about: "The very long horizontal shape of the picture is an effort to give a sensation of great lateral extent. Carrying the main horizontal lines of the design with little interruption to the edges of the picture, is to enforce this idea and to make one conscious of the space and elements beyond the limits of the scene itself."[37]

III.17

Details from Edward Hopper's *Early Sunday Morning*.

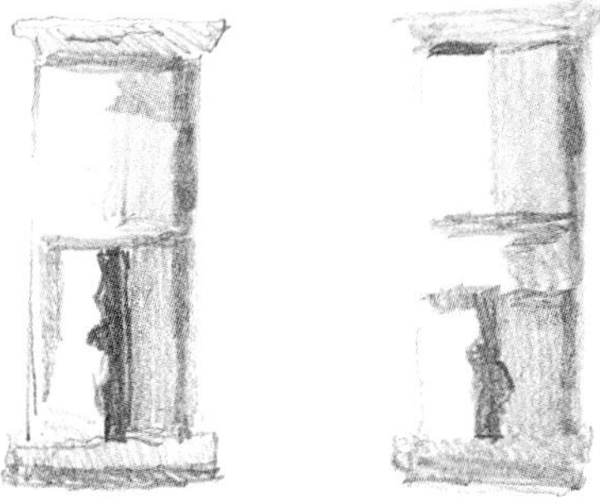

Hopper never painted windows, or any other repetitive elements in his pictures, alike. A curtain is halfway down, the next one is two-thirds down. The black negative between the bottom curtain varies, but note the rhythmical interchange between these shapes. Each detail is received as being significant to the entire composition as Hopper patiently developed his work.

Detail of storefront awning. The light, positive shapes echo the black, negative shapes in the window above.

These details are seen as secondary focal points in the composition, complementing the two primary focal points, the fire hydrant and barber pole. All the focal points pull the eye into the composition. Without them, the eye would be pulled out of the painting at both ends.

Fundamental Principles of Composition

In modern art, painting and composition should be regarded as an integrated process. The goal of composition should be to unify the whole with an understanding that the completed image should be more than the sum of its parts. Composition is, first and foremost, a process of shaping and arranging form to express the artist's feelings. The immediate purpose is to explore possibilities for the development of imagery as it is, inspired first by the vision held by the mind, and second, by the interrelationships of color/forms as they are objectified within the picture plane.

An effective composition is based on an understanding of its limitations and the possibilities for variation. The first brush stroke in a composition, and each additional brush stroke thereafter, is limited by its relation to each other stroke and by the finite limitations of the picture plane. Without these limitations, there is no context for composing form.

There are no laws that govern the way a picture should be composed. There are, however, principles that can be adapted to suit individual expression. Here are some considerations:

- A first objective should be to strengthen pictorial expression. This is best done through a simplification of purpose and its interpretation in the picture plane. The flat surface of the picture plane should be regarded as a finite limitation in composition. The three-dimensional forms in nature must be represented within the two-dimensional entirety of the picture plane.
- This means one must become plane-conscious. A plane is synonymous with flatness. It is a part that exists in space. Form can be developed with any number of planes. Coexisting space can also be seen as a plane or it can comprise multiple planes. The way planes are organized within the limitations of the picture plane determines pictorial order in a composition.
- Since there cannot be real depth in a painting, depth must be created by an interrelationship of planes. Planes advance

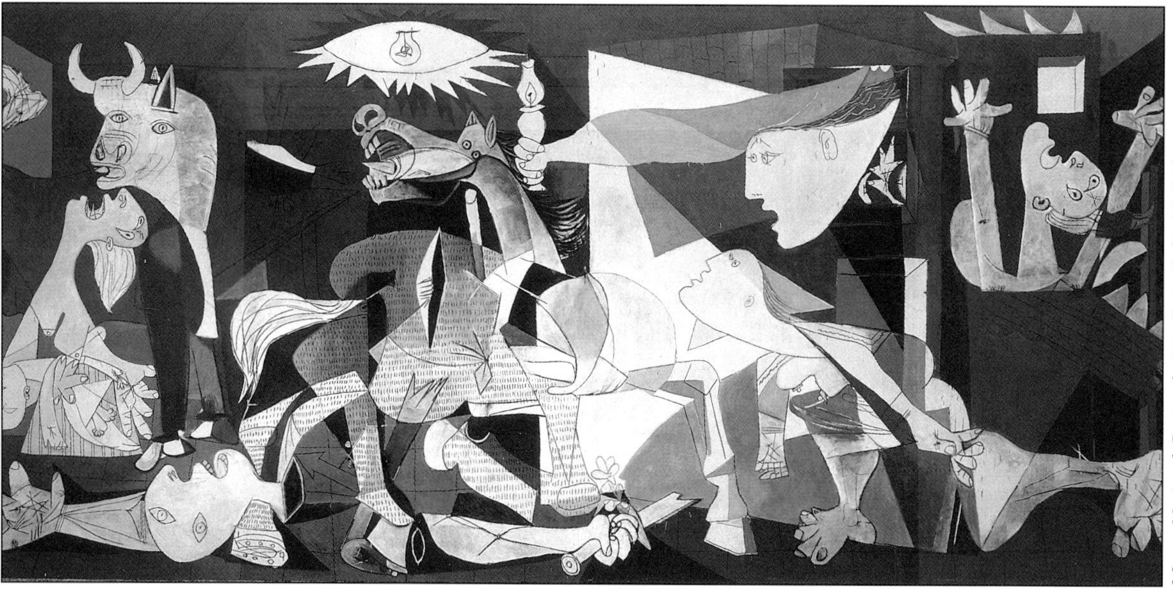

Museo Nacional Centro de Arte Reina Sofia, Madrid.

III.18

Pablo Picasso, *Guernica*, 1937. Oil on canvas, 11'6" x 25'8".

Guernica was motivated by Picasso's outrage at the annihilation of the innocent inhabitants of the ancient Basque town during the Spanish civil war by a fleet of German planes.

During the mid-twentieth century, *Guernica* was vehemently criticized by many well-known American abstract painters for its literary content, i.e., qualities in a painting that can be described better with words than with a brush. All the figures express qualities of rage, horror, or pain, and their anguish is heightened by Picasso's ability to freeze their tortured movement—all taking place in a vast, black interior, lit only by a naked bulb and small oil lamp in the hand of a woman with a profile like an ancient Greek mask. The small window in the upper right is a symbol of the clear light in the outer world.

There are no words that can describe *Guernica* adequately. Its visual power, manifested through Picasso's outrage, provokes the deepest feelings. The composition is incredible. *Guernica* may well be remembered as the dominant work of art in this century.

Museo Nacional Centro de Arte Reina Sofía, Madrid.

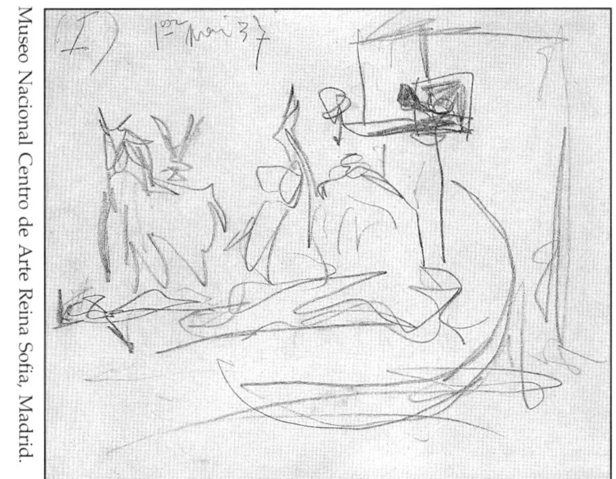

III.19

First sketch for *Guernica*, May 1, 1937.

The beginning of the concept for the composition suggesting the woman with the lamp leaning out the window, the bull on the left, and the fallen horse.

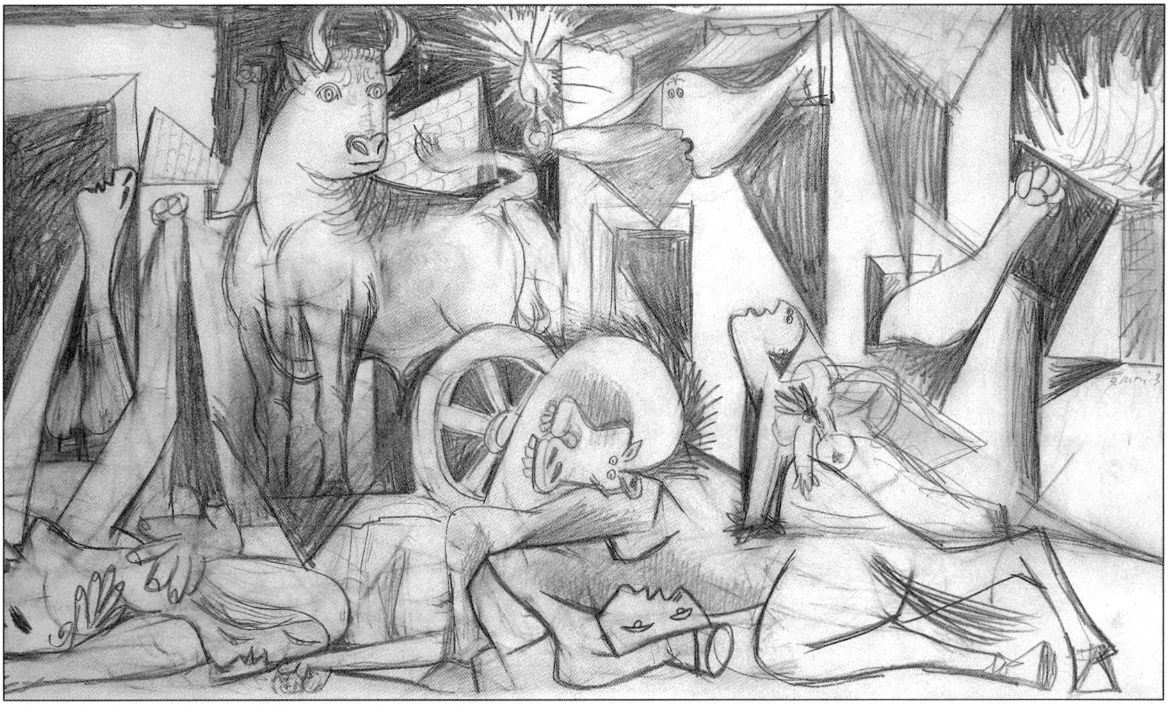

Museo Nacional Centro de Arte Reina Sofía, Madrid.

III.20

Study for composition, *Guernica*, May 8, 1937.

Elements to be used in the painting are defined, including the flames in the night sky, the kneeling, tortured woman, the final head of the woman with the lamp, and the screaming horse seen upside down. At this stage, Picasso draws with pure emotion, establishing content, with lesser thought given to the overall organization.

to the eye and recede away from the eye. To maintain unity, there cannot be holes painted in the canvas, or a sense of deep space created as an illusion of depth that is not consistent with the remaining elements that shape the whole. For the same reason there should not be any forms that jump out of the picture plane and destroy its unity.

- A line is a fragment of a plane. A dot is a point in the picture plane. Generally, neither lines nor points control pictorial order in a composition; however, both lines and points can support and articulate mass relationships that are composed of planes. Composition that is composed solely with lines relates more to drawing than it does to painting.

- Another principal idea should be to reduce form to its essential mass relationships. Forms as they are seen in nature and in painting can be simplified by translating them in the mind's eye into primary forms, secondary forms, and detail. A primary form is the most dominant form in any subject matter. In nature, it can be a mountain or a large field or a large outcropping of rocks. A massive group of trees can be interpreted as a series of planes, much like a wall that is articulated with a variety of smaller planes. As the mind transforms the trees into a massive primary form, their relative weight and relationship to the composition become more apparent.

- Secondary forms support a primary form; they are large forms but are comparatively of lesser importance. The idea is to see component parts of a composition in terms of comparative proportions.

- Details have the function of articulating the larger primary and secondary forms. They should be seen as structural components that add meaning and life to a composition. It is a mistake to think of details in a painting only as the minute forms that we respond to psychologically because of their illusion of reality.

One of the best ways to compose a painting is to work from broad generalizations to specifics. Think about form in the abstract first. Become more shape-conscious. Understand and use the principle that good composition is based on a nonrepresentational underlying framework that is used for composing the actual form.

In order to attain unity, keep your painting in balance as you work. Keep track of where you are, always in the context of the whole. It is all too easy to get lost in a complex series of lines and planes, both in the subject and on the canvas.

Simplify your concept of form in every possible way. Are there any forms that can be deleted? Can the size and shape of any forms be adjusted to gain organic unity and a smoother sequence of movement?

A fundamental principle should be to direct the eye into the picture plane. Primary forms should be used to attract one's vision into the painting and should be placed well within the perimeter of the picture plane because the major forms invariably attract the eye first. It is best to keep energetic forms away from the perimeter. Do not compose forms that are more than halfway out of the painting, because the eye attempts to follow the incomplete form out of the painting.

One or more focal points, or centers of interest, can be used effectively to attract the eye into the painting. The way that focal points are used can vary. One focal point, for example, can be a primary center of interest and can be supported by a number of lesser focal points. Focal points should be balanced within the confines of the picture plane. They should not be placed too close to its perimeter, for they would attract the eye out of the composition. The use of focal points is optional. Paintings can be composed without them to achieve a simpler and unimpaired surface unity.

Do not cut off any corners in a composition. The part that is cut off is isolated from the remainder of the picture and subdivides and weakens the whole.

Do not create static forms. As a general principle, all form, both positive and negative, should be composed so that one side differs from the other, producing an asymmetrical organic relationship in the form and in its corresponding space. Perfect symmetry produces static relationships, re-

III.21

Diego de Velásquez, *Las Meninas (The Maids of Honor)*, 1656. Oil on canvas, 318cm. x 276cm.

The underlying geometrical framework of Picasso's composition in *Guernica* can be compared with the simpler geometry in *Las Meninas* by Velásquez, considered the dominant work of art in the seventeenth century.

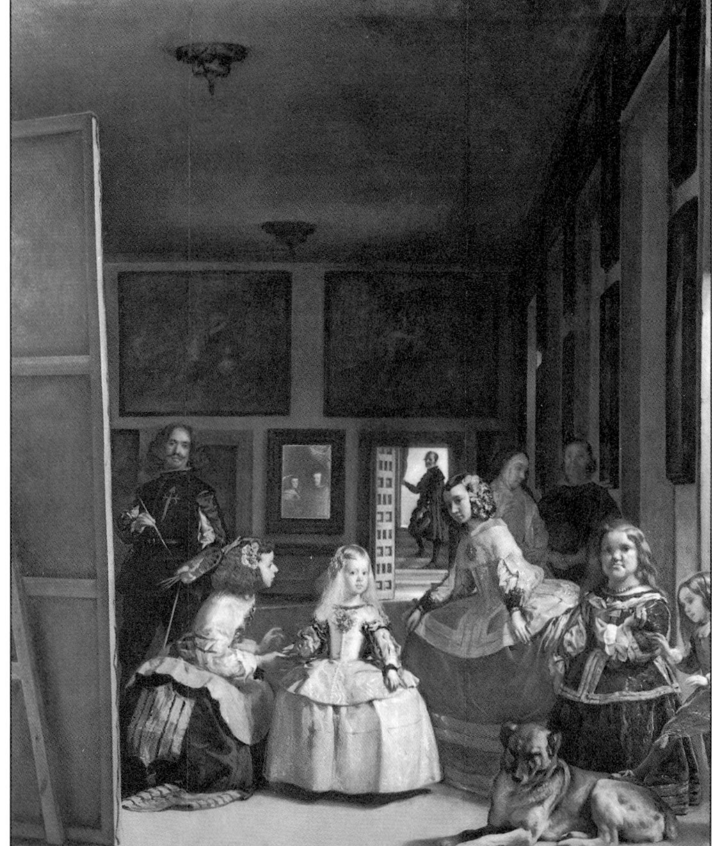

The British Museum, London.

The light dashed line shows the major subdivision of the picture plane as a geometric framework.

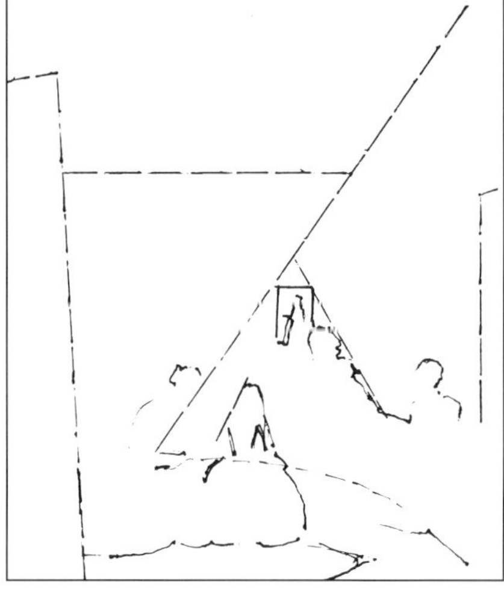

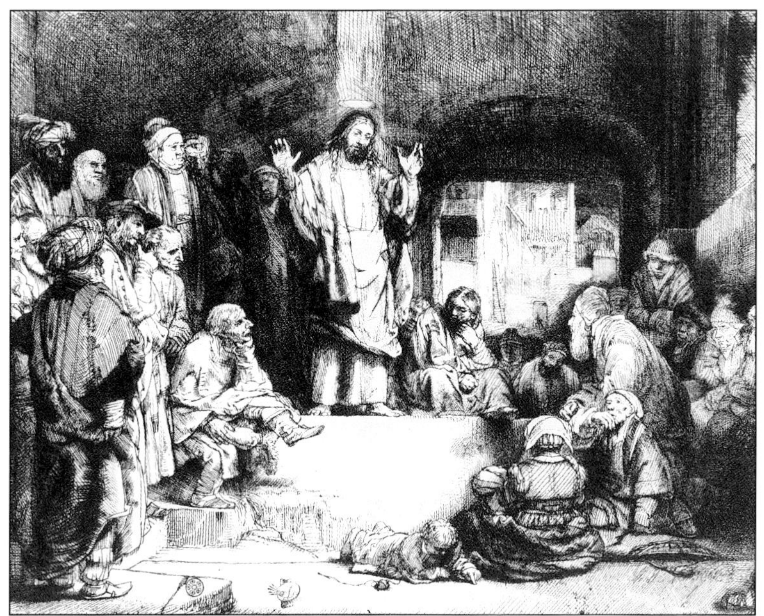

III.22

Rembrandt van Rijn, *Christ Preaching*, circa 1652. Etching and drypoint, 15.5cm. x 20.7cm.

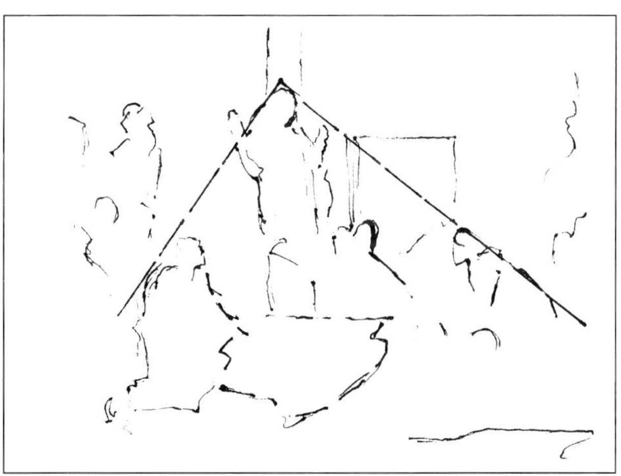

A large triangle and semicircle are used as a simple geometric scaffold for the composition.

III.23

Sketch of Henri Matisse's *Les Aranthes*, 1953. Paper cutout, 122⅜" x 136".

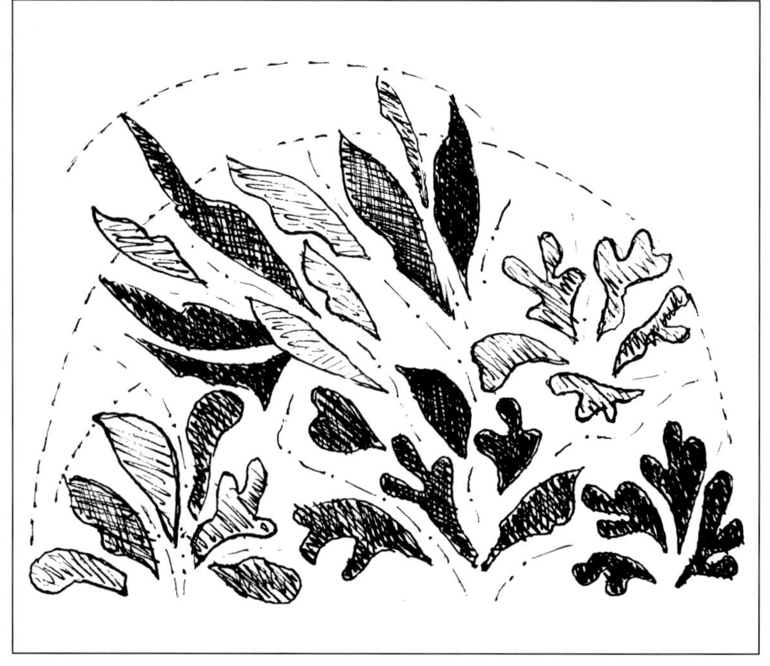

Form can be used to express ideas, theories, and feelings of order. A shape can hover or a space may soar upwards in an arch. Large mass relationships spell monumentality. Diagonals denote speed. Horizontal and vertical dimensions are purely architectural and convey stability and order. Form can be powerful or poetic. If the form is poor, it is too weak to communicate significance.

A combination of curvilinear and diagonal forms. Note how axes of form vary from fairly straight diagonals to curvilinear movements. The flow of negative space between and around the positive forms is the key to controlling the entire arrangement.

gardless of the style of painting. Consequently, a figure, or a head in a portrait, or a dominant form in a still life, should not be centered in a composition because the eye would be attracted equally to the negative space on each side of the form. If a form is centered, one side should be painted differently from the other and in turn the space should be handled so that one side is dominant.

There is much more to painting than surface appearance. The nonrepresentational painter faces the same aesthetic problems in regard to picture making as does the painter who works directly from nature. All visual expression is subject to the same fundamental principles. Good painting is good painting, regardless of style.

The primitive artist starts his pictures by placing all of the particulars first. He has little concern for the importance of mass relationships in painting and their interrelationship to produce unity and strength.

Grandma Moses painted a lot of small details in her pictures, scattered randomly, and always seen from afar, in

The Phillips Collection, Washington, D.C.

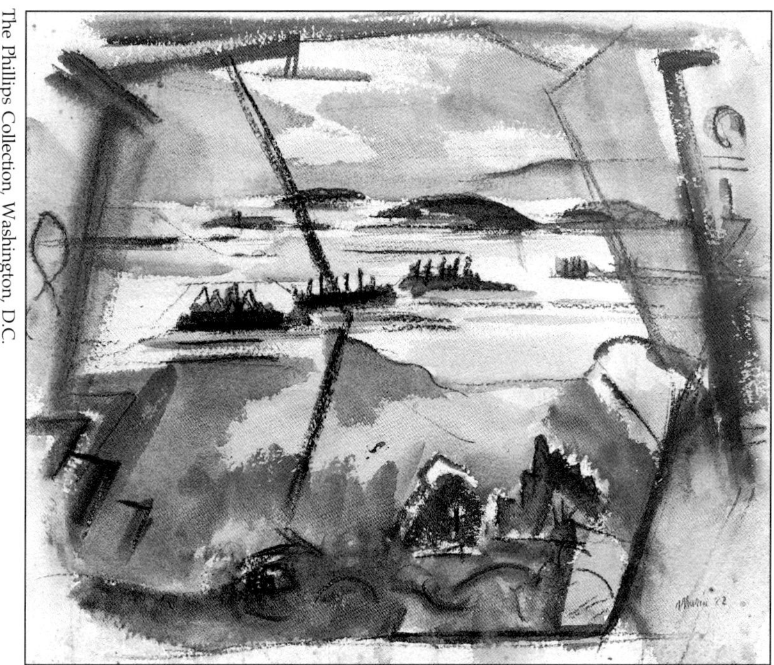

III.24

John Marin, *Maine Islands*, 1922. Watercolor, 16⅞" x 19¾".

John Marin and his corners. John Marin often made an interior frame with lines that skipped and danced around the perimeter of his paintings. Corners were occasionally shaped with diagonals, but these were not drawn to the edges so that the eye was isolated from the remainder of the painting. By merely suggesting this framework, rather than making it concrete, the eye can move in and out, from the perimeter into the image area, and back out.

order to cram in more literal meaning. The famous Pennsylvania primitive painter, Horace Pippin, used innumerable details in his work, all in miniature. He placed a railroad, bridges, a whole town on the side of a mountain, all in a single painting. I feel it safe to assume that most painters who use excessive detail in their paintings are hoping to convey a more comprehensive reality.

The multifaceted drips and fluid skeins of vari-colored paint in a Jackson Pollock painting are the details that constitute its structure, whereas in a Clyfford Still painting the details are seen at the edges of his immense forms. In each instance, the artist's control of the whole was correlated to his perception of negative space. More drips of paint in a Pollock painting would have strangled the space. Inner life, then, would be destroyed. It is all in controlling proportions—proportional interchange is the key. Too much detail becomes profusion rather than clarification of the idea of the work.

Because Matisse was a pure colorist, he relied on color

III.25

Sketch of Henri Matisse's *Nature morte à l'autoportrait*, 1911.

DON'T CUT OFF CORNERS IN A COMPOSITION

minor corner cut off

This corner is cut off and isolated from the remainder of the composition.

entire side of painting isolated

This is a magnificent painting, but it would be even better if Matisse had completely solved the composition without cutting off the corners.

This diagram shows how the composition has been isolated from the perimeter of the picture plane, impairing a unified whole.

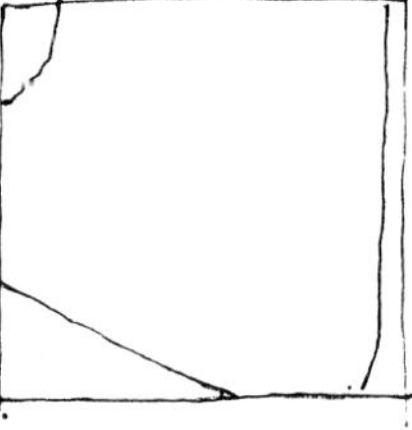

interaction as the primary means to express his feelings, but the way he used color varied considerably. He often suggested gradations of pure color and reinforced these with line. In his later painting, he relied more on flat planes of color, sometimes interspersed with line and other times as hard-edged, concrete mass relationships.

Matisse and Picasso, more than any other twentieth-century artists, experimented with different kinds of visual structure in their painting. The continuity and plasticity in their work, regardless of how it was painted, is self-evident. They understood their painting as structure and how it worked.

Continuity and Plasticity

Continuity in a work of art describes qualities of being connected, of continuation, of coherence and progression.

Continuity is the basis for the harmonic relationships of all the forms in nature. There is an orderly visual sequence from volume to space that is essential for seeing the whole, naturally, without interruption. From nature, we learn how to see the origins of forms, and how they develop and die. We discover that the appearance of each form is related to its function. Each part is indispensable to the whole. The fundamental principle is that form develops from the inside out. As in nature, painting depends on continuity as the foundation for interrelatedness. The search is centered inward to express outward.

The artist depends on his sense of rightness to direct the brush. When it looks right, it *is* right. Each part is indispensable to the whole structure of the painting. When there is doubt or uncertainty based on the mistrust of feelings, the intuitive flow is impeded.

The word plastic, from its Greek origins, means form that can be shaped, extruded, or compressed, or is malleable. The artist's mind searches, inquires, assimilates, selects, and then disperses ideas. As a form is developed, it springs from a progression of visual responses. It is part of an emerging pattern which, like an amoeba, changes shape as it adapts to the expressive needs of the painting. The medium, whether oil, acrylic, or watercolor, is also plastic since it is adaptable to the needs of the artist.

The Selection of Subject Matter

As the flood tide covers the kelp-layered beach, the innumerable forms of life are transformed in perfect harmony as their common denominator is changed from space to water. Deep slate gray and brilliant white stones, rose-tinted starfish, blue-black baby mussels—each has its own asymmetrical perfection that allows the association of thousands to have a natural and harmonious visual accord. Each color and shape is inseparable and each change in light changes all the colors in all the forms.

Beyond the stone beach on the southernmost point of the large island, weathered blue spruce show their years of being buffeted by the unrelenting ocean winds, yet they still stand like sentinels as they overlook massive granite strata extending into the sea. The cool, bluish gray-green of the spruce stands out against a blackish green negative background of deep woods, opposed by an occasional glimpse of wild roses growing in a brighter green sea grass.

The moods of the Maine coast are expressive, varying from the idyllic quiet and beauty of midsummer to the black hell of raging surf during the height of a winter northeaster. We go there each summer to paint, teacher and students as one, in an attempt to understand the extremes of beauty and bleakness. The elemental force of the land opposing the sea is a never-ending subject for our expressive efforts with brush and paint, but each of us, in our own way, must search for and discover on paper or canvas our own imagery and reality.

Let us explore together this particular locale for painting, as if you are with my small group of students. All the senses should be at play. Smell the damp, salty scents of clammy, drenched lichen, barnacles, and seaweed in the deep crevices between the granite ledges as the tide ebbs. Subject matter abounds under every footstep. Tidal pools, formed by the surging waves, are among nature's most beautiful abstractions. Colors in the pools are often startling deep crimsons, blacks, pale yellow greens, streaks of deep burnt sienna and umber. There, right at your feet, is an abstract pattern—flowing kelp at the edge of a tidal pool, broad bands and twisting ribbons of color, a starfish. Cup your hands around these shapes, attempt to isolate them, squint at them to rule out excessive detail. Is this a subject that has possibilities for you? On the weather side of the point, the rocks are bolder and the surf comes rushing in, shooting up cascades of spray. Listen to a breaking wave. Time the sound of its booming crescendo as it explodes against the opposing force of glistening black rocks. There is a hissing as the wave rushes outward beneath the next wave, which rolls rhythmically inshore to boom again.

The art of painting landscape spontaneously with force and emotion is much like practicing Zen Buddhism. Before the great hunter releases the arrow from his bow, it already belongs to its target, the rabbit. The action is involuntary. Rather than a harshly determined effort, it is instead a release of an inner, positive state of being. So it is in the best painting. By feeling deeply the forces at play, the brush does not paint the outward appearance of the wave. It paints the internal force of the wave and the opposing forces of the rocks.

I cannot teach you how to paint! I am merely trying to increase your awareness of these elemental, underlying forces, to invite your mind's eye to see and explore subject matter.

A breaking wave does not just sit there stolidly, like the apples in a Cézanne still life. As it breaks, it plumes upward and shatters, cascading into foam, all in an instant. It has to be one of the toughest subjects to paint. Few artists have succeeded with this kind of imagery. Winslow Homer, for instance, spent many years at Prout's Neck on the Maine coast studying and sketching waves.

Yes, of course, the camera can capture, if you are skillful enough, that instant when the spray is at its highest. But remember: the camera is a mechanized eye; it has no feelings about or empathy with these majestic forces at play.

Nature is our teacher. It is always there for us. And

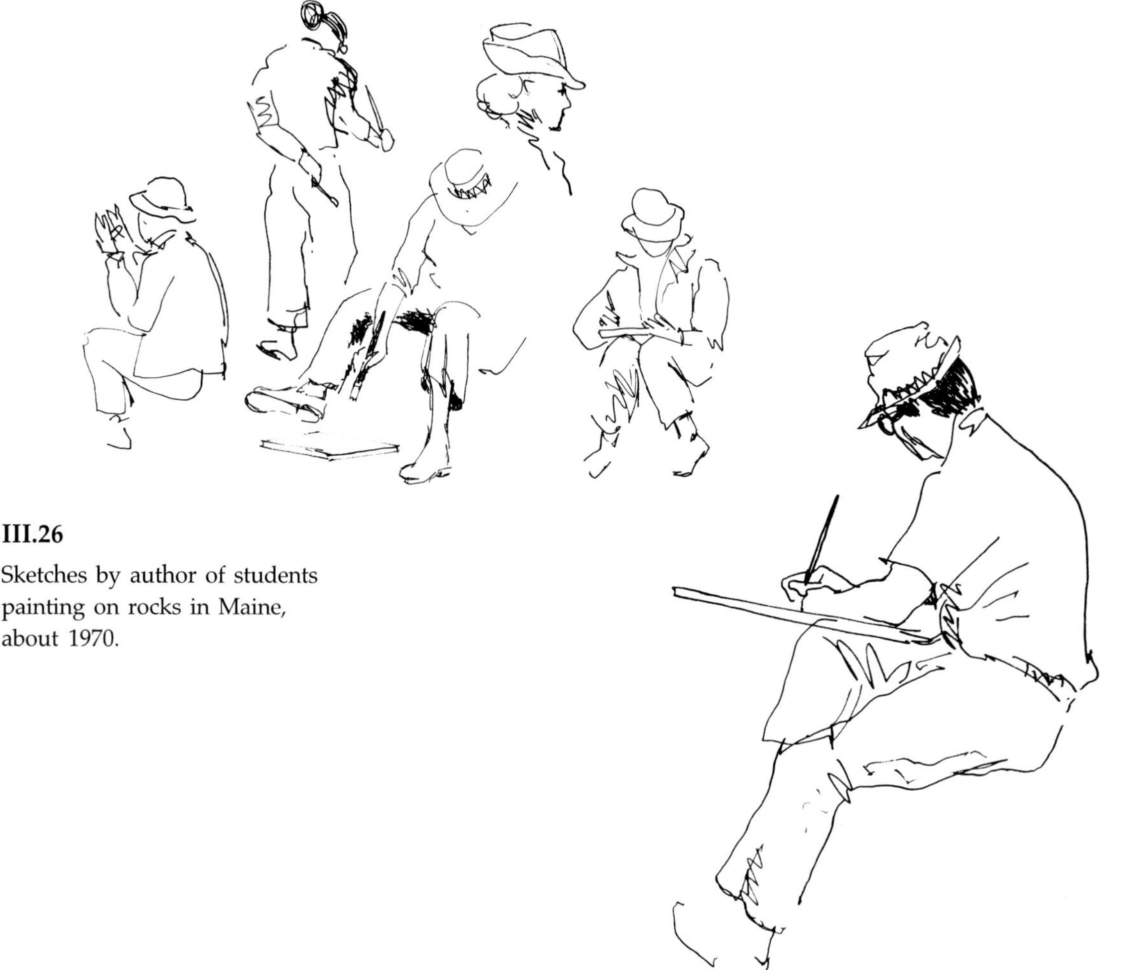

III.26

Sketches by author of students painting on rocks in Maine, about 1970.

Collection of Catherine Reinbold.

yet, in the face of its grandeur and unrivaled immensity, we must adopt an attitude of humility because we cannot equal it with our own work. We must think of ourselves, instead, as extensions of nature and discover through painting how we can interpret it with a clearer understanding of its powerful forces.

On the windward side of the point, the rocks are stacked up. Huge, omnipresent, tilting at odd angles, massive weights, seemingly invulnerable to the savage winter storms. In the more intense light of the later morning, these rocks appear white on the tops and black underneath. Their forms are bold, austere, and unadorned, charged with related energies. To paint these forms is to compose with oppositions, counterbalancing angled thrust lines within their monumental shapes. My "easel rock," so nicknamed by my students because I used one end of its massive form as a table for painting watercolors, perches on the very top of all the rocks. Three miles offshore, suspended in a cobalt blue sea, lies Sequin Island, with its particular bumps and hollows and the lighthouse towering some 400 feet on the highest hill toward the middle—all seen in a glance as a background macrocosm that, by contrast, emphasizes the bold foreground.

Entering the woods behind the point, one actually steps down from the heaped up rocks into a secluded world. The light is transformed at once, filtered, greener, grayer, and cooler. Tonal contrasts are no longer aggressive, as in the outside bright light, but are modulated, the light subdued by the canopy of trees. Sounds are muffled. Breaking waves are murmurs in the distance. Rocks are scattered randomly, all sizes, bluish gray to greenish to purplish gray, in a bed of deep olive green moss, soft under the feet, partially hidden by lighter, cooler green forms. Details abound—broken sea urchin shells dropped by the gulls, scallop and mussel shells blown in by the great winter gales, twigs, branches, larger windfalls, some trunks stripped, bare, silver-tinged gray, an occasional white birch standing out in contrast to spruce and pine, roots exposed. There is a kind of wholly organic profusion.

There isn't any particular "best" subject here. What you choose to paint should be selected intuitively. What you like is important. Trust your vision. That which we are naturally attracted to, our likes, distinguish each one of us from the others. This is the beginning place for singular expression. Take the time to settle in. This is particularly important when the subject matter, exciting as it may be, is unfamiliar. Do not just look at forms. Look into forms. Attempt to feel the sense of place, of light, of shapes and colors.

The first few days are usually nonproductive, besides doing a lot of preliminary, explorative sketches. Usually by the third or fourth day, I find my students scattered at various sites among the rocky ledges, looking almost as natural in these settings as the ever-present seagulls. My best students quickly learn that an isolated, uninhibited, deep involvement with their own ideas produces uncommon results.

At the end of a day's painting session, we often have a group critique back at the camp. Most of the paintings are watercolors. I encourage the artists to show me their sketches and preliminaries, so that their "idea" of subject can be evaluated. In many ways, these group critiques are more helpful than individual critiques. Paintings can be objectively evaluated by making comparisons of subject matter, intentions, and degree of success, or effectiveness of expression. The idea is to have each student see his or her own painting objectively, as if it were exhibited in public. After a few sessions, most of my students lose their self-consciousness about revealing their personal expression, which all good paintings do.

These open critiques also encourage students to see and participate in the evaluation of varied compositional problems that arise when one paints directly from nature. This is a wonderful learning process—learning to see more clearly what makes paintings work. What limitations are prescribed? What are the limits of the picture plane, its size and shape in relation to the particular view of the motif—near, mid-distance, or far away? What are the primary forms and how do they control the overall image? Which is dominant, the positive form or the negative space? Do the secondary forms and details support the dominant forms? Finally, can the color/forms and their movements, which comprise the total image, be further simplified to attain expressive clarity?

The choice of a motif should never be separated from its compositional role. It is one thing to see and admire subject matter, but another to portray it as a meaningful, expressive image.

In the morning there will be a new kind of light, new color/forms, and new ideas of composition. What you have learned has been stored in your mind and is there for you to use. But I advise you, before you confront your subject matter, to forget your intellect and rely on your feelings.

From My Notes

The sheer abundance of subject matter in nature can be confusing, even overwhelming, for some students. Because of the complexity in any motif, your composition must be simplified.

First, some thoughts before you start to paint. You might think of your painting as a small component of a larger view, much like seeing nature through a window. The thought that the view is derived from is important. You should not feel restricted in any way by a subject, either to duplicate it exactly or to adhere to the way that it is structured.

A particular subject can be transposed according to your idea of painting. I cannot emphasize enough the importance of this. Develop an attitude that frees your mind from preestablished criteria and the exact reproduction of objects as they are seen in nature. The selection of subject matter, in turn, is freed from the viewfinder approach—searching with a small piece of mat board through a tiny rectangular opening for a precise arrangement of forms to copy.

You need to be alone, isolated, with your idea of the subject, to be totally receptive to various possibilities. Gain familiarity with your subject, ponder, sketch. Let curiosity take hold: What happens if? Forms and colors are adaptable; they are composed to fit a particular picture plane. Simplify your image. Expressiveness can be increased as the idea of the painting is limited. Can you limit the number of forms? Can you limit the number of colors? Keep track of where you are. Nature, right there in front of you, is your source of information.

If you plan to paint in your studio with a motif derived from preliminary sketches, it is helpful to make color notations on location by identifying them with specific descriptions. Do not think simply in terms of a red or a green or a pink, but rather describe the color as, say, a dark burnt red, a middle, warm olive green, or a pale pink tinged with a pale yellow. In each instance, the tone—dark to light—is used as a prefix to the color to aid your visual memory. Attempt to visualize colors in terms of relative warmth and coolness: a warm cobalt blue, for instance, might be seen against a cooler blackish green.

Consider whether colors seen in your subject can be heightened, because preliminary color sketches done outdoors, if not deliberately strengthened, invariably appear weak and washed out when seen indoors. This effect is usually a result of working in an intense outdoor light. Painting on a gray day is preferred.

As you draw and paint repeatedly with the kinds of forms you are attracted to, you gain an intuitive knowledge of your own response to form—the way you tend to shape curves, angles, masses, and details, and their correspondence to your natural expression. You must learn to trust your feelings as you work. Understand the basic principle that the way you perceive a subject in your mind correlates to your choice of a particular subject. Think about this, long and hard.

A five-year-old child came with her mother to the Strawberry Factory and, after seeing my paintings, asked her: "Do I have to draw before I paint?" Think about this. There is a direct relation between a subject and how it is made.

Pointers for the Simplification of Subject Matter

Choose the simple subject. If you are setting up a still life or posing a model, limit the number of props, choose simple, bold patterns in fabrics, and delete small objects. Position large shapes to carry the eye into the picture plane. Remember to squint at your subject to more clearly perceive mass relationships by ruling out reflected light. This is a way to eradicate unneeded detail.

View your subject as related planes. A field of stones on a beach, for example, can be perceived as a large plane that is articulated by the shapes of the small stones. The idea is to keep details related to the larger forms.

Use large tools whenever possible. If possible, the width of a brush should be commensurate with the width of the form you are painting. A half-inch-wide brush, for instance, can be used effectively to paint a tree branch that is approximately the same width. Large forms that are painted with small brushes usually appear tight (excessively rendered) or they have too much unneeded detail. Remember, each brush stroke is a detail.

Work as directly as possible, always in context with the whole. Stop when you are tired.

> Often the artist seemed childlike and more primeval (in the sense of being closer to the origins) than his contemporaries; thanks to his unique sensitivity he could animate all nature and find echoes and correspondences between all things. Birds, plants, and other objects that surrounded him enticed Matisse to work. (Fishbowls, pewter jugs, mugs, fruit dishes, pitchers, vases, amphorae, tobacco jars, plates, opaline cups, teacups, draperies, textured fabrics, copper cauldrons, glasses—familiar household objects danced a recurrent, elusive saraband in his pictures.) While his eyes carelessly or carefully caressed their well-loved and well-known surfaces, the creative impulse sprang toward a new vision. For him a still life was not a minor theme. Many of his strong works simply depicted artifacts of different sizes, substance, texture, color, and form and their interaction with natural forms. His resourcefulness in combining unusual viewpoints (from above, from below, along a diagonal) matched his fantasy in coupling the most unlikely pairs.[38]

Technique and its Relation to the Intuitive Process

The choice of materials and the way that they are used to make a painting should be regarded as the servants of personal expression. It should never be the other way around, for then the painter becomes trapped by his ideas of technical accomplishment and his paintings will emerge without feeling.

Largely due to the many approaches to contemporary painting, the inherent technical problems in painting are vastly different from those of the Renaissance. The work of the Old Masters was produced with a consistent, highly developed craftsmanship. Techniques were developed and influenced by schools of painting and little, if any, distinction was made between their high standards of craftsmanship and their artistic intentions. Without question, a sound knowledge of materials and how best to use them to ensure quality and permanence is essential to the modern artist, but the extensive amount of available technical information on materials and how to use them should be regarded as neither mandatory nor exhaustive. The development of your expression should be first and foremost; therefore, any technique that you choose should be used to realize and fulfill your feelings. The modern artist discovers his own methods, the potentialities, and limitations of his medium as they relate to and within the context of his particular vision. What is right for Joe is not right for Susan.

One of the major tasks in teaching painting is to overcome the idea held by many students that their creative problems can be solved by technical solutions. This attitude is reinforced by innumerable teachers who emphasize technique as the means for artistic success, the "how-to" books, and the countless workshops that rely on demonstrations to teach painting. Demonstrations can teach conformity, but they can't teach you how *you* should paint.

A few years ago while we were sketching at Pemaquid Point, which is one of the more spectacular formations of vertical rocks on the coast of Maine, my wife and I observed a watercolor workshop in progress. The instructor was surrounded by twenty or so students as he demonstrated how to paint the Pemaquid Point Lighthouse, high upon the point overlooking the ocean. We were curious, so we watched him for a while as he blocked in the image. I remember thinking that this was the usual panoramic view that is so often repeated in calendar art. He worked quickly and with great confidence. His technique was flawless. His students were obviously impressed. They all took notes as he painted, or, I should say, as he copied his subject, and they made little sketches to remind themselves how he painted the scene. After lunch the students set up their easels and they all proceeded to paint the same view. There wasn't a single creative painting done in the entire group, including that of the instructor. Not one of the students had the nerve to innovate nor had they been encouraged to do so. I thought of Edward Hopper and the distinctive ways that he composed subject matter. He painted some grand lighthouses in his day, and I'm sure that he would have been distressed had he been there.

The important thing, regardless of your experience and temperament, is to expand your understanding of the inherent qualities of subjects that have meaning to your world. This is best done through creative painting. The knowledge gained is both visual and technical. It is absorbed by a succession of small and large observations, even abstracted, seemingly inconsequential observations, entangled within the web of useful information. You are involved in a search, particularly in your early stages of creative development, to find solutions to the problems that are inherent to your idea of painting. The way you brush paint on a canvas, whether it is powerful or subtle and refined, dry-brushed or handled wet into wet, blurred or hard-edged, is a result of discovering a private world full of colors, forms, and meaning.

> I sometimes have the impression that it is not me who did my paintings. I feel absolutely detached at first glance. It is absolutely as if they were someone else's. But when I concentrate, then I see a lot of things. I recognize my own quirks, the marks of my style. One's style—it is in a way one's inability to do otherwise. The physical is in command. Your physical constitution practically dictates the shape of the brushmarks, as it does the pen marks in writing.[39]
>
> —GEORGES BRAQUE

Let us go back to the idea of a conceptual image. A conceptual image is related to one's relative creative experience. It is the inspired image held in the mind's eye of how an art form appears. The idea of a wet into wet watercolor with brilliant colors and organic forms, for instance, is a specific kind of image for a painting. The particular technique that is chosen to objectify this concept is a product of both assimilated past experience and the image held in the mind. The artist's skill and craftsmanship are also products of his past experience of using the wet into wet technique, as well as of his acquired knowledge of color and form.

The idea of a large oil landscape painting, for example, can be developed in the studio from preliminary drawing and painting completed at the site. The technical considerations of exactly how the drawing is to be transferred to the larger canvas, whether or not an imprimatura should be used over the drawing, color interactions, surface cohesiveness, the use of a wet into wet technique are all a result of visualizing the finished painting before the work proceeds.

Distinction should be made between technique and vision. Technique is the method by which a work of art is made. It displays the skills of the artist. Vision is the inspiration that determines how to use a technique. Both vision and technique, because they are so closely related, must be learned as interdependent means to develop skills. Skills should not be limited solely to craftsmanship, but must be continually interrelated to one's expanding perceptions. Each new painting has new inherent demands.

The old-timer was asked how he acquired the superb craftsmanship to build exquisite wooden furniture and his answer was, "Just do a little each day." Little by little, the hand comes to know the importance of the balance point in the handle of a brush, the flow and consistency of different colors, or the drag of color on a rough canvas. I do not even try to teach these things. They are personal considerations. When the blade of your palette knife wears thin after countless days of mixing colors, after you have made 300 drawings and 100 watercolors, you will get the hang of it and technique will be regarded as a perfectly natural manifestation of your expression.

> It was in the fall of 1915 that I first had the idea that what I had been taught was of little value to me except for the use of my materials as a language—charcoal, pencil, pen and ink, watercolor, pastel, and oil. I had become fluent with them when I was so young that

> they were simply another language that I handled easily. But what to say with them? I had been taught to work like others and after careful thinking, I decided that I wasn't going to spend my life doing what had already been done.
>
> I hung on the wall the work I had been doing for several months. Then I sat down and looked at it. I could see how each painting or drawing had been done according to one teacher or another, and I said to myself, "I have things in my head that are not like what anyone has taught me—shapes and ideas so near to me—so natural to my way of being and thinking that it hasn't occurred to me to put them down." I decided to start anew—to strip away what I had been taught—to accept as true my own thinking. This was one of the best times of my life. There was no one around to look at what I was doing—no one interested—no one to say anything about it one way or another. I was alone and singularly free, working into my own, unknown—no one to satisfy but myself. I began with charcoal and paper and decided not to use any color until it was impossible to do what I wanted to do in black and white. I believe it was June before I needed blue.
>
> *Blue Lines* was first done with charcoal. Then there were probably five or six paintings of it with black watercolor before I got to this painting with blue watercolor that seemed right.[40]
>
> —Georgia O'Keeffe

Imagine your brush and canvas as substitutes for pen and paper.

> You will write . . . if you will write without thinking of the result in terms of a result, but think of the writing in terms of discovery, which is to say that creation must take place between the pen and the paper, not before in a thought or afterwards in a recasting. Yes, before in a thought, but not in careful thinking. It will come if it is

> there and if you will let it come, and if you have anything you will get a sudden creative recognition. You won't know how it was, even what it is, but it will be creation if it came out of the pen and out of you and not out of an architectural drawing of the thing you are doing. Technique is not so much a thing of form or style as the way that form or style came and how it can come again.[41]
>
> —GEORGIA O'KEEFFE

Form Has Its Own Laws

The more original you are in your approach to composing a painting, the more likely will be your attempt to work out new ways to see the subject and explore your responses to it. This is the essence of creative composition.

Squint. Study your subject with one eye almost fully closed. Now, study the primary forms, their mass relationships, positives, negatives—these will make or break your composition. Then, drawing, arrange the form; simplify; take out what is not needed; rearrange. Be imaginative. Be discriminate.

Because contemporary composition is to a large degree based on the concept of form seen as energy in a reciprocal, negative space, it is a free and exploratory process. Spontaneity is important. Color is important. There is more push and pull of color/form in the picture plane than in traditional painting. The immediate work of painting and composing form are more interdependent. The painting may or may not be developed from preliminary drawings and studies.

One method for developing spontaneous painting is to draw on the canvas only those forms that are essential to the basic composition, suggesting them as a framework for the painting. Drawing can be done loosely with either charcoal or with thinned turpentine washes of color with a brush. Do not draw the forms precisely or in detail. Let the brush take over, so that little by little, you shape the forms more concretely. The brush draws; it sug-

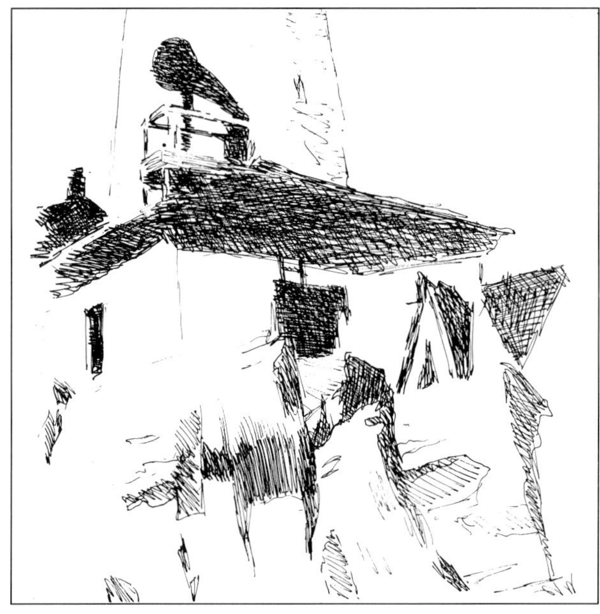

III.27

Sketch of Edward Hopper's watercolor, *Rock Pedestal*.

The brush draws composing with masses.

Hopper composed with masses. He was acutely aware of developing positive and negative patterns as he painted. This sketch of his watercolor of Portland Head Light, painted in 1927, demonstrates how Hopper made each shape count; every nuance is important to the whole. Tonal values are greatly simplified.

gests a contour; feel the rhythm, get into the swing of it; the brush paints in a solid mass, and then the brush draws again, and so forth. Form handled in this way places a greater priority on one's vision for interpreting subject matter directly. Thus, it is less likely to be rendered lackluster in appearance.

In essence, the first stages of drawing on the canvas are nothing more than a scaffold of basic proportions for the masses of color. As the painting evolves, the drawing is further developed with paint. It becomes inseparable from the hue, tone, and substance of the pigment. Since there is a more direct correlation between drawing a form and shaping a form in its entirety, it can be seen more clearly in relation to its coexisting negative space, and one's awareness of the developing composition is constantly expanding. Also, as the composition is developed, its structure is more clearly defined. At a certain point the idea that inspired the painting is replaced by the reality of the interrelationship of color/form.

Now we are at a tenuous point in the composition of

III.28

Sketch of Edward Hopper's watercolor, *My Roof,* 1928.

The brush draws, shaping the negative space.

This sketch shows how the shape of the sky works as a negative field, counterbalancing the powerful, positive forms of the rooftops and chimneys. Hopper distorted the angles of the chimneys and slopes of the roofs to energize this negative field. Note how the axes of all the chimneys vary.

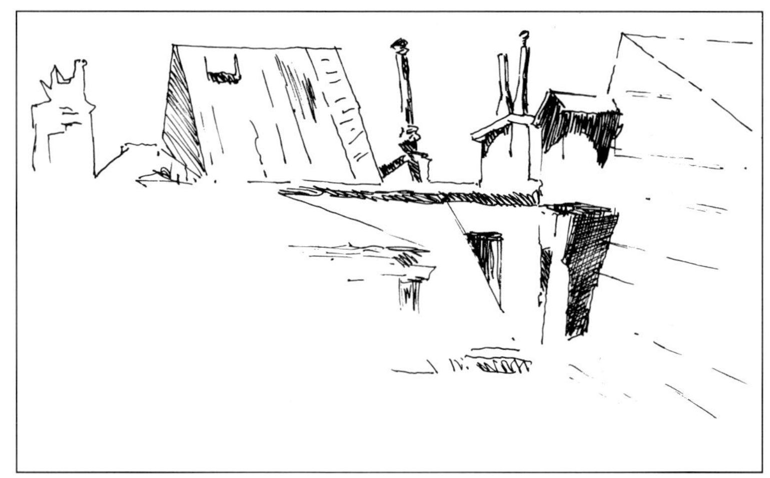

a painting. The generalized concept of the idea has been suggested. The preliminary drawing no longer exists. The stark white canvas has been covered with some paint. The major controlling forms have been at least tentatively established. This means that the relationships between all the major dimensions have been sufficiently developed, so that the entire painting is transposed from the original idea into a new and objective reality.

Something else occurs in the sequence of the work. There is a psychological transformation. The artist no longer asserts his idea of concept into the painting. Rather, at this time, he gives in to its pictorial demands. The painting can be developed in a more meaningful way because the composition is controlled by his intuitive response to its developing structure.

Form has its own laws. Each part of the painting makes its own demands for counterbalancing: movements, color/forms, hues, tones, and intensities—all interacting toward closure.

A rule of thumb is to work into the weakest part of the painting as it is being developed. The idea is to see and paint in context to the whole. If your painting becomes unpredictable, out of whack, fix it. Usually, at this point, there is a sense of uneasiness; the positive, ongoing intuitive process is interrupted. The negative instincts must be obeyed. The work needs to be evaluated and corrected; otherwise, control of the whole is lost and further errors are induced and compounded by lack of recognition of the problem.

Composition, technique, and craftsmanship should be assessed by each artist to determine what is essential to his needs. The process that I have described here is obviously not the only, or even the best, way to compose a painting. The approach I have given here is based on my own experience.

4.

Art as Expression

A Transition to Abstraction

Wassily Kandinsky, who has been credited with the invention of abstract painting, was working toward the elimination of subject matter by the year 1908. By 1910, he had arrived at nonobjective improvisation. He said simply: "I value those artists who . . . consciously or unconsciously, in an entirely original form, embody the expression of their inner life; who work only for this end and cannot work otherwise."[42]

The transition from representational painting to abstraction usually takes place over a period of time and, most often, is the result of dissatisfaction with an earlier style. The artist may feel "bottled up" or frustrated and unable to break away from the restrictions of representation to meet the need for greater freedom. If you wish to change from representational to abstract painting, the question to ask is: What are you giving up and what will you gain?

The Pros and Cons of Representational Painting

The best representational painters transcend nature. Their work is original, creative, well-composed, and expresses their profound feelings for unity and wholeness. The worst representational painters are neither original nor creative and either reject or do not understand the principles of fine composition. Their painting lacks feeling and inner life.

The commitment to reality can become a rigid mindset for many painters; they insist on a precise interpretation of a subject, whether from photography or directly from nature, and proceed to an indiscriminate enumeration of detail. The choice and domination of reality are absolute conditions of thought and expression. Subject matter is frozen by a click of a camera or by the eye because of *a priori* judgment. Composition becomes limited to an imitative reality. Aesthetic harmony and unity are subordinated to illusion and expression is reduced to technical skills. A realistic painting, particularly one with technical mastery, can present the paradox of producing an astonishing degree of reality without being a fine painting. The spiritual content in a painting is found only in its pictorial quality and not in its literary content. The artist must choose between an imitative portrayal of subject matter and an aesthetic realization of color/form.

Modern painting does not have to be purist, abstract, nonobjective, realistic, or of any style that happens to be in vogue. Modern painting is the result of a long, creative evolution and has many alternatives. The best modern painting, regardless of its style, incorporates, in many ways, the synthesis that has evolved during the last century of the Eastern and Western philosophies and ideologies. Modern artists should acquire an understanding of the achievements of the artists who preceded them.

As you recognize more clearly the formal elements of composition, your painting naturally moves toward abstraction. Your objective can change from a literal response to form to a more comprehensive color/form orchestration.

I am not at all sure that the way art is taught conventionally from grade school through college—using realism as the basis for developing visual perceptions—is the best way. Why not turn the process completely around and teach at a very young age the principles of form, space, and composition as the basis for creative art? Young artists would learn at the outset how to think and work in a more abstract mode, starting with the organization of generalizations first, and leaving the specifics to last. The development of the "big picture" first is essential not only for the expression of inner feelings, but also for the resulting unity and wholeness that strengthen this expression. Details are the means to articulate the major elements. Students would not necessarily become abstract painters, but what is real in painting would be seen in a more understandable context, and conditioned concepts of realism in painting would be understood for what they are and how they relate to one's expression.

Some of my students have difficulty overcoming conventional thinking when faced with creative problems. The way they think and work has been ingrained in them since

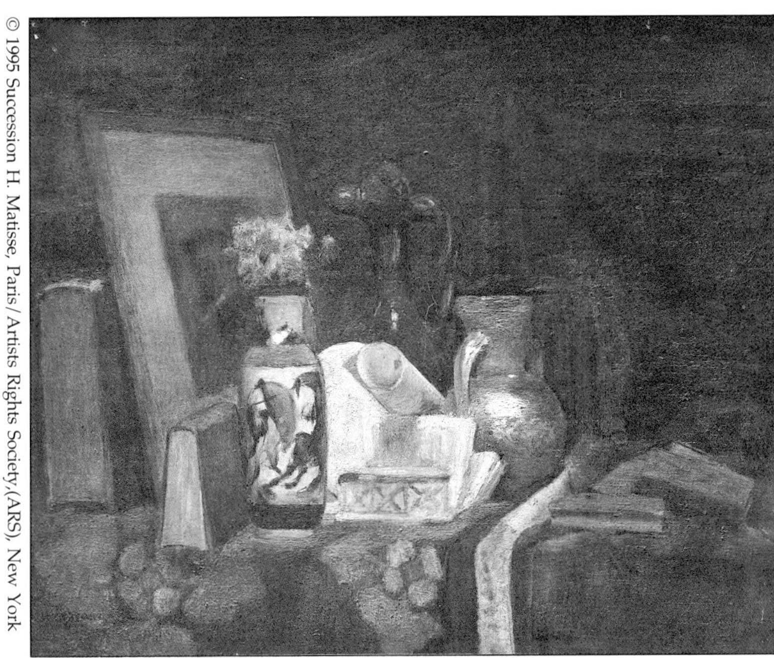

IV.1

Henri Matisse, *Nature morte à l'autoportrait*, 1896. Oil on canvas.

There is an indication in this conservative composition of the bold patterning that was to follow in his later painting. The transition for Matisse from representational painting to highly abstract imagery was part of a creative journey that lasted sixty-two years.

The composition depends on the methods used by the nineteenth-century French traditionalists, which included dull browns and greens painted with a lost and found imagery that simplified the forms and a conventional, true perspective. The general arrangement of the forms and interest in patterns and eye movement reveal an influence from Cézanne's still lifes painted around 1880.

childhood. Their work, invariably, starts at a beginning and then progresses to completion in an ordered way. They experience a sense of satisfaction with a job well done. In contrast, the creative artist depends on thinking, visualizing, and perceiving solutions to problems through imaginative or abstract imagery.

The old axiom, "seek and ye shall find," becomes a requisite. New experience in painting is the reward for a probing, curious mind. An objective scrutiny of your painting will reveal that you naturally emphasize certain qualities in form and color. This is an innate attraction and response to subject matter, and is, as Georges Braque said, "one's inability to do otherwise." The particular characteristics that you discover should be considered fundamental to your expression.

A particular style of painting, then, is not planned or intellectually categorized, but is the consequence of creative experience and the direction that one embarks on to fulfill one's needs for expression. Let the critics define your style.

IV.2

Henri Matisse, *Notre Dame*, 1914. Oil on canvas.

A first view of Notre Dame, seen from a distance. The large negative spaces control the form. True perspective is distorted by emphasizing the geometrical qualities in the design. All the forms are reduced to essential qualities of color tones and lines, which push back and forth in a balanced orchestration. Eye movement is directed from the gravitational base, upward to and across the bridge and then follows the diagonal tree line up to the cathedral. The general eye movement leads predominantly to the right side because of the strong diagonals.

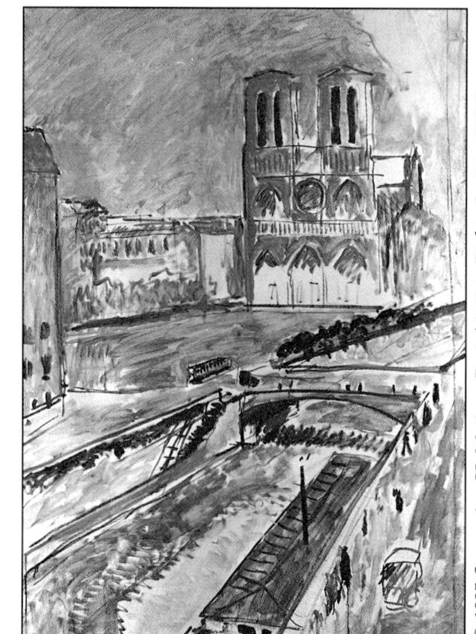

Characteristics of Abstract Painting

As the realistic aspects of subject matter are subordinated, the objectification and unity of color/form and space replace the illusion of reality. Subject matter can be interpreted as planes with coexisting spatial relationships. Both form and space are seen as color. Planes are seen as both surface-related and depth-related movement. Line is also movement. Texture is created optically by dots, lines, marks, and scribbles and can indicate direction as well as depth. Abstract painting emphasizes the flat, two-dimensional surface of the canvas by rejecting true perspective to create the illusion of depth and tonal gradations as a means to create the illusion of volumes in objects and space.

As one's idea of nature becomes less restricted, the eye is free to invent new kinds of relationships. Subject matter can be seen in a new light as it is looked at from above, for example, or flattened by tilting it upwards. Curiosity takes hold: How can this form be simplified; what will happen if I

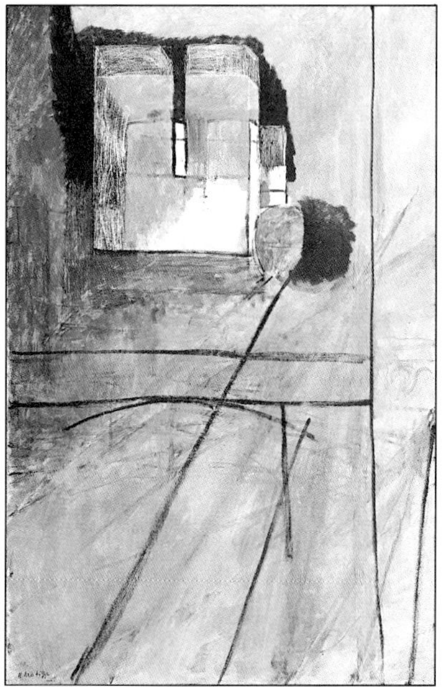

IV.3

Henri Matisse, *View of Notre Dame*, 1914. Oil on canvas, 58" x 37⅛".

The second view of Notre Dame is a geometric abstraction. The elements of true perspective in the first painting are abandoned in favor of simple linear forms in the bottom two-thirds of the canvas, counterbalanced by the suggestion of the cathedral at the top. Since the forms in this painting are not restricted by natural appearance and a gravity-oriented base, they are free to "float" in space, in accordance with their volume, thrust, and relative energy. Matisse "tilted" his subject matter upward, which emphasized the two-dimensional surface of the painting to achieve unity and wholeness.

elongate it to make it fit into a vertically shaped canvas, or strengthen its curvilinear properties? Since colors no longer illustrate objects, composition emphasizes the relationships of color/forms, of shapes, brightness, and luminosity of varying weights, hues, and intensities. The entire reality of painting is changed.[43]

> One day I set up an eggbeater in my studio and got so interested in it that I nailed it on the table and kept it there to paint. I called the picture *Eggbeater* number such-and-such, because it was from the eggbeater that the pictures took their impulse . . . their subject is an invented series of planes which was interesting to the artist. They were then drawn in perspective and light and shade in the same way another artist draws the planes of a human head or a landscape. I invented these geometrical elements. They became the foremost interest . . . I focused on the logical elements. Gradually through this consideration, I felt that a subject had its emotional reality fun-

IV. 4

Stuart Davis, *Eggbeater No. 1*, 1927. Oil, 29⅛" x 36".

The beginning of Davis's geometric abstraction, which depended on brilliant, hard-edged, flat color forms with strongly contrasting tonal values for structural strength.

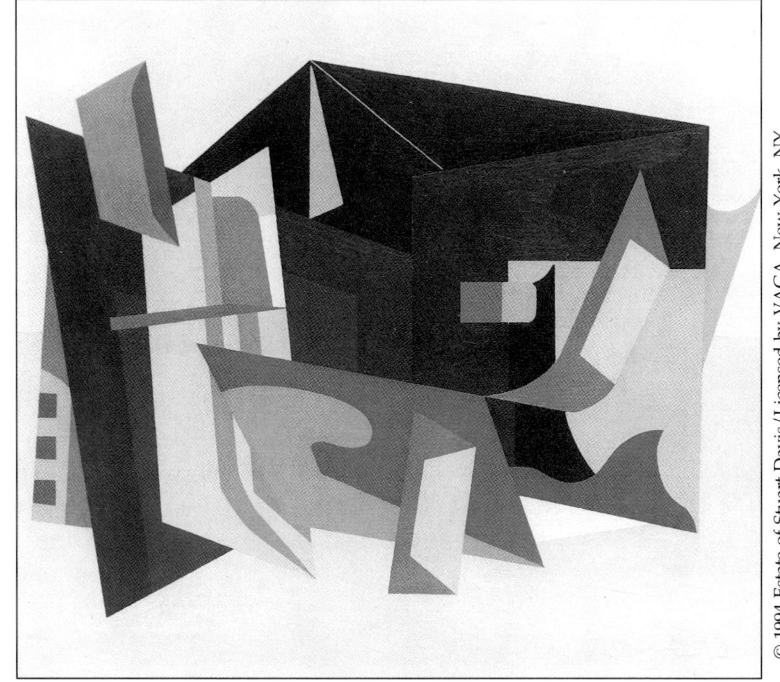

IV.5

Stuart Davis, *Visa*, 1951. Oil on canvas, 40" x 52".

Note how Davis combined curves and angles to shape concise forms. The rhythmical interplay between positives and negatives is pronounced when compared with his earlier, more primitive painting of the eggbeater.

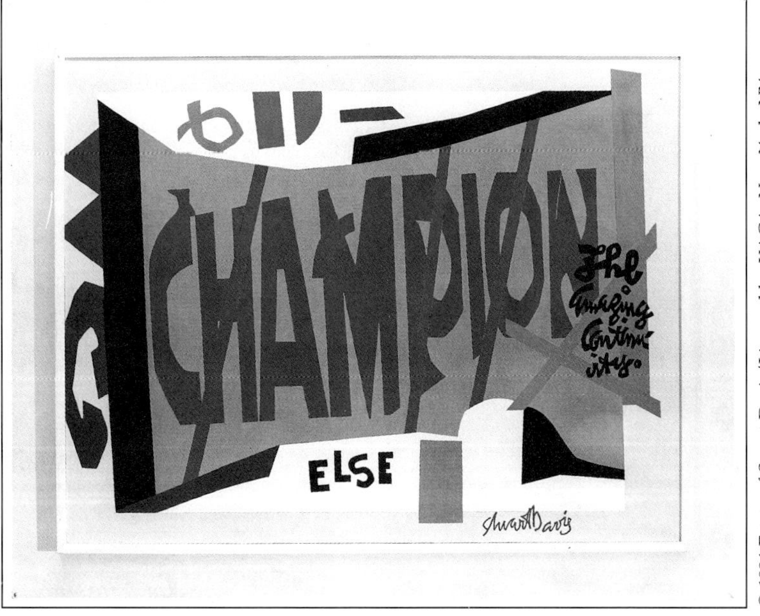

damentally through our awareness of . . . planes and their spatial relationships. My aim was not to establish a self-sufficient system to take the place of the immediate and the accidental, but to . . . strip a subject down to the real physical source of its stimulus. So you may say everything I have done since has been based on that eggbeater idea. I have just tried to carry the idea into greater particularity without abandoning the general scope which interested me there.[44]

—Stuart Davis

From Abstraction to Realism

There is a popular assertion that what you see in modern art is what you are looking at. It should also be understood that what you see is a function of one's creative experience. A good abstract painter learns how to objectify relationships of color and form rather than the relationships of objects. He learns what is essential for his interpretation of form. He attempts a realization of color/form beyond the surface appearance of things and beyond any practice or understanding of most realistic painters.

What then, if any, are the advantages of changing from an abstract style to realism? The answer, on the surface at least, seems to be obvious. Abstract painting experience can serve as a broad, highly disciplined yet relatively free foundational style. The problem for the artist who has worked as an abstractionist and who wishes to express his ideas as a realist is to understand how he can boil down the visual experience that he gained from his abstract painting into what is essential for a new style. If he has been open-minded and creative, he will have gained a new appreciation of the virtually limitless characteristics of colors as they interact with form in composing paintings and, vice versa, of how the inner rhythm and movement of form correspond to color interaction.

These are spatial considerations. In abstract painting, the dynamic energy of color/form can push out beyond the picture plane into physical space, whereas in representational painting the energy of color/form is limited to surface relationships and taking the eye in and out of the interior of the painting. A large area of brilliant cadmium yellow, in an abstract painting, for instance, can interact with other strong colors, yet because of its great energy it advances into physical space. In a representational painting, the same yellow would have to be modified to keep it from jumping out of the picture plane and eradicating the representation of natural form.

Try to discover the abstract qualities in nature and transform them first, in your mind, as relationships between colors, planes, lines, and movements, and then paint them as trees, branches, and sky. Try to relate to nature at a deeper and more profound level, being open to its subtleties rather than trying to imitate its grandeur.

I asked Neil Welliver how his experience as an abstract painter had influenced the way he composed his paintings. His answer was as follows:

> I never paint an area without having visited it many times, over periods as long as five years. I return at different hours of the day, as of course the sun, or lack of it, completely transforms an area. I have on occasion come upon places I painted years ago, and in effect do not recognize them . . . I am never looking for "objects" [and] I certainly am not looking for a "site," but rather just musing, and I would say in all cases it is the "abstract" relationship between the elements there that tells me I should return and return until it reveals its entire structure.[45]

The abstractness in Welliver's landscapes distinguishes them from other realistic painting. Welliver, because of his early influences and abstract painting experience, developed the ability to perceive meaningful relationships of color and form. The forms he chooses to paint become part of his visual world. Because he never paints the same theme in the same way, his creative experience continually expands. To copy nature, for Welliver, would be an act of irreverence.

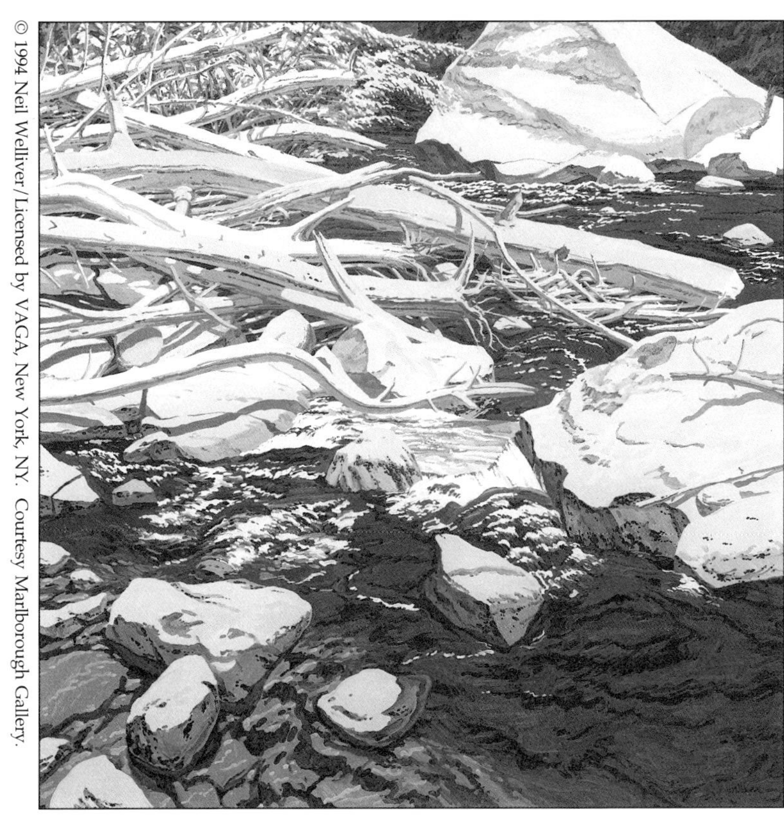

IV.6

Neil Welliver, *High Water Mark*, 1984. Oil on canvas, 96" x 96".

Neil Welliver transforms nature's complex structure into a personal, expressive order. His paint is not attached to his drawing or to an idea of form; it is the form.

As a student in the early 1950s at the Philadelphia Museum College of Art, Welliver was influenced first by Cézanne and later by John Marin. He was broadly assimilating the implications of modern art. After his Cézanne-influenced landscapes and still lifes, he experimented with abstract painting in different ways, under the influence of the cubist painting of de Stijl and Mondrian. He was learning how to see the interrelationships of abstract painting and, at the same time, exploring his emotional relationship to a new visual world. Most importantly, Welliver was establishing a broad visual base for his later work as a landscape realist. His influences were direct, well-chosen intuitively, and meaningful. He went on to study at the Yale University School of Fine Arts under the celebrated colorist, Josef Albers. And it was there, after a lot of experimentation with color/form in various media, that he had a glimmer of his future relationship to landscape painting.

By 1962, Welliver made the decision to paint as a realist directly from the figure and landscape. Abstract painting, for Welliver, had become a dead end. He was dissatisfied with its sameness, with its academic, modernist appearance and with its corresponding loss of originality and vitality. Welliver sought the essence of modern painting—surface cohesiveness, flatness and unity, positive and negative relationships of color/form, and, most importantly, the transformation of all these elements into a new kind of realism. He wanted to achieve a synthesis between the objective aesthetic qualities of his forms and his psychological response to his subject matter.

Welliver portrays space in and around, in front of and behind, trees, meadows, and mountains. He freezes motion as he captures a fleeting shadow, crossing over a distant marsh and meandering river. His air is a cold and clear Maine air. This is Welliver's private world, into which he invites the viewer to share his discoveries.

Developing Your Expression

> We cannot *will* to have insights. We cannot *will* creativity. But we can *will* to give ourselves to the encounter with intensity of dedication and involvement. The deeper aspects of awareness are activated to the extent that the person is committed to the encounter.[46]
>
> —Rollo May

Any painter who is searching for a more elemental and original direction in his work must face the complex problems encountered in the evolving creative experience. The most difficult task is to recognize whatever impedes one's self-liberation and growth.

Through a rigorous process of evaluating your paintings over and over again, you should be able to find the weak visual elements in your work. With the exception of occasional breakthroughs, similar problems tend to crop up in painting after painting. If your comprehension of form is weak, for example, your drawing is probably weak. The solution is to draw from the model and nature, fill sketchbooks, take drawing classes. Be inventive. Explore movements, rhythms, shapes. Little by little, you will gain confidence in your ability to see the proportional interchanges in form that make it come alive. And, as your drawing improves, your ability to master all the relationships of form in your painting will also improve. Regardless of which component in your painting is weak—drawing, color, or composition—the realization that each must have a meaningful relationship to the other as well as to the whole, should help you trace defects.

Psychological obstacles that impede your work are usually more difficult to identify. Most of them are a result of conditioned attitudes that can influence one's entire experience, unknowingly impeding a more creative approach to making art. Fears are difficult to recognize and often are mixed and compounded. For the conservative painter, there can be a very real apprehension over revealing the inner self to others. Closely related is the fear of failure. Because being creative can be a risk-taking process, the artist must accept some failure as a result of trying to achieve more and going beyond what he knows. The conservative painter who risks little rarely encounters failure, but his successes are usually meager. In contrast, the artist who has the will to encounter complexity and who struggles to find an order beyond his immediate comprehension risks failure and regards failure as a consequence of searching for a deeper truth.

> We learn also about our own strengths and limits and extend them by overcoming difficulties, by straining ourselves to the utmost, by meeting challenge and hardship, even by failing. There can be great enjoyment in a great struggle and this can displace fear. Furthermore, this is the best path to healthy self-esteem, which is based not only upon approval from others, but also upon actual achievements and successes and upon the realistic self-confidence that ensues.[47]
>
> —Abraham Maslow

Many artists are better than they think they are. They are smart. They have more than sufficient talent. But they often lack the motivation to commit themselves fully to their work. By evading the direct, personal encounter of self with the complex problems of creativity, their painting remains at the beginning of their expressive potential. The fundamental difference between a confident, successful, professional artist and a less confident and less successful nonprofessional artist can be measured by their degrees of involvement. Developing a work ethic is essential. Understand the premise that one cannot just wait for inspiration. Involvement in the creative process through painting generates a deeper involvement.

Strip off the conditioning that comes from conforming to established standards, which begins at adolescence and continues, unless the cycle is broken, more or less throughout one's lifetime. Teaching in high school art classes, for instance, may emphasize technique, but it impedes the creative responses of a young artist by obscuring subconscious response. An emphasis on technique further separates the artist from nature and the deeper dimensions of his own experience.

Henri Matisse always remembered when he started to paint as a revelation. "I felt transported into a kind of paradise . . . in everyday life I was usually bored and vexed by the things that people were always telling me to do. Starting to paint, I felt gloriously free, quiet and alone."[48] At that point in his life, Matisse was twenty years old. His drawing and painting were straightforward representations of subject matter. Very simply, he was learning how to see. There were no indications of a superior talent or of the remarkable creative images that were to come. Through his work, Matisse discovered that he gained insight to his next step, a vision beyond his immediate knowledge. He had learned from the beginning to place trust in his vision, to work intuitively by using his own feelings to find a natural order in his work.

Matisse's perception was light years ahead of his critics and followers. It did not just happen; it was developed through years of hard work. To a large extent, Matisse shaped his own visual world by constantly expanding his creative experience. The forms he perceived as he developed his work were stored in his visual memory bank, and he used them later as needed to clarify his impressions for new work.

The young Picasso in his native Spain was encouraged to paint by his artist father. By the time he was fourteen he was enrolled in a Barcelona art school. A few of his drawings, saved from this period, show his remarkable vision. Picasso was fortunate to be raised in an open, flexible, and creative environment. His childhood paintings reflect his delight in using his feelings, without fear of nonacceptance. Other than his brief training in art school, his early formative years were never subject to the conditioning so prevalent in most formal art instruction. It was essential for him to find freedom in Paris and to learn firsthand from the nineteenth-century French masters what was new in art to satisfy his quest for creativity.

When we come into this world, each of us is unique. Our vision is untainted. Fear is unknown. There is no one, nor will there ever be anyone, exactly like any one of us. The challenge for you is to regain your original freedom and couple it with your adult faculties and developed perceptions, strengthened by skills developed by painting. Overcoming a dependence on acquired habits can be a painful process. You must learn how to accept your own natural forms of expression.

> Growth has not only rewards and pleasures but also many intrinsic pains and always will have. Each step forward is a step into the unfamiliar and is possibly dangerous. It also means giving up something familiar and good and satisfying. It frequently means a parting and separation, even a kind of death prior to rebirth, with consequent nostalgia, fear, loneliness and mourning. It also means giving up a simpler and easier and less effortful life in exchange for a more demanding, more responsible, more difficult life.[49]
>
> —Abraham Maslow

To anyone familiar only with his later work, few of the pictures painted by Cézanne before 1872 would appear to exhibit any of the qualities characteristic of his fully developed style. Nearly all of his early canvases were painted with an excessively thick medium. He often used a palette knife to flatten and spread the heavy blobs of color, cutting into and modeling the paint with bold strokes. He called this method of painting "couillarde"—a word that is difficult to translate exactly, but that may be rendered approximately as vigorous, bold, hearty, or daring. Nothing could be more unlike the "couillarde" technique of his youthful pictures than the slow, carefully placed small brush strokes of his mature years, laid thinly and with infinite patience one over the other, touch by touch.

> There is a strange, somewhat repellent mysticism about some of these early pictures that is almost entirely lacking in Cézanne's later work. The wildness of many of these imaginative compositions, the tortured attitudes of the figures, betray the feverish turmoil of his spirit at this time; the furious strokes and slashes of colour reveal the intensity of his struggle to express his emotions in a recalcitrant medium.[50]

I began to develop my own expression only after graduating from art school. I worked hard, struggling with color, painting crudely with a palette knife on innumerable small canvases. I discovered an unexplained expression that I saw as forceful, primitive, overworked, and not wholly acceptable. It was as if I were at war with myself. I remember feeling frustrated and angry because I could not make better pictures. I discarded canvases; my knee punched through one; I threw another in a rage out of my fourth-floor studio window on a snowy night, and I watched it float down, gracefully, until it landed on top of a passing trolley car. Now, I wish I had saved those canvases. They were elemental and immature, but they were strong and original and were probably better than I thought they were.

Clyfford Still wrote of his quest for self-expression in

a letter to Gordon Smith, Director of the Albright Knox Art Gallery in Buffalo, New York:

> It was as a journey that one must make, walking straight and alone. No respite or shortcuts were permitted. And one's will had to hold against every challenge of triumph or failure, or the praise of Vanity Fair. Until one had crossed the dark and wasted valleys and come at last into clear air and could stand on a high and limitless plain. Imagination, no longer fettered by the laws of fear, became as one with vision. And the act, intrinsic and absolute, was its meaning, and the bearer of its passion. The work itself, whether thought of as image of idea, as revelation, or as a manifest of meaning, could not have existed without a profound concern to achieve a purpose beyond vanity, ambition, or remembrance for a man's term of life.[51]

Influences

> The arts have a development which comes not only from the individual, but also from a cumulative force, the civilization which precedes us. One cannot do just anything. A talented artist cannot do whatever he pleases. If he only used his gifts, he would not exist. We are not the masters of what we produce. It is imposed on us.[52]
>
> —Henri Matisse

In the modern world, it is almost impossible to be separated totally from the cultural influences that infiltrate our lives and surround us every day. Certainly, we have been inculcated in the ideology and vision of this century. The chances are that during our formative years we were influenced by other paintings. Consequently, influences should be seen first in the broadest possible way. To the creative artist, art history is a visual, not intellectual, appraisal of the past; it is made up of one's visual response, first to one's own time with all its implications, and then to the past to clarify direction.

All too often, painters are unconsciously influenced by second-rate painters and teachers of painting. The young painter, particularly, should seek out and study the masters first. Try to see other paintings in the context of your own development. Recognize that your creative growth can be impeded by commercial success as well as by the influence of other successful painters. Commercially successful art often comes into vogue, lasts for a while, and then disappears.

If you are honest as you develop your painting, your work will be influenced not by intellect but by your subconscious responses, by what moves you, a creative and natural state on which your whole approach depends. Trust your instincts; your "likes" are positive. Any fear of dominance by another painter can disrupt the inner flow of feeling outward. Focus on your own ideas. Understand that changes in art are never wholly new; they have all occurred somewhere before to some degree. What comes first is life, then art, and then an interdependency; each thrives on the other. Your art must be open to all that you experience. The imagery that has value to you is entirely your own affair, whether it is expressing a savage fury or peace and harmony.

One of my students had fled Nazi Germany in 1939 to start a new life in the United States. During the early 1930s she had been an illustrator for a German newspaper, and was obviously skilled in representational, commercial drawing. Some twenty-five years later, she joined my class and began to paint. Although she had had no drawing experience during those intervening years, her skill and direct approach to drawing were readily apparent, but she had had little experience painting expressively. She greatly admired Georgia O'Keeffe's painting and believed that art should be fully contemporary in every sense; much as she tried, however, her painting had little to do with the American concepts of the 1950s, although she had obviously studied and had gone to many exhibitions. Regardless of subject matter, her painting evolved expressively, with an inner strength, in a style reminiscent of the German expressionist, Franz Marc, who had influenced her young mind while she had been in art school, in about 1910. Her use of color, particularly, was influenced by Marc.

There is a simple lesson to be drawn from this example: personal expression reflects one's origins (in this case, Germany) and experience (in this case, a brief experience in art school). Most importantly, during the twenty-five years that she did not paint, she acquired no new *expressive* experience.

Some years ago I had an advanced student whose work was gradually developing toward a more original use of form and color. She voiced her fears to me about going to see a major retrospective exhibition of Arthur Dove's paintings; she was afraid her work would be further influenced by Dove. I strongly urged her to see Dove's paintings and to look closely at them—not to seek similarities, but to look for the differences that would distinguish her painting from Dove's. After seeing the exhibition, she conveyed her excitement about seeing her own painting in a much more objective way. Her work was more original and more forceful than she had presumed. Seeing the differences was the key.

The painting of Clyfford Still is the best example I know of how dynamic art, no matter how original it is, is a product of its time. Still studied Vermeer and copied Velásquez when he was a child. At age 12, while living on a Canadian farm, he knew the prints of Botticelli and Van Dyke and he spent all the time he could drawing, painting, and studying color, light, and perspective. In 1925, he enrolled in the Art Student's League in New York City but left after forty-five minutes, saying: "The exercises and results I observed I had already explored myself some years before and had rejected most of them as a waste of time."[53]

During the summers of 1934 and 1935, Still painted at the Trask Foundation in Saratoga Springs, New York, where he began an intense review of his painting until he felt he had mastered his "recording of visual phenomena." He said, "From then on, I realized I would have to paint my way out of the classical European heritage. I rejected the solutions of antic protest and parody (Picabia, Duchamp, and the theorist Breton) or the adaptation of the idioms of exotic foreign cultures (Picasso, Modigliani) which became popular manifestations through the 1910s and 1920s in the publishing and educational worlds." By the late 1930s, Still felt he had worked through his influences, which he referred to as "the idiomatic means to which my culture had subjected me":

> By 1941, space and figure in my canvases had been resolved into a total psychic entity, freeing me from the limitation of each yet fusing into an instrument bounded only by the limits of my energy and intuition. My feeling of freedom was now absolute and infinitely exhilarating.[54]

From then on, Still's painting evolved freely as an affirmation of his own daring, original vision. Yet it is not mere coincidence that his painting, in some respects, was being paralleled emotionally by the work of Mark Rothko, Franz Kline, and Willem de Kooning. The fact that their work was a product of the same era and similar avant-garde values provides the basis for their conclusions concerning a whole new vision.

Jackson Pollock, the fifth painter in this highly original group of artists of the 1950s, was particularly impressed with the European concept of the source of art being the unconscious. The artists he admired the most were Picasso and Miro. Pollock said, "The idea of an isolated American [style of] painting, so popular in this country during the thirties, seems absurd to me, just as the idea of creating a purely American mathematics or physics would seem absurd . . . An American is an American and his painting would be naturally qualified by this fact, whether he wills it or not. But the basic problems of contemporary painting are independent of any one country."[55]

Matisse should hearten any painter concerned about being influenced by others: "I have never avoided the influence of others. I would have considered this a cowardice and a lack of sincerity toward myself. I believe that the personality of the artist develops and asserts itself through the struggles it has to go through when pitted against other personalities. If the fight is fatal and their personality succumbs, it means that this was bound to be its fate."[56]

Distortion: How Far and to What End?

> A consciousness of limitations is paramount for an expression of the infinite. Beethoven creates eternity in the physical limitations of his symphonies.[57]
>
> —Hans Hofmann

How far can an artist take his expression and still communicate with his viewers? There is no clear answer because, for the creative artist, clarity of expression must be based on faith in his personal beliefs, and it is this faith that enables him to communicate at a deeper, more meaningful level. The alternatives offer less.

Yet there remains the question of how far to pursue one's expression and to what end? Can an artist explore unlimited forms of expression with total freedom from restricting conditions? Are we not all bound together by our era, yet separated by our individual circumstances?

In creative painting, the imagination operates in juxtaposition with form. When this interaction is successful, it is because imagination infuses form with its own vitality. But how far can we let our imagination loose? Can we give it unfettered rein? Will we lose sight of the boundaries that enable us to orient ourselves to what we call reality?

And yet I am sure that the master painters of this century were not conscious of any boundaries to their expression as they worked. As Matisse said when he was in his early sixties, "After an entire life as a harried laborer, I was able at last to sing like a child . . . at the top of the mountain I had climbed."[58] Where is new reality, but from within us? There are no laws when you work with your feelings; there is only the privilege of self-expression.

I see Jackson Pollock's painting as an extreme, bound only by the limitations that he encountered. He probably would have worked on larger canvases if the two-car garage that he used as a studio had been larger. He probably would have used longer flowing lines if his arms had been longer. Shortly before his tragic death in a car crash, Pollock told his wife, Lee Krasner, that during some of his visits to his psychiatrist he was able to communicate only by making drawings.

IV.7

Jackson Pollock painting *Number 32* in the summer of 1950 in his studio at Springs, Long Island.

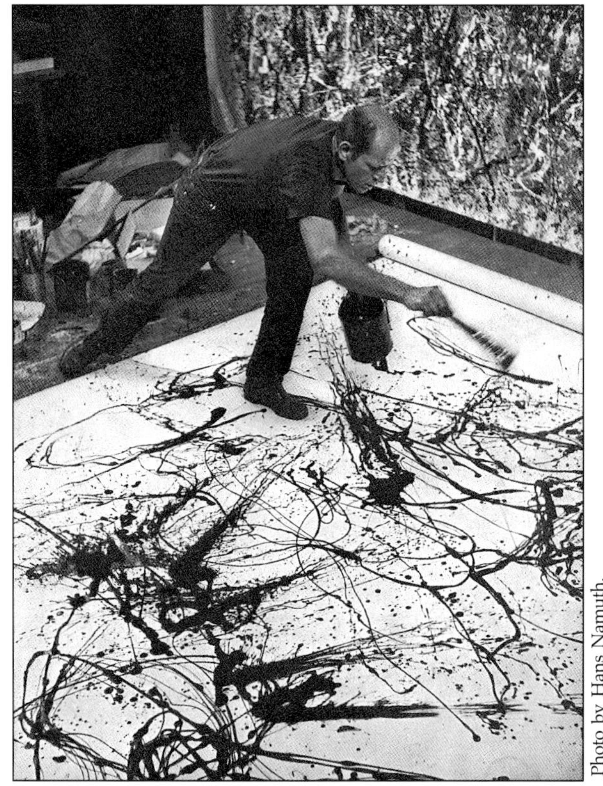

Photo by Hans Namuth.

Pollock's painting, however, is lucid, direct, and has clarity. His art is much like a window open to the universe; it communicates facets of our existence. His work goes well beyond the relativity of humans commonly found in traditional paintings.

In September, 1932, Picasso was honored with an imposing retrospective exhibition of his paintings at the Zurich Kunsthaus. One of the twenty-eight thousand visitors was Carl Jung, and the result of his confrontation with an overview of Picasso's *oeuvre* was a devastating piece that appeared in the *Neue Zuricher Zeitung* on November 13, 1932. Struck by the similarity between Picasso's work and the drawings of his schizophrenic patients, Jung declared him a schizophrenic, expressing in his work the recurrent, characteristic motif "of the descent into Hell, into the unconscious,

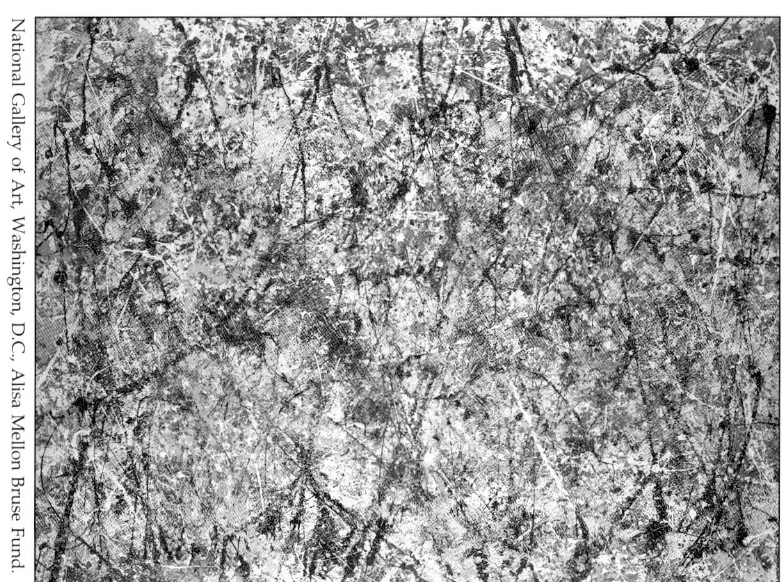

National Gallery of Art, Washington, D.C., Alisa Mellon Bruse Fund.

IV.8

Jackson Pollock, *Number 1, 1950 (Lavender Mist)*, 1950. Oil on canvas, 87" x 118".

Many people are offended by Jackson Pollock's paintings because they cannot relate to an image that is devoid of representational form. A visual prejudice blinds the viewer to the appreciation of real qualities beyond their visual experience. Hence they rely upon a response to painting in the context of their views of reality. The interaction of Pollock's dripped skeins of colors in his painting, *Lavender Mist*, and the sensation of their existence in a deep space produces the aura of a lavender mist, which is a purely aesthetic response. Pollock did not think his painting was being influenced in any way by nature; rather his role as an artist proceeded from his assertion: "I am nature!"

and the farewell to the world above." Comparing the images produced by his patients with those produced by Picasso, he wrote:

> Considered from a strictly formal point of view, what predominates in them is the character of mental lacerations, which translate themselves into broken lines, that is, a type of psychological fissures which run through the image . . . it is the ugly, the sick, the grotesque, the incomprehensible, the banal, that are sought out—not for the purpose of expressing anything, but only in order to obscure; an obscurity, however, which has nothing to conceal, but spreads, like a cold fog, over desolate moors; the whole thing quite pointless, like a spectacle that can do without a spectator.[59]

IV.9

Francis Bacon,
Study for Portrait of van Gogh III,
1957. Oil and sand on linen,
78⅛" x 56⅛".

Painted flesh, sinister, hair-raising, and beautiful.

Francis Bacon's awesome, fiercely expressionistic paintings were motivated by his memories of a miserable childhood in revolution-torn Ireland, and by his deep fear and hatred of World War II. His painting is scary, angry, and ghoulish. The paint is twisted, screaming in color, movement, and texture. His distortions transcend his early influences from Picasso and move toward a paint quality that bears comparison to Goya and Velásquez. His paintings echo Cézanne's youthful and compelling aggression, such as in *Portrait of Achille Emporaire*.

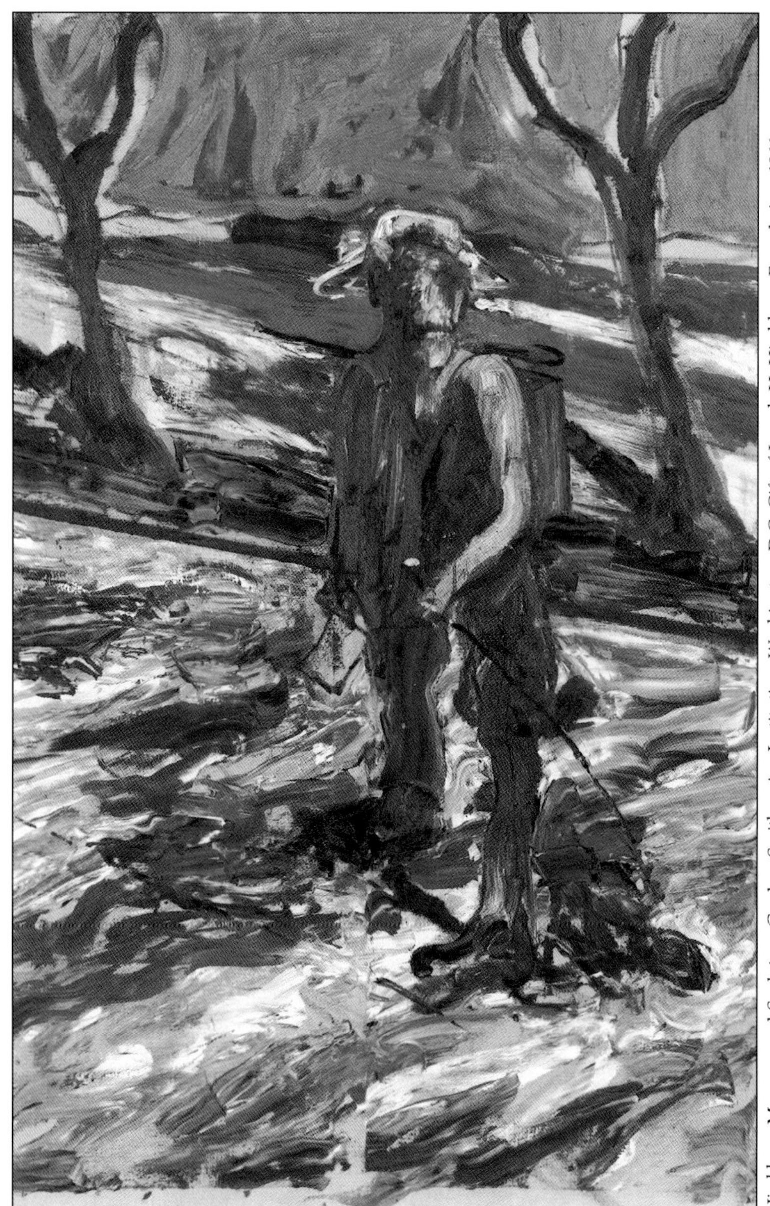

Hirshhorn Museum and Sculpture Garden, Smithsonian Institution, Washington, D.C. Gift of Joseph H. Hirshhorn Foundation, 1966.

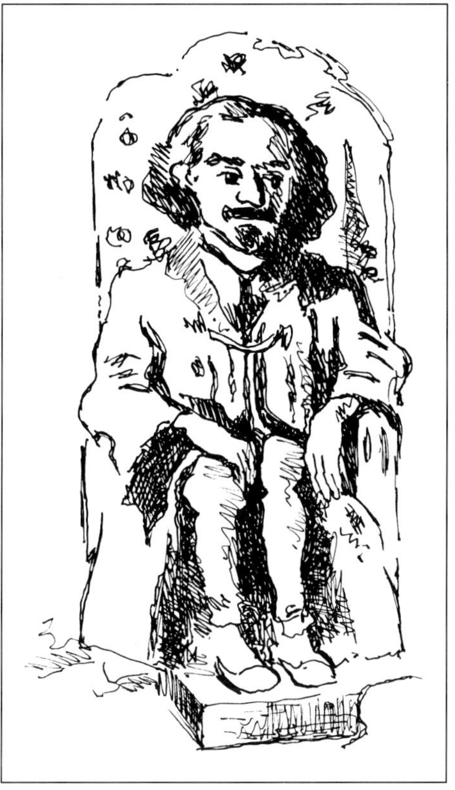

IV.10

Author's sketch of *Portrait of Achille Emporaire*, by Paul Cézanne, about 1868.

Cézanne's early paintings were inspired by his powerful psychological responses to form. In his later, more mature, work, he strove for a more stabilized and pictorial abstract order that denied his highly emotional vision.

The way a painter sees Picasso's paintings is quite different from the way a psychiatrist sees them. I see Picasso as living and working on the edge. His enormous expressiveness changed twentieth-century art.

> When I am alone with myself, I have not the courage to think of myself as an artist in the great and ancient sense of the term. Giotto, Titian, Rembrandt and Goya were great painters; I am only a public entertainer who has understood his times and has exhausted as best he could the imbecility, the vanity, the cupidity of his contemporaries. Mine is a bitter confession, more painful than it may appear, but it has the merit of being sincere.[60]
>
> —Pablo Picasso

Picasso's fierce independence was the source of the unusual originality of his painting. His life was an act of defiance of the world, and his paintings revealed his complex nature. There were no limits to Picasso's emotional involvement with his life and art. One was the other. In contrast, Matisse restrained his emotions. His joy of life was simple, self-rewarding, and clearly evident in his work. Peace and harmony were reflected in his paintings.

The way an artist chooses his lifestyle, his environment, his relationships, and all the things that surround him, the way he goes through life, is fundamental to his work. He wins his way to freedom.

Discovery and Experience

> . . . to know that what is impenetrable to us really exists, manifesting itself as the highest wisdom and the most radiant beauty.[61]
>
> —Albert Einstein

There is little question that true credibility in a work of art is the result of an inspired synthesis of intuition and experience. The psychologist, Abraham Maslow, refers to this kind of happening as "the cognition of being in a peak experience" that takes into account "a sense of wholeness (unity . . . integration . . . rightness . . . uniqueness . . . self-sufficiency . . . and completeness)." He notes that this experience also features "playfulness, exuberance and effortlessness."[62]

The creative process is structured, never isolated, and is part of an ongoing, procreative evolution. Meaningful originality in a work of art does not just happen. Our intuition takes into account all our past creative experience (including dissatisfaction with existing insights as the mind constantly searches for the right solutions to new problems), and the understanding and confidence gained from our earlier accomplishments. There is no such thing as perfection for the creative person. The process is endless.

The dilemma many artists face over the apparent choice to be made between using their reason, logic, and experience or their subconscious when painting can be resolved with the recognition that each can support the other. As a generalization, do not think when you paint, and think all you like when you are not painting. Following one's intuition when painting fulfills one's inner demands, whereas knowledge, reason, and logic clarify creative synthesis. As Braque said of his painting, "I like the law which corrects emotion."[63]

The comparisons and judgments artists make about their work are both abstract and highly objective— abstract in the sense that they respond emotionally to the whole field of play as they paint, followed by an objective evaluation of what happened with the paint. It is almost impossible to determine the point at which the intuitive process of painting freely—with full control, without conscious thought—is replaced by the conscious process of evaluation.

Which is more significant— a total trust in our feelings to complete a painting, or trust in a more objective and logical critique of the painting as it is being developed by the use of those feelings? I do not believe there can be a single answer. The intuitive process for Braque depended on the support of conscious evaluation, but for a highly emotional painter like Jackson Pollock the same process would have been disruptive. The bottom line, however, is that any work of art, regardless of one's approach to painting, must be subjected ultimately to a conscious evaluation. Without the support of our critical faculties, the intuitive act may transcend the thin line that separates meaningful reality and the meaningless.

You may complete a painting and be highly pleased with it and not want to change a single brush stroke. Yet the painting may provide an idea for a new painting, or a variation of it; each completed painting can be a step in a continuing process of expansion. Dissatisfaction, then, is used in its broadest sense—as the motivation to expand one's awareness beyond a narrow frame of reference related to the conclusions in any one painting. A complete trust in your intuition can lead to a new understanding of what was, until then, incomprehensible.

Expression as Life

> The art experience can only be an experience in being . . . being a human organism doing what it must and what it is privileged to do . . . experiencing life keenly and wholly, expanding energy and creating beauty in its own style . . . and the increased sensitivity, integrity, efficiency, and feeling of well-being are by-products.[64]
>
> —Abraham Maslow

I form at random a group of letters, t-m-o-r-b-c-a. Since they do not form a word, they have no meaning. Indirectly, we learn the value of limitations. We do not think in terms of single letters and only on occasion in terms of single words. Our thoughts depend on an association of words to develop meanings.

Similarly, one does not draw an isolated line disassociated from the development of a form. Meaning is developed as one visualizes and draws. How I draw is related to my awareness, which, in turn, is related to my sense of expression at that instant.

> Everything I can possibly experience begins and ends with awareness; every thought or emotion that captures my attention is a tiny fragment of awareness; all the goals and expectations I set for myself are organized in awareness. What the ancient sages termed the self can be defined in modern psychological terms as a continuum of awareness, and the state known as unity consciousness is the state where awareness is complete—the person knows the whole continuum of self without masks, illusions, gaps, and broken fragments.[65]
>
> —Deepak Chopra

We must rethink what is basic, what is elemental to our expression. We must be unafraid to ask questions. Each of our visual expressions is an answer to visual questions posed by our subconscious. My role is to motivate you to ask questions.

The gestalt psychologists believed that visual chaos is not possible because of the insatiable human drive for order and completeness. Chaos, however, abounds in human activities. I have seen hundreds of chaotic paintings. It is commonplace in nature, in volcanoes, earthquakes, floods, and twisters.

When a work of art is limited solely to a concept of unity and wholeness, its meaning is also limited. Expression in a work of art generates a meaning implicit in its form. I believe that humans have an insatiable drive to express meaning, and only when their art is meaningful to themselves can they consider it complete. When unity and wholeness are the objectives of painting, the end result can emerge as complete, but devoid of emotion. The process of making art should not be confused with design or intellectual theories.

Children have an unquenchable thirst to express themselves, a natural part of the expanding process of simply being. What a delight it is to witness the effects of the mind of a child—so naturally exuberant, playful, demanding, serious—all happening so quickly and effortlessly. We, as adults, must continuously reinvent our expressions. There is a primitive, unlearned, elementary consciousness that remains ingrained within us.

"I do love." These words by a valued ex-student profess how she feels about life and about all people of all colors, ages, and beliefs, and also reflect her simplified feelings about what painting is. A small portrait that she painted of her grandson is stored in my mind, showing a small black face as a focal point, the eyes aglow with the wonder of the world. The child is sitting among vertical spikes of purple-blue lupin, marching up a steep, green hillside in Oregon. My student is elderly now, but her mind is keen and she still paints. Her paintings are primitive, charming, full of her love of life.

> The truth about each of us is that our life spreads out in larger and larger fields of experience. There is no limit to the energy, information, and intelligence concentrated in one person's existence.[66]
>
> —Deepak Chopra

The assimilation of nature's beauty is a basic need within the larger order that has sustained us to this time and place. We are subservient to its natural laws and indebted to creative ancestors of the past who established and embellished the foundations of our knowledge and expression. Life sustains life, and beauty sustains and reassures each of us as we seek meaning in our search for order. Without beauty, life degenerates into despair, and the instinctive needs of hope, dignity, and the expansion of spirit are denied.

A startling Chinese-red flower seen against a dark summer green, the sweep of a white gull wing in a blue sky, a shock of bitterness, or a knot of fear are all parts of our assessment of life. Nothing is too small. As our consciousness grows, we become more aware of the inner life and organic origins of all existence.

At one time I felt that there must be a balance among all my experiences. I tried to separate them so as to place each in an order of time and events. But now they come together in increasing unity, and this is as it should be. Our lot is simple enough; it is in the finding.

No one can predict what art will be like in the twenty-first century. There will be many forms, of chaos, of divergence, and of synthesis. New boundaries will be established. The art of this century will be used to evaluate what is significant. The choice for the creative person who wants to make art must be one of security or growth. It takes courage to discover new meanings. If you need to express yourself, you must recognize your inner nature and accept the consequences of going onward.

> The surface of the earth is soft and impressible by the feet of men; and so with the paths which the mind travels. How worn and dusty, then, must be the highways of the world, how deep the ruts of tradition and conformity. I did not wish to take a cabin passage, but rather go before the mast and on the deck of the world, for there I could best see the moonlight amid the mountains. I did not wish to go below now.[67]
>
> —Henry David Thoreau

Sources and Notes

1. Sacks, Oliver, "A Neurologist's Notebook," *The New Yorker Magazine*, May 10, 1944, p. 59.
2. Sun-Tzu, *The Art of Warfare*, translated with introduction and commentary by Roger Ames, New York, Ballantine Books, 1993, p. 49.
3. Lao-tse, as quoted in *The Family of Man*, The Museum of Modern Art, New York, 1955, p. 124.
4. Hans Hofmann, as quoted in Weeks, Sarah T., and Bartlett H. Hayes, eds. *Search for the Real*, Cambridge, Mass., MIT Press, 1948, p. 66.
5. Matisse, Henri, *Jazz, the Text*, Paris, Teriade, 1947.
6. Ibid., unnumbered pages.
7. This list is by the Ch'ing critic Chou Hsing-lien, translated by Ch'en Chihmai in *Chinese Calligraphers and Their Art*, Melbourne, Melbourne University Press, 1966, p. 202.
8. Letter from Welliver to author, undated, 1994.
9. Smith, David, "Second Thoughts on Sculpture," Washington College Art Journal, Spring 1954, in Rose, Barbara, ed., *Readings in American Art Since 1900*, New York, Praeger, 1968, p. 192.
10. From address by Robert Henri to School of Design for Women, Philadelphia, 1901, in Rose, *op. cit.*, p. 36.
11. Liberman, Alexander, *The Artist in His Studio*, New York, Viking, 1960, p. 13.
12. Goodrich, Lloyd, *Edward Hopper*, New York, Harry N. Abrams, Inc., 1974, p. 132.
13. From "Notes of a Painter" by Henri Matisse, as quoted in Barr, Alfred H., *Matisse, His Art and His Public*, New York, The Museum of Modern Art, 1951, p. 122.
14. Goodyear, Frank, Jr., *Welliver*, New York, Rizzoli International Publications, 1985, p. 75.

15. Barr, *op. cit.*, p. 75.
16. Mack, Gerstle, *Paul Cézanne*, New York, Alfred A. Knopf, 1935, p. 377.
17. Ibid.
18. Ibid., p. 380.
19. Gowing, Lawrence, *Matisse*, New York, Oxford University Press, 1979, p. 114.
20. Ibid., p. 117.
21. Ibid., p. 150.
22. There cannot be a standardized way to mix color. The intent of the color chart is to help develop an artist's sensitivity to color as a language. I have found that the way my students selected their palettes and mixed their colors varied considerably according to their degree of experience as colorists and generally to how they regarded color—i.e., traditionally, conservatively at one extreme, or openly, more creatively, at the other.
23. Rose, *op. cit.*, p. 68.
24. O'Keefe, Georgia, *Georgia O'Keefe*, New York, Viking Press, 1976, p. 58.
25. Many artists are led to believe by the art establishment, i.e., art critics, historians, gallery owners, etc., that one's style should not vary. This is particularly true after one attains recognition.
26. Goodrich, *op. cit.*, p. 85.
27. Katherine Kuh, as quoted in O'Neil, John P., ed., *Clyfford Still*, New York, Metropolitan Museum of Art, 1979, p. 11.
28. Goodyear, *op. cit.*, p. 75.
29. Barr, Alfred H., *Matisse, His Art and Public*, New York, The Museum of Modern Art, 1951, p. 136.
30. From lecture by Frank Lloyd Wright, "To the Young Man in Architecture," undated, Chicago, Art Institute of Chicago, p. 59.
31. Einstein, A. and L. Infeld, "The Evolution of Physics," 1938, from Edwards, Betty, *Drawing on the Artist Within*, New York, Simon & Schuster, 1987, p. 3.
32. Lines of the drawing are perforated by running over them with a perforating wheel. The design is then "pounced" through the perforations with a small muslin bag of dry color. The dots are then connected with thin paint or other media to complete the cartoon.
33. Liberman, *op. cit.*, p. 40.
34. Mack, *op. cit.*, p. 378.

35. Georgia O'Keefe, *Georgia O'Keefe*, New York, Viking Press, 1976, p. 107.
36. Quoted from *Interiors*, May, 1951, by Barbara Rose, *Readings in American Art Since 1960*, New York, Praeger, 1968, p. 160.
37. Goodrich, *op. cit.*, p. 104.
38. Gilot, Francoise, *Matisse and Picasso: A Friendship in Art*, New York, Doubleday, 1990.
39. Liberman, *op. cit.*, p. 40.
40. O'Keefe, Georgia, *Some Memoirs of Drawing*, New York, Atlantic Editions, 1974.
41. From a conversation with Gertrude Stein in Ghiselin, Brewster, ed., *The Creative Process*, New York, A Mentor Book, 1952, pp. 159–60.
42. Cheney, Sheldon, *The Story of Modern Art*, New York, Viking Press, 1947, p. 409.
43. Abstract painting often is derived from, or suggests, subject matter, whereas subject matter is totally eliminated in nonobjective painting.
44. Goosen, E.C., *Stuart Davis*, New York, George Braziller, Inc., 1959, p. 21.
45. Letter from Welliver to author, August 6, 1992.
46. May, Rollo, *The Courage to Create*, New York, Norton Co., Inc., 1975, p. 46.
47. Maslow, Abraham, *Toward a Psychology of Being*, New York, D. Van Nostrand & Co., 1968, p. 200.
48. Gowing, *op. cit.*, p. 9.
49. Maslow, *op. cit.*, p. 204.
50. Mack, *op. cit.*, p. 139.
51. O'Neil, *op. cit.*, p. 196.
52. Gowing, *op. cit.*, p. 107.
53. O'Neil, *op. cit.*, p. 177.
54. Ibid., pp. 177–78.
55. Karpe, Bernard, "A Selected Bibliography," *Art and Architecture*, Vol. 61, No. 2, February 14, 1944.
56. Barr, *op. cit.*, p. 101.
57. Weeks and Hayes, *op. cit.*, p. 43.
58. *Life Magazine*, August 28, 1970, p. 42.
59. Attributed to Carl Jung by Arianna Stassinopoulos Huffington in *Picasso: Creator and Destroyer*, New York, Avon Books, 1988, p. 202.
60. *Life Magazine*, Vol. 65, No. 6, December 27, 1968.
61. Albert Einstein, as quoted in *The Family of Man*, New York, The Museum of Modern Art, 1955, p. 156.

62. Maslow, *op. cit.*, p. 83. He says the trick is to make the unfinished painting appear effortless.
63. Liberman, *op. cit.*, p. 13.
64. Maslow, *op. cit.*, p. 46.
65. Chopra, Deepak, *Ageless Body, Timeless Mind*, New York, Harmony Books, 1993, p. 36.
66. Ibid., p. 40.
67. Henry David Thoreau, as quoted in *Walden*, Babcock, C. Merton, ed., Peter Pauper Press, Mount Vernon, N.Y., 1966, p. 62.

Glossary

Abstract expressionism. An abstract style of painting and sculpture that is based on pure emotion during a creative experience.

Aesthetic response. Reaction to beauty as perceived in form, color, and space. An apple is seen as a pleasing shape, composed of volume, curves, and color, rather than seen as a fruit to eat (*see:* Psychological response).

Aerial perspective. The effect of atmosphere and distance on the appearance of objects, i.e., objects close to the eye are in focus, seen as a sharper image and clearer than objects in the distance that are seen as blurred, paler in tonal value, and bluer in color.

Axis or **Thrust line**. The center line of any form, the direction of which is determined by measurement to or away from the horizontal or vertical edges of the picture plane.

Base tone. The fundamental tonal value as observed in an object.

Chalky. An unnatural appearance in a color due to its undue cool temperature as it is seen next to a darker, warmer color of the same hue.

Color field painting. A style of nonobjective painting in which large fields of color dominate the composition.

Color/form. In modern painting, color is seen as form rather than as illustrating a form. A brush stroke of color, for example, has a specific form.

Color/space. In modern painting, color is also space.

Composition. The arrangement and developed organization of a painting. In modern painting, the process of composing based on immediate perception is all-important.

Conceptual image. Visualization of a painting as it is seen by the mind's eye.

Continuity. In painting, a connected and unbroken stream of thought (visual imagery), response, and action.

Cubism. An early twentieth-century style of painting and sculpture, characterized as flat, overlapping planes and linear continuation used to create an illusion of depth in the picture plane. Georges Braque and Pablo Picasso are credited with the invention of cubism; it's origin, however, was in the painting of Paul Cézanne.

Depth. Traditionally, pictorial depth in a painting is an illusion made by conveying naturalistic form in deep space, as in Renaissance painting and photo-realism. Depth in the contemporary plastic sense is revealed by the relative energy of color/form as it advances or recedes within the spatial field of the picture plane.

Distortion. Any change from normal appearance. In painting, form and color are distorted to make them more pleasing, more unified, or more expressive (aesthetic response), or are distorted to make the form and color more convincing (psychological response).

Energy. *see:* Visual energy.

Expressive medium. The means by which the artist portrays his inner world of feelings.

Form. The appearance of something as it is defined as size and shape by its surrounding negative space.

Free form. A form that is shaped without mechanical aids such as a ruler or compass, and which, subsequently, has a sense of inner life or is seen as organic rather than static (*see:* Organic, static form).

Focal point. A center of interest in a painting. Some painters use various focal points in a single painting; they can be called the primary focal point, secondary focal point, etc.

Flat color. A color of a single hue and tonal value.

Geometric abstraction. Abstract painting that relies on geometric forms in its composition, i.e., is usually hard-edged, based on straight lines, angles, and curves and any combinations thereof.

Gestalt. In psychology, an integrated group of acts and experiences that function as a whole over and above the sum of the parts.

Ground. The arbitrarily defined area in which the interaction of colors or forms as defined by space, takes place, e.g., the surface of paper or canvas.

Hue. The name of a color and one of the three main attributes of color. Hue is determined by the interaction of the wavelength of light and the characteristics of the surface upon which it falls.

Hiding power . The degree of opacity in a paint correlated to its ability to conceal underlying color.

Hold together. A term used to describe a painting that appears united, with all of its parts interrelated and essential to the whole.

Impasto. Thick, heavy painting that stands out in relief, composed with pronounced bristle brush strokes or dragged palette-knife applications.

Intensity. The amount of hue or lack of grayness in a color, or, in simpler terms, the relative purity of a color.

Kinetic. Energetic, dynamic (cf. stable).

Limitations. The most extreme amounts permitted. Awareness of boundaries is both elementary and indispensable to one's expression of feelings in painting. The inherent problem of time and relativity are restricting factors in painting. The size, substance, and shape of the picture plane and all the materials used to create a picture are also restrictions.

Limited palette. A palette restricted by the artist to a finite number of colors. For example, earth colors such as indian red, burnt umber, yellow ochre, and terre verte, and black and white. (With the exception of the neutral black and white, all of these are warm colors from the same family.)

Literary content. Content in painting that can be better described in writing or seen as story value.

Lost and found. The contours of a form are either lost in the deepest shadows or in the brightest light and then clarified as needed for definition; often referred to as a method of simplification used to unify positive form and negative space, i.e., as a contour or edge is lost, eye movement transverses form and space.

Mass. A description of form or color/form that appears weighty and solid.

Medium. 1) The liquid with which paint is thinned. 2) The mode of expression of an artist: painting, sculpture, etc. 3) The material used by an artist: oil paint, acrylic, tempera, watercolor, etc.

Minimal art. Styles of painting based on the concept that more is less.

Modulated colors. Colors that have minute spatial intervals and are in harmony (hold together).

Monochromatic. A composition based on the exclusive use of a single hue in gradations of intensity and tone.

Movement. The eye is able to distinguish the place and position of a form by means of comparison toward or away from a vertical or horizontal axis.

Negative field. The two-dimensional surface of the picture plane seen as negative space in the mind's eye. A negative field of color is a large area defined by its relationship to positive form.

Negative space. The space surrounding a form that defines its size, proportions, and shape. The creation of any form simultaneously creates a surrounding space.

Neutral. Any tone of white, gray, or black.

Nonobjective. A style of painting that has its own indigenous reality and is not related to objects or any kinds of natural appearances.

Objective, objectivity. Something real and observable. When form, color, and space are fully realized as in a meaningful relationship to composition, they are objectified and have their own reality.

Organic. A description of natural inner life in form, i.e., not manmade, geometric, or static in any way.

Painterly. A description of rich surface qualities of pigments and the skillful way they are manipulated.

Paint quality. The skillful handling of paint and its surface characteristics. This term does not refer to the physical quality of the ingredients in paint.

Pattern. An arrangement of contrasting forms and colors as seen in nature and in composition. A relationship of parts that achieves a predictability based on repetitive occurrence.

Perception. The process used to identify one thing from another. The power of being aware through the senses.

Photo-realism. A style of painting that depends on photography for its composition, content, and illusions of reality.

Picture plane. The two-dimensional surface of a painting as it is defined as a particular size and shape by its limiting horizontal and vertical dimensions. The essence of the picture plane is flatness.

Plane. A flat surface of a material body. In modern painting visual structure is based on a plane concept.

Plastic, plasticity. A form that can be molded, extruded, or compressed. The whole process of creation is plastic. A painting is fully plastic when the form as seen on its two-dimensional surface works in concert with its depth relationship to create a unified whole.

Pop painting. A style of realistic painting based on objects from American commercial culture, i.e., Andy Warhol's Brillo boxes and Coke cans.

Positive form. Form seen as a plane, mass, or volume as defined by negative space.

Primary negative. The deepest space perceived in a painting.

Primary positive. Form seen as closest to the eye in a painting.

Process. The practice of modern painting depends on an immediate perception of the effects of form and color in relation to expressive intentions. Also progress, development, and continuation of one's feelings for the purpose of composing a work of art (*see:* Composition).

Proportion. The size, shape, and extent of any part of a form, or a whole form relative to another form or to its coexisting space. Space also has a proportion that is determined by comparison to its coexisting form.

Proportional interchange. The way one proportion affects another proportion in composition.

Psychological response. A reaction to the basic identity of a form as affected by prior knowledge of it. For example, an apple is identified as a fruit to eat (cf. aesthetic response).

Reality. Awareness of existence. In painting there are two kinds of reality: material reality as it is seen visually, and spiritual reality as it is felt emotionally by the conscious or subconscious response in the mind.

Representational painting. An all-inclusive definition for any style of painting that represents objects or nature.

Simplification. The reduction of form, color, and space to only those elements that work together to form a unified whole.

Simultaneous contrast. Seeing two colors equally at the same time. The eye does not know which one to look at first because of identical shapes, tonal values, and intensities.

Space. The unlimited expanse within which all forms are contained. A distinction should be made between physical space, i.e., the actual expanse in which we exist, and pictorial space, i.e., the inner and outer expanse of depth perceived in a painting.

Space frame. The picture plane as it is defined by its horizontal and vertical limitations.

Spatial interval. The optical interval between two colors. The interval between a hot color and a cold color is an extreme. As the color temperatures come closer, the interval between them is decreased and the colors become more harmonious.

Stable. A description of equilibrium in a form. A stable form has either a vertical or horizontal axis and is at rest (cf. kinetic).

Static form. A form that is devoid of inner life (cf. organic). There are no static forms in nature. Symmetrical, manmade shapes such as a square, a perfect circle, or oval are static shapes. A form that has one side drawn or painted identically to the other side is a static form. A symmetrical shape of space, created by a corresponding symmetrical form, is also static.

Structural adequacy. Describes qualities that hold up and are time-tested. This is a good way, for example, to describe a drawing or a painting that has good flow and good balance between the positives and negatives, as well as alive, organic qualities in all of its relationships.

Structure. Something that is built. Also, anything composed of parts arranged together as defined by their coexisting space. Structure also means the manner of building, or the way the parts are made and hold together (*see*: Visual structure).

Support surface. A term that is used to describe the surface of a stretched canvas or paper.

Surrealism. A style of painting that represents imagery of subconscious thought patterns that are characteristic of dreams. The illusion of time and vast space are often emphasized.

Temperature. The degree of warmth or coolness of the colors in a painting as determined by the extent of reds and yellows (hot) or greens and blues (cool).

Texture. Either an apparent surface quality or one that suggests surface qualities by means of dots, marks, squiggles, etc.

Tonal painting. Any painting that relies on dark and light values rather than color for its composition. A tonal painter typically uses tones rather than color to create an illusion of volume in form. A black and white photograph of a painting will reveal its tonal structure.

Tonal values. The relative lightness or darkness of colors or forms. White is the lightest form and black is darkest. A middle tone exists halfway between the lightest and the darkest form. Any color has a hue, intensity, and a tone, each of which determines its appearance.

Unity. All of the parts, which are not necessarily equal, work together to form a whole.

Visual balance. The equilibrium of all the forms in a composition as they are perceived, first as weight relationships and relative movement on the surface of the picture plane, and, second as forms perceived with relative energy as advancing to, and receding from, the eye within the picture plane.

Visual energy. Color/forms, perceived in terms of their

comparative depth relationships within the picture plane, are translated in the mind's eye as forms with relative amounts of energy. A color / form that advances to the eye has greater energy than another that recedes from the eye.

Visual structure. The interrelationship of parts composed or arranged together as defined by their coexisting space. Structure also means the manner of building or the way the parts are painted and hold together.

Visual weight. Color / forms on the surface of the picture plane are translated in the mind's eye as weight relationships. Light or heavy is determined by comparison to other forms in relative size, hue, intricacy, and tonal value.

Volume. A quantity or a mass. In drawing and painting, the gradation of tonal values from light to dark creates an illusion of volume.

Bibliography

Albers, Josef. *Interaction of Color*, New Haven, Yale University Press, 1971

Ames, Roger. *Sun-Tzu, The Art of Warfare,* New York, Ballantine Books, 1993

Barnhart, Clarence L. *The World Book Encyclopedia Dictionary,* Chicago, Field Enterprises, Educational Corp., 1966

Barr, Alfred H. *Matisse, His Art and His Public*, New York, The Museum of Modern Art, 1951

Cheney, Sheldon. *The Story of Modern Art,* New York, Viking, 1947

Choay, Francoise. *Le Corbusier,* New York, George Braziller, Inc., 1960

Chopra, Deepak. *Ageless Body, Timeless Mind,* New York, Harmony Books, 1993

Edwards, Betty. *Drawing on the Artist Within,* New York, Simon and Schuster, Inc., 1987

Giedion, Sigfried. *Space, Time and Architecture,* Cambridge, Harvard University Press, 1967

Gilot, Francoise. *Matisse and Picasso: A Friendship in Art,* New York, Doubleday, 1990

Goodrich, Lloyd. *Edward Hopper,* New York, Harry Abrams, Inc., 1978

Goodyear, Frank H. *Welliver,* New York, Rizzolli, 1985

Goossen, E.C. *Stuart Davis,* New York, George Braziller, 1959

Gowing, Lawrence. *Matisse,* New York, Oxford University Press, 1979

Henri, Robert. *The Art Spirit,* Philadelphia, J.B. Lippincott, 1923

Huffington, Arianna Stassinopoulos. *Picasso: Creator and Destroyer,* New York, Simon Schuster, 1988

Ketcham, Howard. *Color, Its Theory and Application,* London, International Textbook Co., 1956

Liberman, Alexander. *The Artist in His Studio,* New York, Viking, 1960

Mack, Gerstle. *Paul Cézanne,* New York, Knopf, 1935

Maslow, Abraham H. *Toward a Psychology of Being,* Princeton, Van Nostrand, 1968

Matisse, Henri. *Jazz, the Text,* Paris, Teriade, 1947

May, Rollo. *The Courage to Create,* New York, Norton Co., Inc., 1975

Mayer, Ralph. *The Artist's Handbook of Materials and Techniques,* New York, Viking, 1982

Metropolitan Museum of Art. *Clyfford Still,* New York, Harry Abrams, 1979

Miller, Dorothy C. *Fourteen Americans,* New York, The Museum of Modern Art, 1946

O'Keeffe, Georgia. *Some Memoirs of Drawing,* New York, Atlantic Editions, 1974

O'Keeffe, Georgia. *Georgia O'Keeffe,* New York, Viking Press, 1976

Rowland, Benjamin, Jr. *Cave to Renaissance,* New York, Shorewood Publishers, 1965

Rose, Barbara. *Readings in American Art Since 1900,* New York, Praeger, 1968

Schweitzer, Albert. *Out of My Life and Thought,* New York, H. Holt, 1949

Symmons, Sarah. *Goya,* London, Oresko Books, Ltd., 1977

Weeks, Sarah T., and Bartlett H. Hayes, eds. *Search for the Real,* Cambridge, MIT Press, 1948

Index

Titles of illustrations and the pages on which they appear are shown in Italics.